The Mediterranean

THE

MEDITERRANEAN

Richard Carrington

Weidenfeld & Nicolson   5 Winsley Street London W1

Designed by Behram Kapadia
for George Weidenfeld & Nicolson Ltd, London.

Maps and line drawings by Claus Henning;
fossil reconstructions by Crispin Fisher and Maurice Wilson.
Printed in Italy
ISBN 0 297 00443 3

(*Title page*) View of the Mediterranean from Eze, on the
French Riviera.

Contents

Photographic Acknowledgements

Figures in **bold** refer to pages carrying illustrations in colour

Aerofilms Ltd, 87; Alinari, 134, 140a, 146a, 150r, 151l, 151r, 158l, 158r; Anderson, 104, 108, 111, 144r, 144b, 148-9, 150l, 159, 160, 182; Arthaud, 189b; Associated Press Ltd, 34; Bodleian Library, Oxford, 188; British Museum (Natural History), 66, 69; Camera Press, 13, 196, **27, 28-9,** 45r, 82, 95, 206, 219, 233, 270, 271; Chapelle du Rosaire, Vence, **185**; Franco Cianetti, 12, 36; Bruce Coleman Ltd, 220, 221, 224, **232,** 234-5, 238-9, 240, 241, 245, 254r; Deütsche Archäologisches Institut, Athens, 121; Deütsches Archäologisches Institut, Rome, 153, 174b; Werner Forman, 122l, 123, **126-7,** 129, **137, 138, 156**; Fototeca Unione, 135, 140r, 176; French Government Tourist Office, 209; Gabinetto Fotografico Nazionale, 143; Photographie Giraudon, 96, 100a, 101, 184; John Hillelson Agency (Photo Erich Lessing), **front jacket, 39**; Hirmer Bildarchiv, 118, 122r, 130, 172; Inter-Communications Ltd, 212; Behram Kapadia, title page, **30,** 124, **214,** 248, 266; Keystone Ltd, 41, 49; Landesmuseum, Trier, 142; Frank W. Lane Ltd, 25, 32-3, 38, 229, **231,** 244, 253, 258b, 262, 272; London Express News, 275; Mansell Collection, 110, 179, 181; Mas, 113l; Leonard von Matt, 201; Metropolitan Museum of Art, New York, 103; Ministry of Public Buildings and Works, 193; Montreal Museum of Fine Arts, 152; Ann Münchow, Aachen, 180; Musée de l'Homme, Paris, 70; Musée National du Bardo, Tunis, 112, 113a, 113fl; Janine Niepce, Paris, 183; Novosty Press Agency, 276; Picturepoint, **204,** 207, **213**; Paul Popper Ltd, 216r; Josephine Powell, 106, 119, 120, 177; Reuter Photos 19r; Scala, **115t, 115b**; Rodney Searight Collection, 202; Service de Documentation Photographique, 91, 100b; Ronald Sheridan, **17,** 24, **40, 116,** 117, 191, **203**; Staatliche Museen, Berlin, 164; Victoria & Albert Museum, 192; Weidenfeld and Nicolson Archives, 44, 45l, 89, **97b,** 102, 105, 114, **125,** 144-5b; **146r, 155,** 157, 173, 174a, 175, **186,** 189a, 190; Roger Wood, **19,** 43, 93, 94, **97t, 98, 128,** 133, **165, 166-7, 168,** 171; World Wildlife Fund, 225, 243, 247, 252, 258l, Photo Yan, 20-1, 47, 162a, 162r, 197, 198, 199, 216l, 218, 267.

For my good friend
Edward Hindle
zoologist, geographer and humanist, whose
generous help contributed so much to the
magical times my wife and I have spent on
Mediterranean shores.

Author's Acknowledgements

At the completion of a book there have always been helpers and supporters to whom one owes the greatest debt.

My acknowledgements go, as always, to my good friend and publisher Sir George Weidenfeld, with whom I have shared a long and happy collaboration, and to all the members of his staff, especially Mr Behram Kapadia and Mrs Enid Gordon, who helped so much with the present book. The work of the photographers, artists, and cartographers who contributed to the visual presentation is also greatly appreciated.

A special word of thanks is due to my friend Group Captain John Malcolm, Professor of Surgery to the Royal Air Force, and Director of the Surgical Department of the Royal Air Force Hospital at Ely, Cambridgeshire, who is mainly responsible for enabling me to finish the manuscript with morale and sense of humour intact under the threat of serious ill health. My secretary, Mrs Mora Hammerton, has been indefatigable in typing and retyping notes and drafts with infinite patience and tolerance.

The debt to my wife, Mary Eden, who has shared the whole of my writing life, is as always too deep to be becomingly expressed. Any merit this book may have is due to the many happy years we have spent exploring the Mediterranean together, sometimes with frustrations and difficulties but always with gaiety and mutual understanding.

R.C.

Preface

This book is not intended to be a 'guide' to the Mediterranean. Many excellent guide books already exist and I have no intention or desire to add to their number. My own contribution is meant to be a 'companion' for those who have made the Mediterranean their home or come there in increasing numbers as visitors each year.

With this aim in view, I have, of course, nothing to say about schedules of transportation or detailed itineraries of visits. Nor, although much general geography, geology, and natural history is included, have I given a comprehensive key to every rock formation, animal, or plant to be seen in this or that Mediterranean country. For this detailed information, and such matters as the dates of festivals and the relative merits of hotels, the reader must go to the more specialised sources to which the Appendix is intended as a guide. What I hope to have produced instead, in a light-hearted but not superficial spirit, is a background, a framework, to enlarge the perspective of the more curious person who comes to some part of the Mediterranean to make his home, or wishes to learn something of its history and customs as well as to enjoy some days or weeks of relaxation. I have therefore concentrated on giving a description of some of the most interesting physical and biological facts about the region, its history through geological time, the nature of its pre-human inhabitants, the story of the main Mediterranean civilisations, and some aspects of the modern Mediterranean which may arouse the curiosity of thoughtful people of all ages and interests.

One of my special objects has been to stimulate thought by asking questions. Not all these questions have been answered, or are even answer-

Preface

able, but some readers may perhaps be led to dig deeper in other books or, better still, to acquire first-hand knowledge by making wider explorations in Mediterranean lands. Both in outlining facts and posing questions I have particularly wished to appeal to the reader's sense of the romantic as well as to his intellect. How many people know, for example, that the early ancestors of man were exploring the Mediterranean at least a million years before the Egyptians established their civilisation? Or that the present sea is a remnant of a vast ancient ocean called Tethys which more than 300 million years ago extended across the whole of the modern Sahara desert and central Asia, with the rocks of the present Himalayan mountain chain forming its bed? Less dramatically, but just as intriguing, how many of us understand why the Mediterranean is more salty than the Atlantic or know that rice can be cultivated as successfully in the Rhône valley as in the Far East, or that the exotic greater flamingo rears its young in colonies in southern France and Spain, or that on the French Riviera you are nearer to Africa than the English Channel? It is by reflecting on such facts that our imaginations are stimulated and can take us beyond the limitations of pedantic description. If this companion succeeds to some extent in clothing facts with colour without damage to their authenticity, and thereby enriches the reader's appreciation of this sea-centre of the civilised world, it will encourage me to believe that I have at least partly succeeded in my object.

Nice, France, and Ely, England, 1970-1   R.C.

PART I

INTRODUCTION

Profile of the Mediterranean

My friend the late Professor Frank Debenham, until shortly before his death the Director of the Scott Polar Research Institute at Cambridge, used to say that 'geography is the pursuit of wisdom through the spirit of place'. A fellow Cambridge scholar, the late novelist E. M. Forster, has written, 'it is in the Mediterranean that humanity finds its norm'.

The Aegean is dotted about with islands. (*Above*) Mykonos. (*Opposite*) The lagoon of the volcanic island of Santorin.

Although wisdom and normality are qualities that are none too apparent in the modern world, the attempt to link these two ideas to my theme does not seem to need any excuse. Meanwhile in this opening chapter I intend to give a framework for the purely physical scene by stating some simple geographical and geological facts.

The word 'Mediterranean' means 'Middle of the Earth', and it is well named, lying as it does between the three great continents of the Old World. An eastern extension of the Atlantic, it forms a great gash between the sophisticated peninsula of Asia we know as Europe and the vast and as yet only half-tamed plateau of Africa to the south. At its eastern extremity, lying some 3,720 kilometres (2,320 miles) east of the Straits of Gibraltar, begins Asia itself, represented on the Mediterranean by those political groupings of mankind known as Syria, Lebanon, and Israel, with Turkey, or 'Asia Minor' to the north. The southern seaboard of the Mediterranean has a comparatively smooth outline, although there are large continental promontories in Tunisia and Cyrenaica. The northern seaboard is much less regular, including great bays such as the Gulf of Lions and the Gulf of Genoa, the long inlet of the Adriatic between Italy and Yugoslavia, and the Aegean Sea between Greece and Turkey. The Aegean has also a north-eastern extension, the Sea of Marmara, which is a kind of 'anteroom' to the Black Sea, but neither the Sea of Marmara nor the Black Sea will be dealt with here as they are not integral parts of the Mediterranean as it is generally conceived.

Throughout the length and breadth of the Mediterranean are scattered many hundreds of islands of varying degrees of size and importance. The largest are Sardinia and Sicily which lie respectively to the west and east of the Tyrrhenian Sea off south-west Italy. Next in size comes Corsica, just north of Sardinia, and Cyprus and Crete in the eastern Mediterranean, while smaller, but better known and more accessible, are Majorca, Minorca, and Ibiza, comprising the Balearic Isles off eastern Spain. Finally there are the hundreds of small islands of the Aegean and such scattered groups and single islands as the Dodecanese and Cyclades in the Sea of Crete, the Dalmatian Islands off Yugoslavia, the Ionian Islands off western Greece, Djerba off Tunisia, Malta and Gozo south of Sicily, Corfu off Albania, and the volcanic islet of Stromboli in the south-east Tyrrhenian.

The area of the Mediterranean is of some 2,965,000 square kilometres (1,145,000 square miles). It falls into two distinct parts, the Western and Eastern Basins, divided by comparatively shallow water between south-western Sicily near Marsala and the tip of Cap Bon in Tunisia. Except for the waters just east of the Straits of Gibraltar, where the Mediterranean begins to open out into its Western Basin, the sea is here at its narrowest – the Sicilian Channel, as it is called, being less than 160 kilometres (100 miles) across.

The two basins differ considerably in shape, size, and character. The Western Basin, which comprises about 38 per cent of the whole, is roughly bisected by the 40th parallel of latitude; it is thus some six degrees further north than the Eastern Basin, which is roughly bisected by the 34th parallel. This is one of the explanations of the higher surface temperatures and greater aridity and salinity of the Eastern Basin as compared with the Western. The shapes of the two basins also differ considerably. We can fancifully compare the Western Basin as seen on a map to a twin-peaked mountain, with eastern Morocco, Algeria, Tunisia, and northern Sicily as its base and the peaks represented by the Gulf of Lions and the Gulf of Genoa. The Eastern Basin, on the other hand, is much more uniform in shape, a sort of contorted sausage with irregular northern projections in the Adriatic and Aegean, and Cyrenaica pressing in like an intrusive thumb from the south.

The special atmosphere of the Mediterranean is apparent to all those who know the region well, and is unique in the world, but it is difficult to say exactly what character, or interplay of character, confers this elusive quality. In the prosaic language of academic geography the region may be regarded as a transition zone between the temperate regions to the north and the tropics to the south, characterised, as we were all taught at school, by 'hot dry summers and warm wet winters'. But in fact this is only an over-simplified generalisation, a useful starting point, not the whole truth of the matter. The real Mediterranean is a region where not only climate, but a widely varied relief, contrasted vegetation and animal life, and above all the influence of human associations and historical traditions, have created the possibility of an astonishingly varied range of emotional and physical experiences.

To begin with, the Mediterranean is composed of two major natural regions which to some extent grade into one another but which from the point of view of geology and physiography are quite distinct. The first of these regions consists of the folded mountains which characterise the whole northern coast of both basins and, except where they fringe such comparatively large tracts of flat land as the Rhône delta and the plain of Lombardy, are seldom more than a few miles from the coast. In fact in such dramatic parts of the littoral as the French Riviera east of Nice they plunge directly into the sea.

The western extremity of these folded mountains lies, however, not on the northern, European, coast, but in Africa. The High Atlas in Morocco is the starting point, and the African branch of the chain disappears in Tunisia some seventy miles west of the coastal plain running southward from Cap Bon to Gabès. Its northern branch in Europe is much more extensive, however, and forms part of a system which is connected geologically (although in a controversial way) with the still vaster mountain systems of western and central Asia. The regions which will concern us in this book consist of the coastal *sierras* of south-eastern Spain; the Alps (which are continued into central Europe by the Carpathians); the Apennines of Italy, which extend south-westwards through Sicily and, after a submarine journey across the Sicilian Channel, meet the eastern Atlas; and the mountainous regions of the Aegean peninsula and Turkey. All these are interrelated but their exact history is confused, and there are almost as many theories of their formation as there are geologists.

This book is meant to be a pleasurable companion, however, not a textbook for geological students, so we may content ourselves with a simple bird's eye picture of the relief. To reassure any reader who feels cheated by this degree of generalisation I repeat a statement current even among experts on the region: 'the evolution of the mountains and basins of the Mediterranean is the Enigma Variations of tectonic geology.'*

Turning now to the second of the two major natural regions which make up the Mediterranean seaboard, we find ourselves in a quite different setting. East from Gabès lies Libya, then Egypt, then, turning northwards, the Levant. Here, especially in Libya and Egypt, the Sinai peninsula and Israel, the desert is the dominant influence. Except for the little oasis of green hills known as the Djebel el Akdar in Cyrenaica, the African shores of the Mediterranean east of the Atlas are typically Saharan. Temperatures rise to 49°C (120°F) and more, rain scarcely ever falls, and in the heat of summer the *sirocco* and other furnace-hot winds from the heart of the desert reduce everything living to dessication and periodically scour the coast with dense clouds of wind-blown sand. These searing winds from the Sahara not infrequently reach the Italian, and sometimes the French, coasts, especially in spring and autumn. They often carry red or yellow particles of sand which fall as the so-called 'red rain' or 'yellow mud', an

* *A Million Years of Man*, Weidenfeld and Nicolson, London, 1965.

unpleasant phenomenon experienced especially in Sicily, Calabria, Campania, and Basilicata. Sometimes freak air currents carry these African winds still further afield; for instance, in the late 1960s Londoners and Parisians were startled one morning to find their cars left parked at night in the streets encrusted with Saharan sand. A similar effect is produced in parts of the Levant by winds from Egypt and beyond, of which the *khamsin* and the *shlouq* are well-known examples.

A modification of the desert landscape of eastern North Africa and the southern Levant occurs, as stated above, in north-western Cyrenaica, where the Djebel el Akdar forms a comparatively fertile limestone table-land, and also in the northern coastal section of the Levant from southern Lebanon to Turkey, where the transition to more typically 'Mediterranean' conditions is made. The mountains of Lebanon, known as the Lebanon range, are particularly spectacular. The range begins in the north just below the lava flows between Tripoli and Homs, and extends southward to merge near the northern frontier of Israel with the Hills of Galilee. This coastal massif is over a hundred miles long, and despite its comparatively low latitude (33 degrees N) the imposing height of its peaks gives it the special character of a mountain zone rather than the typically Mediterranean atmosphere of southern Europe and north-west Africa. The highest peak, Cornet es Sauda, rises to 3,085 metres (10,100 feet), which is about two-thirds the height of Mont Blanc and some 600 or 700 metres (1,900-2,300 feet) higher than most other peaks behind the Mediterranean area. Mount Sannin, the spectacular backdrop to Beirut, is only a little lower, and snowfalls and deep frosts are common along the whole of the Lebanon range in winter. On the other hand, oven-like temperatures may occur in summer on the westerly slopes of the range when the scorching *khamsin* and *shlouq* blow in from the Sahara. The Levant, in fact, presents more startling variations of climate than any other part of the Mediterranean.

The difficulty of defining the particular character of the Mediterranean has already been alluded to. Having made the standard generalisation about 'hot dry summers and warm wet winters', and then shown its limitations by reference to the desert zones and the special climate found in the Levant, we may perhaps come nearer the truth by describing the Mediterranean as 'the land of the olive'. In fact the possibility of cultivating the olive is the most convenient single way by which a typically Mediterranean country may be defined. It has for long been regarded as such by the great majority of geographers and has successfully defied the efforts of innovators to substitute the holm, or evergreen, oak as the more characteristic Mediterranean tree. This is mainly because the holm oak is not found in the greater part of southern Turkey, southern Tunisia, or the Levant – all olive-growing regions. It is also present on the French Biscayan coast and will even grow in Britain and other northern regions totally un-Mediterranean in climate, relief, and vegetation, where olives could not possibly survive.

The reasons why purists attempted to demote the olive from its honoured position as the typical plant of the Mediterranean is that it is not indigenous to the region but was introduced there from Asia in

(Opposite) The Hoggar, central Touareg massif in Algeria, is made up of crystalline rocks surmounted by extinct volcanoes and dominating sandstone plateaux.

(*Opposite*) A sandstorm in the Wadi-el-Sheikh, Sinai. Sandstorms are a common and sudden occurrence in the Sinai peninsula.

(*Right*) The Pharan oasis in the Sinai; about ten miles long and one mile wide, it contains gardens of date palms, pomegranates and tamarisks. (*Below*) Wind-sculptured dunes in the Sahara. (*Overleaf*) A dried-up swamp in the Camargue.

Profile of the Mediterranean

pre-classical times purely for cultivation. The Phoenicians are reputed to have brought it to Provence when they founded Marseilles at the beginning of the sixth century BC, where it may have become well established even before it was introduced into Italy. However, an alternative theory is that it was not first transplanted westwards by man, but arrived through the natural agency of blackbirds and thrushes, which both feed on olives. This idea is poetically (if not scientifically) supported by a belief, held by some Mediterranean peasants in less sophisticated times, that an olive-stone would not germinate unless it had passed through the body of a bird.

More will be said about the olive in Chapter 8, but meanwhile, whether it spread naturally or was introduced by man, its value in defining the boundaries of the true Mediterranean is that it will only grow in the regions where it is now found. From the distribution map below it will be seen that, apart from two desert zones in Libya which belong to the second, and more atypical, of our two natural divisions of the Mediterranean, it is cultivated along the whole of the littoral and to varying depths in the hinterland. Except for the shores of the Sea of Marmara and the Black Sea (where the olive occurs on the southern coast) and the olive-growing country in the interior and west of Spain – which is excluded as being not strictly Mediterranean in character – the regions enclosed by the 'olive-line' as shown in the map coincide almost exactly with the coverage of this book.

Latitude and the relief of the surrounding lands are not the only features that determine the regional variations of the characteristic Mediterranean climate. As a sea it is itself sufficiently large to exercise an important barometric influence, and it is a focal point for the interaction of many large air masses which advance and retreat seasonally according to fluctuations in temperature and other climatic factors. The dynamics of Mediterranean meteorology are too complicated to deal with here, but a few generalities may encourage the reader to study the subject in greater depth by reference to some of the sources mentioned in the *Guide to Further Reading* given in the Appendix.

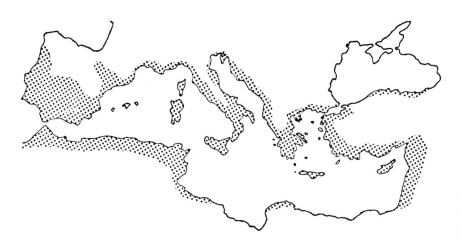

Map of the Mediterranean showing the distribution of the olive.

Profile of the Mediterranean

There are four main air masses which affect Mediterranean climate, two polar and two tropical. The first source of cold polar air that flows in at certain seasons is the moisture-charged polar maritime wind which originates over the north-east Atlantic. When this comes in contact with the warm air of the south a thermal inbalance is created, generally known as the 'Mediterranean front', which by causing depressions has an important effect on the rainfall in Italy and Greece. The front generally forms between the Bay of Biscay and the central Adriatic and is a common feature of southern France and northern Italy in winter. The second source, which mainly affects the Eastern Basin, is the cold, dry, continental polar air flowing south across the Russian steppes. The interaction of this air with the warm, comparatively moist, air of the Aegean peninsula is probably another cause of the local depressions which form in the Adriatic and also farther east in the vicinity of Cyprus. The two tropical influences are the reservoir of intensely dry air lying over the Sahara and tropical maritime air from the Gulf of Guinea. This last, however, reaches the Mediterranean very rarely in its original form owing to the distance involved and the desert character of Africa north of the western rain forests; in most cases the moisture is extracted long before it reaches the Mediterranean basin, and so the original properties of this air are lost.

These major movements of the atmosphere all play a part in the formation of the local winds, each with its own special name and character, which are so familiar to all visitors to the Mediterranean. Such winds, as much as the sunshine or rain, may make or mar a visit to the region, and their behaviour is a perennial theme for the expression of delight or grievance in every Mediterranean café. They do not simply lead to the general grumbling provoked by the vagaries of northern weather; they stimulate more personal reactions, and their names are introduced into the conversation almost as if they were the descendants of primeval nature gods. For instance no one driven off the streets in Aix-en-Provence by the violence of a strong *mistral* (Latin *magister*: master), a wind which blows periodically with enormous force in western Provence and Languedoc, would dream of just commenting 'terrible today'; rather it would be '*quel coup de mistral affreux*!' followed by much serious and voluble discussion of the wind's effects and particularly the disasters it may have caused, such as the blowing of cars off the roads, the destruction of cypress wind-breaks, and so on. And indeed these are seldom exaggerated. I personally have several times seen cars, and even great French *camions*, thrown so violently out of control by the *mistral*'s assault that they have left the road; and when I lived in Beaucaire on at least two occasions foolhardy fishermen, refusing to give up their afternoon's relaxation for the *mistral*, were blown bodily into the Rhône by exceptionally powerful gusts.

Another personal experience, this time in North Africa, underlines the special character of a second type of Mediterranean wind. My wife and I were making the crossing of the northern Sahara from Tunis to Cairo and, nearing the end of our journey, decided to spend the night at Sollum before driving on to Alexandria. It was August and extremely hot, still, and humid, the kind of humidity in which one wishes to take a continuous

cold shower as a protection from the sweat that pours off one, soaking one's clothes in a few minutes and filling ones eyes with salty rivulets. We were making the best of these uncomfortable conditions when suddenly from the direction of the desert came a rush of oven-hot air. I cannot say exactly how long the transition from extreme humidity to extreme aridity took, but certainly not more than five minutes – it seemed even less. My body and clothes dried out like magic and my face flannel, till then a soggy, soaking, sweat-covered rag, turned as stiff as a board within ten minutes. The wind increased in violence all night and the hotel was noisy with

(*Opposite*) Although traditionally known for its mild climate the Mediterranean region can occasionally have dramatic extremes of temperature such as a heavy fall of snow in Jerusalem.

(*Left*) A waterspout, a column of mist and water whipped up by a whirlwind, rising on a September day over San Feliù de Guixols, Spain.

slamming doors and creaking windows through the cracks of which sand poured in to cover the floor and furniture with a thin film of grit. In the morning when the sun rose we found visibility in the outside world cut off as by a blizzard. Sand was piled up against the walls of the hotel in great drifts and the air was so laden with particles that even the nearest houses were invisible. This was my first experience of the *khamsin*, already alluded to, which is the cousin of the *chili*, the *leveche*, the *ghibli*, the *sirocco*, and the *shlouq* – the local Saharan winds which mainly affect different parts of the North African coast or the southern Levant in a similar way.

The difference between the local winds of the European and African shores is, of course, that in Europe they are injecting cold northerly conditions into the region whereas in Africa they import the influences of the tropical Sahara. However, winds from both sources are actuated by the same climatic cause – the formation of depressions over the Mediterranean itself. The *mistral* and its more easterly cousins, the *maestrale* of Liguria, the *bora* of the northern Adriatic, and winds of similar type which flow from the Balkans to the sea, blow when deep depressions build up over the Gulf of Lions, the Gulf of Genoa, the Gulf of Venice, and off the Albanian and Greek coasts. At these times the high-pressure air over the mountain ranges and massifs of the interior rushes violently southwards, often being funnelled by valleys between high ground so that its force is concentrated as in an air-jet. For instance, the *mistral*, which blows mainly in winter, uses the Rhône valley as a channel to bring down the cold air of the Massif Central and the Alps. The wind fans out over the Rhône delta, where it makes its biggest show of force on the coast, but its influence extends as far to the west as Spain.

Nor is it a particularly rare phenomenon. Six meteorological stations in Provence have recorded it as blowing for 105 days a year with a speed of 27 knots; a seventh for 101 days with a speed of 21 knots. Much higher speeds than this are of course reached, and Force 8 gales (which have a mean wind speed of 37 knots) are not uncommonly caused on the Mediterranean as a result of the *mistral*'s assaults. Fortunately, to the east the coastal regions of Provence are largely protected from the wind by the Basses Alpes and the Alpes Maritimes, and this accounts for the favourable microclimate of the Côte d'Azur, especially between Cannes and Menton. Nevertheless, as far east as St Raphael it remains a scourage and the related winds already referred to produce an equally unpleasant effect over the greater part of northern Italy.

The same depressions which produce these disagreeable European winds also give rise to the inflow of the hot, dry winds from the Sahara; when the depressions form, the high pressure air over the desert rushes northwards to redress the balance, creating over the North African coast the oven-like conditions already described. These desert winds, beginning with the *chili* of Tunisia in the west and ending with the *shlouq* at the coast's easternmost extremity, do not normally blow at the same time; their onslaught is sequential as the depression moves along the sea. Their effect, as already stated, is also felt in southern Europe in different ways. For example, when the sea passage is comparatively short – as in the Sicilian

(Opposite) The crater of Mount Etna. *(Overleaf)* A caravan in the Moroccan Sahara.

Channel – the *chili* may arrive in Sicily in the form of a dessicating blast producing temperatures of well over 35°C (100°F). Where the Mediterranean is wider the winds have time to absorb a great deal of moisture from the sea surface, with most unpleasant results in the regions they affect. In Italy south of Naples, for example, a series of excessively humid hazy days frequently occurs and life becomes a misery; often at these times the 'red rain' referred to earlier, which is caused by the condensation of moisture round airborne particles, adds nothing to the attraction of the experience. The legendary laziness and apathy of the southern Italian is at least partly accounted for by these climatic factors. In fact the Mediterranean depressions provide striking evidence of the effect of climate on human character, an effect which is of more basic importance than is sometimes supposed and has played a key role in the evolution of social traits in both historic and prehistoric times.

Among other physical factors which have had a more obvious if less sustained effect than climate on human geography in the Mediterranean is vulcanism. The word volcano is itself Italian and derives from the name of the ancient Roman deity Volcanus or Vulcanus, the god of fire. In classical times, as is well known, nature was thought of as being composed of four elements — earth, air, fire, and water – of which fire was regarded as being for the most part violent and destructive. Even in its most sublime manifestations and its metaphorical applications in such phrases as 'the divine fire', it was seen to be an all-consuming force to be feared as much as revered.

Those who live in northern Europe and other regions where eruptions, earthquakes, and other dramatic large-scale earth movements are rare, are apt to overlook the fact that the Mediterranean is a region of considerable seismic instability. Long before Vesuvius on the Bay of Naples engulfed the Roman city of Pompeii in AD 79, there were numerous active volcanos in the region, and accounts of their eruptions and the legends connected with them are found in many classical writers. Vesuvius, although at least temporarily quiescent, has been intermittently active for several millennia, and during the last thirty years I have seen it give several spectacular displays.

Even more dramatic than Vesuvius is Etna in Sicily, one of the greatest volcanos on earth, whose summit rises to 3,295 metres (10,705 feet) and for most of the year it is covered with a thick blanket of snow. This is the volcano where the Greek philosopher Empedocles of the fifth century BC, a disciple of Pythagoras and Parmenides, is alleged to have thrown himself to his death in the crater; tradition has it that he became obsessed with the delusion that he had miraculous and supernatural power, and to prevent these claims being questioned he sought to persuade posterity by his sudden disappearance that he was, in fact, a god.

Aptly nicknamed 'the bonfire of Europe', Etna has a base that occupies an area of 966 square kilometres (600 square miles) and its smoking cone is visible from 209 kilometres (130 miles) away in clear conditions. Since ancient times it has erupted disastrously on numerous occasions and more than 135 such incidents have been recorded. The famous eruptions of 1329

(Opposite) Driftwood on a Camargue beach.

31

The eruption of Vesuvius in
1873

Airview of the volcanic island of Stromboli, part of the Lipari group of islands, during an eruption.

and 1381, which wrought havoc on the island, were only exceeded in violence by that of 1669. In that year a series of cataclysmic explosions were followed by an outpouring of lava which cascaded down the slopes of the mountain into the Ionian Sea, devasting Catania, and causing disastrous destruction of life and property. In the present century eruptions have occurred at frequent intervals, notably in the years following the Second World War and, although less lethal in their effect than their predecessors, they have caused great suffering and anxiety among the peasants who cultivate the rich soil of the mountain's middle and lower slopes. Etna is still the liveliest and potentially most dangerous volcano in Europe, liable to erupt at any time on the same gigantic scale as in 1669.

Among other active Mediterranean volcanos two of the most celebrated are Stromboli and Vulcano, both islands in the Lipari archipelago in the extreme south-east of the Tyrrhenian Sea. There are seven main islands in the group, which is also termed the Aeolian archipelago because in classical times it was thought to be the home of Aeolus, the god of the winds. By comparison with the slopes of Etna these volcanic islands are wild and uncultivated, due mainly to lack of water; their main industry, apart from some small but high quality vineyards, is the collection of the frothy solidified lava known as pumice, and fishing. To geographers and especially geologists, however, they are of great interest. The primeval effect of Stromboli as seen at sunset from a passing ship, its gaunt silhouette crowned with red and black plumes streaming from the crater, is a memorable aesthetic experience which greatly enriches one's purely scientific appreciation. Stromboli is also a volcano where the drama of vulcanism

34

can be appreciated directly at far closer range than is possible with many other volcanos. It presents a regular mini-eruption every two hours, and the imaginative visitor who is prepared to climb to the crater in the company of a guide can obtain in a few minutes an understanding of the majesty of terrestrial processes far more vivid than could ever be produced by a textbook description.

Other Mediterranean volcanos exist outside the Italian zone, but most of these had their period of maximum activity in the Pleistocene epoch of geological time – that is to say between approximately a million and ten thousand years ago. Although the history of this period of vulcanism, and of many others in still more remote ages can be read in the rocks, most of these volcanos are now extinct and seismic activity in the western and eastern Mediterranean is mainly represented by earthquakes. Volcanic eruptions and earthquakes are, of course, closely interrelated, the latter triggering off the former in places where the earth's crust is sufficiently weak to permit the extrusion of gas and molten rock.

This heated matter is discharged through the typical volcanic cone, which is connected with the interior by a chimney-like tube that carries the white hot lava and its accompanying gases to the surface. Here they emerge either in a series of coughing explosions, followed by an out-pouring of lava or, if the build-up of pressure is sufficient, a cataclysmic blast which may tear away the summit of the volcano itself and cause a disaster of the greatest magnitude.

The pressure that leads to these events is built up partly by the super-heating and consequent expansion of gases and molten rock beneath the surface and partly by the shuffling and settling of the substratum of the crust in regions of structural weakness. These subterranean rock move-ments cause the characteristic earthquake tremor at the surface and even when insufficient force is generated to produce a volcanic eruption they can themselves cause enormous damage, especially in densely populated areas where there is a heavy concentration of large buildings.

The whole Mediterranean region is subject to earthquakes, and minor tremors detectable only by instruments are an almost daily occurrence. There are also quite frequent but comparatively harmless quakes which can easily be felt by direct experience. These sometimes cause no more vibration than would be created by the passing of an exceptionally heavy lorry and their effects are more usually inconvenient than menacing; for instance, the possible fracture of a water main, a narrow crack or two in a macadamised road surface, or a minor leak of gas. Sometimes, however, more sinister quakes occur, causing the warping of railway and tram lines, the fall of pediments and other facings from stone buildings, the disruption of public services, and possibly loss of life.

The Mediterranean has had its full share of major earthquake disasters. Particularly tragic were the Lisbon earthquake of 1775 which wiped out the medieval and Renaissance areas of the city overnight, the famous Messina earthquake of 1908, and the quakes which occurred at Avezzano, Irpina, and Partanna in 1915, 1930, and 1968 respectively. Still more recently than Partanna, in the spring of 1970, the disastrous earthquake at

(*Above*) Ash formation, remains of
an earthquake of 1956, on the east
coast of the island of Santorin.

(*Opposite*) Diagram showing
the process of eruption of a
volcano as explained on p. 35.

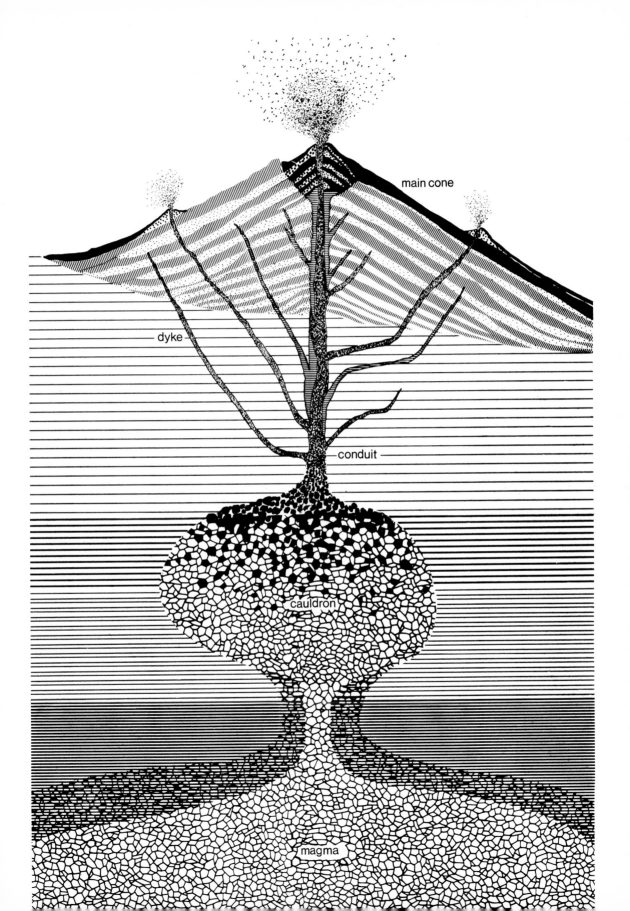

(*Above*) The same hotel before and after the Agadir earthquake of 1960 in which over 10,000 people lost their lives.

(*Opposite*) The bay of Ermonais, Corfu, supposed by many to have been the landing place of Ulysses when he reached the land of the Phaecians.

Gediz in Anatolia claimed over a thousand lives as well as destroying the finest Temple of Zeus in Turkey, which dated from the second century. The modern answer to these calamities, in which thousands of people have lost their lives, is to rebuild areas devastated by earthquakes with shock-proof buildings, but it must nevertheless be disquieting for residents in a region of seismic instability to feel that their home may fall about their ears during the night. Fortunately, however, the major quakes have occurred at irregular and fairly long intervals and advances in seismic technology have made it possible to predict at least to some extent the likelihood of a major quake and the region where it will probably take place.

A strange seismic phenomenon which occasionally disturbs the Mediterranean lands as it does other regions is the so-called 'slow earthquake', known in scientific language as 'bradyseism'. This is characterised by sub-crustal activity and tensions over a fairly wide zone which instead of causing dramatic or immediate vulcanism lead to a gradual uplift of the land. This process may or may not be followed by more violent manifestations but in any case can have dangerous, or at best inconvenient, results. The latest example of bradyseism – a particularly remarkable one – occurred at Pozzuoli on the Bay of Naples in 1970. Instruments detected during the second half of 1969 that this city of 70,000 inhabitants, built on the site of an ancient Roman town and acquiring a different order of distinction more recently as the birthplace of Sophia Loren, was rising above sea-level at what, in geological terms, was a remarkable rate. In fact the rise was estimated at 76 centimetres (2 feet 6 inches) in six months and was apparently continuing. Although damage was being done to drains and sewers the rise was uniform and there were as yet no fissures in the earth. However, in March 1970 a state of panic was reached as cracks began to appear in buildings, and arrangements were hastily made to evacuate the entire population. Seismologists and vulcanologists from as far afield as Japan and the United States converged on the region to collaborate with their Italian and French colleagues in predicting what might happen. Numerous different theories were proposed by different savants but fortunately before

(*Above*) The wrecked mosque of Gediz, in Turkey, after the earthquake of April 1970 which wiped out most of the town.

any dramatic evacuation had to take place the situation became stabilised and by the beginning of April only very slight earth movements were detected. With surprising phlegm everyone went back to work and, for the time being at any rate, the excitement is over.

Turning next to the fresh waters of the Mediterranean region, we find that the sea is fed by a rich variety of rivers and streams. These include the mighty Nile, the second-longest river in the world; the Rhône, with its dramatic hydrology; comparatively small but historically significant rivers such as the Tiber; and a whole host of lesser streams of varying character and interest. By far the greater number of Mediterranean rivers flow in from the European coast, but I shall start with the Nile for its unique importance in actually creating out of the desert sands the possibility of human life in a whole Mediterranean country, and for its role in fathering one of the three most ancient civilisations in history.

The country which the Nile has given to the Mediterranean is, of course, Egypt, which were it not for the waters of the river would be as barren and infertile as the rest of the Sahara desert. In Egypt it scarcely ever rains, and when the fractional amount of water falls, sometimes with a gap of more than a year between each short-lived shower, the people come out in

41

the streets as if to see the passing of a comet. The river, not the sky, is the country's life-blood.

The total reliance of Egypt on the Nile can best be understood from a vegetation map, or, better still, by imagining a flight from the country's southern frontier to the sea. Except for the section above Aswan, where even cultivation of the banks is limited, a narrow strip of fertile land averaging only 10 kilometres (7 miles) across represents by far the greater part of Egypt's fertile land. Admittedly this is greatly augmented in Lower Egypt by the delta, and springs and water channelled from the Nile allow the Fayum depression in the Western Desert to support a million people, but the fact remains that less than 4 per cent of the country's entire surface can be cultivated. The remainder consists of sand, bare rock, and a few scattered oases that will only support a limited amount of vegetation, mostly unsuitable for human consumption.

Egypt then, as has been well said by Herodotus, is 'the gift of the Nile', and as in this respect it is unique among Mediterranean lands a few words are necessary to explain its special hydrology. Although the lower reaches of the Nile are the source of Egypt's only fertility, the factors controlling the seasonal flow of water in the country, and therefore dictating the appropriate irrigation procedures, operate far higher up the river. The irrigation of the fertile strip of Egypt is, as is well known, dependent on the Nile flood, the amount of water flowing in from the south causing the height of the river to fluctuate very considerably at different times of the year. The flood is at its height at Wadi Halfa on the Egyptian-Sudan frontier in late September and early October after a build-up lasting six weeks or more; it reaches its peak at Cairo about a fortnight later. In ancient times the Egyptians used to believe that the flooding of the river was caused by the tears of Isis, goddess of the Earth and the Nile, mourning her husband Osiris, who was treacherously murdered by his brother Set. Nowadays we must fall back on a more prosaic scientific explanation.

By far the greater part of the Nile system lies in north-east, north-central, and central Africa. The two main branches of the river, the White Nile and the Blue Nile, rise respectively in Lake Victoria (some 5,600 kilometres or 3,500 miles from the sea as the river flows) and Lake Tana (about 4,600 kilometres or 2,887 miles from the sea), joining at Khartoum. In determining the behaviour of the Nile in Egypt these two branches have different functions. The White Nile is the comparatively slow-flowing and steady regulator of the water supply; the Blue Nile produces the seasonal floods. Very simply, what happens is this. The White Nile flows from Lake Victoria through Lake Kioga and the great southern papyrus swamps known as the Sudd region, to Khartoum, whence it traverses the

View of the Nile valley at Beni Hassan. The fertile strip of land averages only seven miles across in Upper Egypt.

Submerged palm-trees
during the autumnal flooding
of the Nile.

Nubian desert and enters Upper Egypt at Wadi Halfa. Its progress during
this long journey is for the most part leisurely and assured, the main exceptions being its passage of the Murchison Falls – where the whole river is
compressed into a rocky gap – its traverse of the famous five cataracts in
Nubia, and the man-made obstacles it encounters in the form of barrages.
Imposed on this steady-flowing stream are three main influences from
the east: the Blue Nile itself, locally called the Bahr el Azrak, and the
great tributaries known as the Sobat and the Atbara, the former above
Khartoum, the latter below it. Unlike the White Nile, all three of these
rivers are susceptible to powerful seasonal floods caused by the monsoonal
rains of Ethiopia, where they all rise. These rains begin in June and the
flood reaches Wadi Halfa in July, where it roughly follows the time-
table set out previously until it reaches the sea. Especially in the Atbara
the descent of the water is a most dramatic event. The famous British
geographer and explorer Sir Samuel Baker described in his book *The
Nile Tributaries of Abyssinia* (1867) how the river rose from a parched
trickle to a magnificent stream some 500 feet across literally overnight. The
approach of the water, first heard like distant gunfire, turned in a few
minutes to a thunderous roar and some of Baker's Arabs, who had elected
to sleep on the bed of the river instead of above high water mark, barely
escaped the wall of advancing water which almost engulfed them.

When the floods produced by these three eastern rivers abate, the White
Nile – which during the flood is partially ponded up above Khartoum by
the water rushing down the Blue Nile from the east – takes over again
and, reinforced by water from the Sobat, maintains the steady flow of

44

water to the coast. However, it creates no floods, and it is therefore the eastern rivers which are responsible for maintaining the fertile strip on either side of the Egyptian Nile. In the early nineteenth century and before, they did this simply by causing inundations of the flood plain on either bank, so that it was covered once a year with a layer of rich silt where crops such as wheat and flax could be easily cultivated. But in general one crop a year, sown immediately after the flood water ran off the land, was the most that could be obtained. When the low-water season came it was only by the use of such time-honoured aids to irrigation as the *shaduf* (a scoop pivoted on a pole which lifted water with manual aid into a network of small canals), the water-wheel, and the Archimedean screw that a very limited amount of land could be kept under cultivation. It is odd to reflect that little more than a century ago Egypt's hydraulic technology was still limited to three devices invented well before the dawn of the Christian era.

As hydraulic engineering developed, however, the situation changed. There was a growing demand for irrigation in the low-water season, especially when the profitable results of introducing cotton cultivation into Egypt on a large scale began to be realised. The result was the construction of the Mohammed Ali barrage across the two delta distributaries of the Nile just below Cairo. This structure became operational in 1861 and has been followed by many much more ambitious barrages, culminating in the recently-completed High Dam at Aswan. As a result of this human endeavour the Nile flood has now been successfully controlled, water being held back or released according to the needs of cultivation. The High Dam even makes it possible to store reserves for several years

(*Above, left*) The time-honoured irrigation system of *shaduf*, still used extensively in Upper Egypt. (*Right*) The development of hydraulic engineering in Egypt has made it possible for areas hitherto infertile to be cultivated.

Profile of the Mediterranean

so that an exceptionally low flood can be compensated for by drawing supplies from this great 'water bank'.

Apart from the Nile, with its unique desert environment, the most interesting and dynamic river flowing into the Mediterranean is without doubt the Rhône. The river, of glacial origin, rises in Switzerland between the Bernese and Lepantine Alps, whence it descends through Lac Léman and then west to Lyon, where it is joined by the Saône, coming in from the north. Much increased in volume from this source it flows almost due south to form the great delta of the Camargue, now a nature reserve, which is one of the most evocative coastal zones on the Mediterranean, the home of semi-wild horses and black bulls, and one of the few breeding grounds of the greater flamingo. During the river's southern progress from Lyon it is joined by numerous tributaries from the Massif Central in the west and the Alps in the east, but these are too far from the Mediterranean to concern us here. The Mediterranean section of the Rhône begins at the famous Défilé de Donzère, just below Montélimar, where the river has cut a narrow passage 3 kilometres (2 miles) long through a limestone formation separating the plains of Montélimar from the plains of Tricastin; this is sometimes referred to as the '*robinet*', or tap, of Donzère, sometimes as 'the gateway to Provence'. South of the défilé the character of the country changes abruptly; poplars give way to cypresses, and the broad river valley begins to take on the wild and arid aspect so typical of this part of the Midi.

But the unique feature of the Provençal Rhône from the point of view of hydrology lies in the behaviour of its tributaries south of Donzère. On the right bank these are the Ardèche, the Cèze, and the Gard, which rise in the Cévennes; on the left bank the tributaries are the Lez, the Aygues, the Ouvèze, and the Durance, which rise in the Basses Alpes. The Cévennes are famous for their torrential rains which, although highly concentrated and totalling only between fifty and seventy days a year, are of extreme violence (the figure of 94 centimetres [37 inches] in 24 hours appears in the record book for 15 June 1950). These rains render the western tributaries of the lower Rhône liable to dramatic floods which strike on occasion with catastrophic suddenness. The Ardèche is particularly affected and the flow may rise to the huge figure of 7,800 cubic metres (275,557 cubic feet) a second when the flood is at its height – that is, some twelve times the mean rate of flow of the Seine at Paris. At such times the level of the tributary may rise as much as 20 metres (65 feet), in a single day, and although floods of these proportions are fortunately rare a rise of 9 to 17 metres (30 to 55 feet) in under 24 hours is quite normal. The impact of these masses of flood water on the Rhône may be imagined. When a '*coup d' Ardèche*', as it is called, occurs, the waters emerge from the tributary's mouth with the force of a projectile and make deep inroads into the Rhône's left bank. Downstream at Avignon the water may rise over 4 metres (15 feet) or more in a few hours, and only begins to fall when it becomes partly absorbed by the marshes of the delta.

The flooding of the western tributaries fortunately happens in autumn and winter when the tributaries of the left bank are at their lowest. The

The Rhône at Tarascon.

46

reason for this difference is that the latter are not fed as much by rain as by the melting snows of the Alps and so attain their maximum flow in late spring and early summer. These two complementary systems tend to keep the level of the water in the Rhône fairly constant except when the balance is disrupted by exceptionally violent cloudbursts in the Cévennes. Nevertheless it can be a very fickle and dangerous river for navigation, and one can understand the sentiments of French writers such as Madame de Sévigné who refers to it as 'this devil the Rhône', or Michelet who compared it to a furious bull descending from the Alps.

Imbalance in the hydrology of rivers is not the only cause of inundations and other disasters in the Mediterranean region however. Sometimes

47

exceptionally heavy rainfall in places normally thought of as arid, such as the North African coast, can cause widespread havoc. The outstanding example in recent years was the flood that devastated Tunisia in the late summer of 1969, referred to by the Arabs of the region as 'the flood of a thousand years'. After many months of drought the skies suddenly opened and for eight weeks there was almost continuous rain. At first, in a country where water is highly prized, the inhabitants were delighted, but as day succeeded day their joy turned to panic. The parched *wadis* turned swiftly into uncontrollable torrents and millions of tons of valuable topsoil, the capital of the agricultural community, was swept as mud into the Mediterranean. Some 14 per cent of the country's livestock and the greater part of its important olive and date crops were entirely destroyed. The whole of central Tunisia was transformed in a few days into a vast lake, and more than a quarter of a million terrified people had to flee from their homes. Between five and six hundred Tunisians were drowned and many more who had saved themselves by taking to isolated patches of high ground suffered from near starvation or from violent food poisoning due to eating the putrefying raw flesh of drowned sheep and goats. Apart from the total destruction of many homes, the damage to public works was enormous. Countless miles of roads, including two Roman highway bridges which had stood for 2,000 years, were swept away. Some 80 per cent of the whole of Tunisia was ravaged by the flood, and the estimated cost of repairing the damage was 200 million dollars.

To turn now from fresh water to salt, what of the Mediterranean itself as a sea? I have already briefly referred to its dimensions and shape and pointed out why it is convenient to regard it as consisting of two basins of rather different character, but this is not enough. A few details must now be filled in concerning its topography, physical characteristics and dynamics.

One misconception must be removed at the outset, namely that the Mediterranean is a universally calm and peaceful sea where the more violent displays of the elements are seldom if ever encountered. This rosy picture, instilled by a flood of travel posters featuring sleepy fishing ports and half-naked girls and bronzed muscle-men skipping along sandy beaches, is very far from being accurate. The Mediterranean hides beneath its placid image the unpredictable character of any sea and, as all mariners will tell you, its storms can be as angry as those in the Atlantic when the depressions are deep and the full violence of the winds is felt. However, storms are no more typical of the Mediterranean than of any other sea, and between their infrequent appearance the blue waters do indeed offer an image of sun-drenched tranquillity unmatched by any maritime environment in the world.

Beneath the surface lies a whole new world less familiar but quite as intriguing as the lands which enclose it. The floor of the sea has a richly varied relief and the movements of currents, the gradations of temperature and other physical characteristics of the waters greatly influence the behaviour of the atmosphere above, having therefore a basic effect on the whole economy of Mediterranean man.

The two major basins of the sea differ in character and are divided into a number of subsidiary basins. The Western Basin can be broadly regarded as consisting of three parts. The most westerly is the tiny Alboran Basin, extending from the Straits of Gibraltar to a longitudinal ridge from which the little Spanish island of Alboran rises abruptly about mid-way between southern Spain and the tip of the Cap des Trois Fourches in Morocco. Eastward from this ridge, extending to Corsica and Sardinia, lies the largest of the subsidiary basins, known as the Balearic Basin. At its deepest point, off western Sardinia, this basin reaches more than twice the depth of the Alboran Basin – 3,149 metres (10,390 feet) compared with 1,500 metres (4,950 feet). With the exception of stretches of comparatively shallow coastal water to the west of the Rhône delta and off north-eastern Spain south of the mouth of the Ebro, the exposed land plunges here in a steep slope beneath the waves with only a very narrow fringe of continental shelf. This is especially true on the Côte d'Azur of France and in northern Algeria where the continental shelf is virtually non-existent. The third subsidiary region of the Western Basin is that containing the Tyrrhenian Sea. Here again the rocky shores plunge abruptly beneath the surface and half of the basin lies below 2,000 metres (6,600 feet). An area at its centre which is larger than Sicily is deeper still – over 3,000 metres (10,000 feet) – and a sounding of 3,731 metres (12,300 feet), made 80 kilometres (50 miles) from the Isole Ponziani near Naples, is the greatest depth so far discovered in the western Mediterranean.

In spite of being thought universally to be a calm and peaceful sea, the Mediterranean can cause extensive damage as shown in the photograph above, taken after wintery high winds and storms at Cagnes-sur-Mer on the French Riviera.

Profile of the Mediterranean

But when we turn to the Eastern Basin we find that these figures are still further exceeded. The deepest waters lie to the north-west between southern Italy and Greece. This region is known as the Ionian Basin and soundings of well over 4,000 metres (13,200 feet) have been made here. The remainder of the Eastern Basin cannot be so neatly carved up into subsidiary basins as the Western Basin. Off the North African coast between Tunisia and Cyrenaica the water is comparatively shallow and covers a broad continental shelf. Eastward lies the Egyptian Basin where 2,000 metres (6,600 feet) or so is the maximum depth. To the north of Crete the waters are still shallower and geologists believe that the Aegean Sea was created by the foundering of land that some ten million years ago was fully exposed. The innumerable islands of the Aegean, which are among the most beautiful and historically important features of the eastern Mediterranean, are therefore the mountain peaks of an ancient land which once joined eastern Greece with the west coast of Asia Minor. Finally there is the inlet of the Adriatic, whose origin is something of a geological mystery. This sea is extremely shallow, and its bed seems to have been formed by a variety of geological processes too complex to outline here. The sediment brought down by the Po has shrouded the underlying rock with a uniform covering however, so there is very little obvious variation in the relief of the bed. Despite this, the distinct character of the eastern Italian and Dalmatian coastlines emphasises their different origins and also has historical significance. For example, the deep inlets of the Dalmatian coast provided perfect lurking places for the pirates who harassed the comparatively vulnerable shores of eastern Italy from the first century of the Christian era to the time of the Venetian Republic.

Within the great geological vessel of the Mediterranean basin, with its deeps and submarine mountains and canyons, the waters pursue their dynamic rhythms. Among the controlling forces, apart from the shape of the basin itself, are the sun, the moon, and the flow of currents in and out of the sea at the Straits of Gibraltar and the Dardanelles. The sun determines temperature and hence evaporation rates, which in turn effect the behaviour of the waters themselves. The moon, as everywhere, is the main controller of the tides, but in the Mediterranean the results of its magnetic pull are only very slightly apparent. In fact the Mediterranean is virtually tideless, the reason being its enclosed character which is comparable to that of a land-locked lake. It does not present a large enough surface for the pull of the moon to have more than a minimal effect on its level, and although it communicates directly with the world ocean where it meets the Atlantic, the Straits of Gibraltar are too narrow for the great tidal variations of the main to influence it significantly.

The movements of the Mediterranean waters are therefore mainly due to currents. Their dynamics are extremely complex, but a few general remarks should be made about their origin and character. The main current flows in from the Atlantic to compensate for the really astonishing rate of evaporation in the Mediterranean which exceeds 115,400 cubic metres (4,274,074 cubic feet) per second. To compensate for this loss of water rivers, rainfall and the inward flow of water through the Dardanelles provide only limited replacements – 4.9, 21.3 and 3.2 per cent respectively. The remaining 70.6 per cent comes through the Straits of Gibraltar and were it not for this source of supply it would not take many millennia for the waters of the basin to dry up completely.

The current from the Atlantic is a surface current that sweeps in like a lion, travelling at some 2½ mph. It rapidly slows, however, and flows leisurely along the North African coast to turn north at the Levant and west when it encounters the southern shores of Asia Minor. This anti-clockwise movement, controlled by the earth's spin, is universal in currents in the Northern Hemisphere. There is a sill at the Straits of Gibraltar preventing the inflow of the colder, deeper Atlantic waters, so the chilling influence of this source of supply is reduced to a minimum. The surface of the Mediterranean being largely exposed to the sun and subjected to the hot Saharan winds, now evaporates water at the astounding rate referred to above. This water does not, of course, carry its burden of salt with it when it turns into gas, so the water left behind has a very high salinity indeed – about 38 per cent. The extreme saltiness of the Mediterranean, which is noticeable even to a bather who accidentally takes in a mouthful of water, can therefore be traced directly to the action of sun and wind.

Other more local currents occur in the Aegean and the Adriatic. The waters of these inlets, although to some extent isolated from the Mediterranean proper, obey similar laws, their motion being generally anti-clockwise. In addition to the inflowing currents at Gibraltar and the Dardanelles, the Mediterranean also loses heavy saline water by outflowing currents at these points. They run into the Sea of Marmara and the Atlantic, only at greater depths than their inflowing counterparts. The reasons for this counterflow and the details of the sea's behaviour in many other respects cannot possibly be explained in a book of this kind. I hope I have said enough, however, to show that the Mediterranean is not just a simple pond of sparkling blue water but a region of dynamic physical activity – a fitting centre-piece, in fact, to the dramatic tale that has unfolded itself on its ancient shores.

PART II

THE MEDITERRANEAN
IN THE PAST

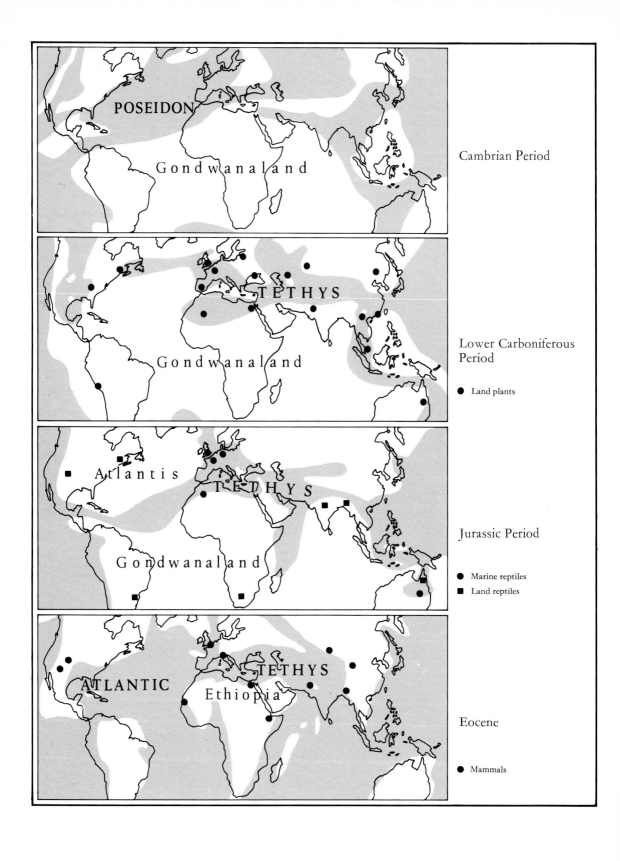

Cambrian Period

Lower Carboniferous
Period

● Land plants

Jurassic Period

● Marine reptiles
■ Land reptiles

Eocene

● Mammals

2

Life before Man

For the purposes of this chapter the term 'Prehistory' will take us far beyond the advent of Mediterranean man, into those distant geological ages when the sea that was the parent of the Mediterranean was going through the early stages of its evolution: this sea was known as Tethys. Tethys as a sea is quite unimaginably old. It was already in process of formation in the Lower Carboniferous period of geological time some 300 million years ago, and was itself derived from the still more ancient sea known as Poseidon which ran from the present eastern Pacific across the North Atlantic and most of Europe and Asia in the Cambrian period. This is now believed to be at least twice as old as the Tethys of the Lower Carboniferous.

The stage of geological evolution in which Tethys becomes more obviously identifiable as the forbear of the modern Mediterranean occurs in the era of Earth history popularly known as the Age of Reptiles. At the middle of this period, some 150 million years ago, Tethys extended not only over the existing Mediterranean but right across Central Asia to join the Pacific on the north-east side of the Indo-Chinese peninsula. In Europe it covered all but the north-west tip of Spain, Ireland, Scandinavia, the north of Greece, and Russia. The sea also covered a broad belt in north-west Africa, Cyrenaica, northern Egypt, and the Levant. Mountains such as the Alps, the Atlas, the Hindu Kush, and even the mighty Himalayas at that time formed part of the sea-bed.

The explanation of these odd facts lies in the operation of geological forces. Contrary to poetic fancy, the 'eternal hills' are far from permanent. Even the greatest mountains are constantly being eroded, flattened, and

(*Opposite*) Maps showing the geographical history of the world, including the Mediterranean area, from the Cambrian to the Eocene Period.

covered by water, while in other regions coastal tensions and vulcanism raise formerly submerged land above the level of the sea. These processes operate over many millions of years, but with the inevitability of the movement of the stars in their courses. Sometimes the results are exceedingly spectacular, as for instance in the Himalayas where the folding of the crust has produced in Mount Everest the earth's highest mountain (8,840 metres or 29,000 feet). The fact that the Himalayas and the Alps once formed part of the floor of Tethys is demonstrated by the existence of marine fossils at their summits. No less a person than Voltaire was among the first to remark on the presence of marine shells high up in the Swiss Alps, although unfortunately instead of drawing the correct conclusion that they were ancient fossils he explained them away as the refuse left by pilgrims picnicking off shell-fish on their way to Rome.

In the Age of Reptiles, when the ancestral Mediterranean was going through these geological transformations, no mammals as we know them had yet evolved on Earth. The waters of Tethys were dominated by giant marine reptiles, while dinosaurs ruled the surrounding shores and pterosaurs, or 'flying lizards', made gliding sorties from the cliffs, in search of fish and other smaller prey.

A study of fossil remains shows that among the inhabitants of the ancestral Mediterranean were such strange animals as ichthyosaurs, plesiosaurs, and mosasaurs. The word ichthyosaur means 'fish-lizard' and typical members of the group were comparable to large dolphins; they had streamlined, torpedo-shaped bodies and sharply pointed skulls with bony, saw-like jaws and enormous eye-sockets. The larger ichthyosaurs reached a length of 9 metres (30 feet), but despite their size could propel themselves with great speed and grace through the water by lateral movements of their twin-fluked tails. Their remains have been found far inland from the existing boundaries of the Mediterranean, for Tethys spread far to the north in those days. In one fossil find in southern Germany the imprint of the animal's skin was even found preserved in the black shales of the region.

The plesiosaurs were likewise large animals, and some attained a length of $12\frac{1}{2}$ metres (40 feet). Their name means 'near-reptiles' because when their fossils were first discovered it was thought they represented a transitional stage between fish and marine reptiles. This was erroneous however. It is now known that plesiosaurs, like all marine reptiles and mammals, are animals that had returned to the sea after a period of evolutionary development on land. Plesiosaurs were built on quite a different plan from ichthyosaurs, being much less fish-like in appearance. They had comparatively stocky bodies and long necks. Their limbs were modified into paddles with which they could make their way strongly through the water, although somewhat more slowly than the ichthyosaurs.

Mosasaurs, although no larger than the bigger members of the two groups mentioned above, were even more spectacular in appearance. They were lizard-like animals about 9 to 12 metres (30 to 40 feet) long, of which half was made up of the bony, laterally-flattened tail. The head was pointed and a powerful battery of teeth gave the jaws a most fierce and voracious appearance. The limbs, presumably webbed in life, were very short and were used for steering. The exceptionally long tail was the propelling organ and must have enabled the mosasaurs to rush through the water after their prey with a remarkable turn of speed.

In the brackish waters of the estuaries of Tethys giant members of the crocodile group flourished. One species has been given the apt scientific name of *Deinosuchus*, from the Greek *deinos* 'terrible' and *souchos*, an Egyptian name for the crocodile. A fossilised skull of this animal preserved in the British Museum (Natural History) is 2 metres (6 feet 3 inches) long, and just under $1\frac{1}{4}$ metres (4 feet) broad. This means that in life the total body length from nose to tip of tail could have been in the region of $15\frac{1}{2}$ metres (50 feet), or nearly 6 metres (20 feet), longer than the largest recorded measurement of a modern crocodile. Another crocodile of the ancestral Mediterranean is known scientifically as *Geosaurus*, which rather misleadingly means 'earth-lizard'. In fact the animal, which had a long pointed snout and a very narrow body and tail, probably ranged more widely in the open sea than the estuarine *Deinosuchus*.

The extinct flying reptiles commonly known as pterodactyls, but more accurately termed pterosaurs, were common along the shores of Tethys 100-150 million years ago. These strange animals, which looked like ungainly living umbrellas, did not have true wings as are found in birds. They progressed by a gliding, rather than a flapping, motion supported by a bat-like membrane, or *patagium*, of skin which joined the body with an immensely elongated finger projecting from the forelimbs like a boom. A well known example was *Rhamphorhynchus*, or 'hook-beak', with a body little bigger than a starling's but possessing an exceptionally long tail terminating in a flattened oval rudder; its beak was filled with a battery of sharp teeth. The giant of the pterosaur group, which could make long gliding flights over the sea, was known as *Pteranodon*, or 'toothless wing', and had a wing-span of nearly 9 metres (30 feet). This appeared much later on the scene than *Rhamphorhynchus* and did not become extinct until some 76 million years ago. It had a long bony crest which projected from the back of its head like a weather-vane and presumably acted as a counterpoise to the large, toothless beak.

The famous dinosaurs are associated by most people with North America and Africa rather than the Mediterranean, but they were also widespread in Europe and Asia, and the fossilised remains of many species have been found where the coasts of the Tethys sea once lay. Such plant-eating dinosaurs as *Brachiosaurus*, *Cetiosaurus*, and the famous *Iguanodon* and *Brontosaurus* all roamed across the plains and wallowed in the swamps and lagoons, while such carnivorous forms as *Ornithosuchus* and *Megalosaurus* preyed on the smaller and more vulnerable vegetarians of the region. One of my most memorable experiences in the Mediterranean was a visit to the dinosaur beds near Aix-en-Provence where the huge fossilised bones and even eggs of these strange reptiles are excavated from the rocky matrix.

The vegetation that clothed the shores of Tethys during the Age of Reptiles would have been more familiar to modern eyes than the animals,

(Overleaf) Composite drawing of animals of the Age of Reptiles. The animals shown here did not all exist at the same time, but range from the Triassic to the Upper Cretaceous. Across the drawing is a brontosaur (*Apatosaurus*), wading in shallow water. On the left-hand page, two rhamphorhynchids are flying; at top left, *Megalosaurus* lies in wait, with, below it, *Ornithosuchus*. Swimming on the left is a mosasaur, and to its right are two ichthyosaurs. On the right-hand page, two *Pteranodons* are flying, one in pursuit of fish. On land is an *Iguanodon*. At the water's edge lurks a *Phobosuchus*, and below it swims a plesiosaur.

although many thousands of modern plant species had yet to evolve. But already at the dawn of the era some 200 million years ago the ancestors of our modern flowering plants were beginning to blaze forth from the sombre background of evergreens that had previously composed the vegetational covering of the earth. Towards the end of the period the first deciduous trees appeared and in the mild conditions the sweet perfumes of many plants that now grow in the region were already scenting the air. The plane tree, so common on the European shores of the Mediterranean today, was already well established there 100 million years ago and the tall shapes of poplars and cypresses broke the horizons of the flat, fertile ground.

Then some 70 million years ago an extremely dramatic series of events took place along the shores of Tethys, paralleling similar processes in other parts of the world. For reasons not yet fully explained, the great ruling reptiles of earlier times all became extinct. Dinosaurs, pterosaurs, and the dragon-like mosasaurs, ichthyosaurs, and plesiosaurs of the oceans disappeared entirely from the face of the earth. Although this disastrous change did not take place cataclysmically, as the more sensational interpreters of the process once liked to assert, it did occur in what geologically speaking was a very short space of time – perhaps little more than a million years. Nor can a sudden climatic change fully explain the phenomenon (although it undoubtedly played a part), for the plants were little affected, and many of the smaller reptiles ancestral to our modern forms survived the period quite well. But whatever the reason, there was without doubt a sudden change in the cast. The ruling reptiles were almost entirely superseded by the mammals, which had hitherto been comparatively small and inconspicuous, existing in hidden places and never coming into obvious conflict with the more powerful and successful reptile dynasty.

The Age of Mammals, which preceded what we may now aptly call the Age of Man, saw the final moulding of the Mediterranean basin into its modern form. This Age, known to geologists and palaeontologists as the Cainozoic, or 'era of recent life', is technically divided into two major Periods, the Tertiary and the Quaternary. As their names suggest, these represent the third and fourth divisions of the whole history of the earth as seen in geological terms. Each Period is itself divided into a number of Epochs. Thus the Tertiary consists of the Eocene ('dawn of the recent'), Oligocene ('few of the recent'), Miocene ('less recent'), and Pliocene ('more recent'), while the Quaternary consists of the Pleistocene ('most recent'), and the Holocene ('wholly recent'). Examples of the fossil mammals of all these divisions occur in the Mediterranean region as do examples of the ancestor of man who migrated there from his evolutionary cradle in Africa.

During the first part of the Tertiary the European and North African land masses went through many changes, being sometimes covered by shallow seas spreading out from Tethys, at other times fully exposed. Rivers often formed vast deltas and freshwater lagoons. But Tethys itself, narrow and deep, generally preserved its character until the end of the Oligocene, when parts of its floor began to be compressed by movements of the earth's crust. Thus gradually the great folded mountain chain of the Alps began to appear, together with its extensions in Spain, North Africa and eastern Europe. The process was continued even more dramatically in the Miocene, when the land connection between Europe, Asia, and Africa was finally established. By some 15 million years ago the western end of Tethys had become reorganised in outline by these titanic earth processes and was recognisably the Mediterranean of today.

As a result of these geological transformations the character of the climate was also changing. In the comparatively low-lying landscape of the early Tertiary, subtropical conditions prevailed in the western Tethys basin. But as the mountains gradually emerged and the sea surface contracted in area the whole circulation of the atmosphere was revolutionised and the cycles of evaporation and rainfall radically changed. Subtropical vegetation gave place to temperate, forests were reduced in size, and grassy plains covered much of the northern Mediterranean shore. In places, especially in the lee of highlands, a decrease in the rainfall saw the establishment of local deserts.

To describe the geological and climatic cycles to which the Mediterranean has been subject during the last 12 million years would take us far beyond the scope of this book, although a few major episodes relevant to the development of man in the region will be touched on later. However, no companion to the Mediterranean would be complete without some mention of the animals, and particularly the mammals, that invaded its waters or roamed its shores before the advent of man. These not only included creatures ancestral to many of the Mediterranean animals of today, but a number of grotesque forms that flourished for many millions of years and then became extinct.

In Tethys itself in Eocene times lived a number of early whales. One of the most remarkable of these was known as *Zeuglodon* or *Basilosaurus*, whose fossil remains have been found in North Africa. This animal measured

The *Zeuglodon* was the ancestor of the whale and its fossil remains have been found in North Africa.

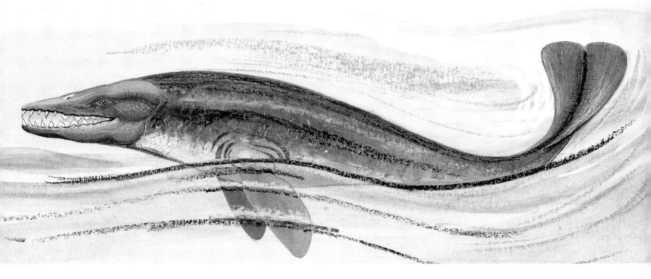

some 21 metres or 70 feet, in length and had a slim, tapering body pro-
pelled by a single pair of flippers at the forward end. So remarkable was
the skeleton that some people suggested that a living descendant of the
animal might be the original of the sea serpent legend, and in fact the
bones were assembled as those of a sea serpent in New York in 1845 by
an unscrupulous showman known as Koch. An equally remarkable land
mammal of North Africa which appeared in the next Epoch, the Oligocene, was known as *Arsinoitherium*, or 'the beast of Queen Arsinoe' of
Ptolemaic Egypt. This was so called because its fossil bones were found
near the remains of the Queen's palace in Egypt, where it must have
roamed along the southern shores of the Tethys sea. It was the size of a
rhinoceros and possibly a marsh-dweller, for there were no deserts in
Egypt in those days. Its strangest feature was two huge horns on the nasal
bones, fused at the base to support them more strongly.

The Mediterranean is of particular interest to students of evolution
because it is the region where the elephants went through the earliest
stages of their development. It is not generally known that African
elephants, now restricted to the lands south of the Sahara, lived in the
Atlas mountains in historic times and were used by Hannibal in his
armies. Still less appreciated is the fact that some 70 million years ago on
the southern shores of Tethys dwelt a variety of small ancestral elephant
closely related to its giant descendants of today.

The earliest representative of the elephant dynasty to be unearthed by
fossil hunters is known as *Moeritherium*, 'the beast of Moeris'. The bones
of this animal were found in the early years of the century by H. J. L.
Beadnell, of the Egyptian Survey Department, in the Fayum, a depression
in the desert south-west of Cairo which contained a lake known to the
ancients as Lake Moeris. The animal was small, being about the size of a
large pig, and its bone structure showed that in all probability it had no
typical elephantine trunk. The earliest deposits in which it was found date
from the Eocene, when this part of Africa consisted not of deserts but of
vast swamps and fertile plains. It seems likely that *Moeritherium*, like
Arsinoitherium, was a swamp-dweller and spent much of its time in the
water as hippopotamuses do today.

On the same expedition Beadnell turned up two other collections of
bones belonging to early members of the elephant group. These are known
to scientists as *Phiomia* and *Palaeomastodon* respectively and they date from
the Oligocene Epoch which ended some 35 million years ago. Although
Moeritherium also survived into this Epoch it was probably already dying
out and the two new types gradually replaced it. Again going on the
structure of the bones it seems possible, but by no means certain, that both
animals had rudimentary trunks, rather like the 'blackish, bulgy nose'
possessed by Kipling's Elephant's Child in the *Just So Stories* before it was
grabbed and elongated by the crocodile.

Between the end of the Oligocene and the beginning of the Pleistocene,
which saw the dawn of the modern world, the shores of the Mediterranean
were occupied at various times by a rich assortment of elephantine types.
Particularly grotesque was *Dinotherium*, or 'terrible beast', whose remains

have been found in the Rhône valley and further to the east. This animal was quite as large as a modern elephant but its tusks, instead of pointing forward, curved downwards and inwards towards its chest like gigantic hooks. Some scientists maintained at one time that *Dinotherium* must have been an aquatic animal that used these odd-shaped tusks to anchor itself to the shore when not swimming; others that it was a marine mammal generally inhabiting the Mediterranean itself but coming ashore from time to time and using its tusks for pulling itself along the ground. These rather wild speculations, which show that men of science can be as human and romantic as the rest of us, have since given place to more sober interpretations. It is now assumed, less dramatically but more plausibly, that *Dinotherium* was simply a land-living form that probably used its tusks both to protect the delicate trunk and on occasion to tear the bark from trees for use as food.

These early elephants of bizarre shape were mainly cousins rather than antecedents of modern elephants, but the Mediterranean also saw, in an elephant named *Palaeoloxodon*, a direct ancestor of elephant species that were contemporaries of the first men. *Palaeoloxodon* was smaller than its successors, however, the largest of the three forms discovered standing less than 2 metres (6 feet 3 inches) at the shoulder compared with 2 to 3 metres (7 to 11 feet) for living elephants. The remains of these animals, which date from the Pleistocene, were found on the island of Malta in the 1860s by an enterprising British surgeon named Andrew Leith Adams. With them were the fossils of other animals of the time, including an extinct hippopotamus, an extinct swan, an extinct freshwater turtle, and a giant dormouse. Adams reconstructed these, not very accurately but rather charmingly, in an illustration to his book *Notes of a Naturalist in the Nile Valley and Malta* (1870).

An example of ancestral elephants. (*Left to right*) *Moeritherium, Palaeomastodon* and *Phiomia*.

Dinotherium giganteum, a Pliocene side-branch of the true elephants.

Also appearing in the fossil record of the Mediterranean at this time are the remains of mastodons, mammoths, and the so-called straight-tusked elephant, which were contemporaries of Stone Age man and much-prized quarry in his hunts.

Apart from elephants, the forests and plains bordering the Mediterranean were the home of a vast array of animals, both herbivores and carnivores, which have long since vanished not only from southern Europe and North Africa but from the whole face of the earth. The giant wild ox, or aurochs, the giant cave bear, the sabre-toothed cats, and many other animals lived on into early human times, but others were extinct before man came on the scene. Particularly interesting were the forerunners of the horse, whose evolutionary history can be traced right back to the little *Eohippus,* or *Hyracotherium* as it is correctly called, of the Eocene. This 'dawn horse' was no larger than a fox-terrier and possessed five toes on each limb instead of the single hoof of the modern horse. Lions, hippopotamus, rhinoceros, and strange three-horned deer were among other members of the cast which occupied the Mediterranean stage in those days, as well as many extinct species of birds, reptiles, and amphibians.

64

But we must now consider one group of animals, not so far mentioned, which is of particular importance to our story. This is the Order Primates which in the apes and monkeys contains man's nearest living relations as well as his common ancestors. First, however, it must be made clear that man himself as a biological organism did not originate in the Mediterranean region. The centre from which our ancestors first radiated has now been almost conclusively proved by the work of Dr L. S. B. Leakey and his colleagues to be situated in East Africa. The Mediterranean's importance in the history of man, therefore, is as the scene of his development when he migrated to the north, and then west and east, not as the place of origin of man himself. Nevertheless some Mediterranean fossil monkeys of much earlier geological times are worth a passing mention because they represent a phase of evolution parallel to our own.

Apes and monkeys are not very common as fossils for a number of reasons. First, being highly intelligent, they seldom met death by drowning, and it is the preservation of drowned animals which become covered by waterborne sediments that has been one of the main causes of fossilisation. Again, many species live in forests and woodlands where the soil is rich in organic acids which rapidly destroy their remains. Nevertheless Tertiary apes have on occasion been found in the Mediterranean region in a good state of preservation and some of these show by their structure that they were fairly close to the main human stem.

The most ancient apes and monkeys began to appear in the Oligocene Epoch and the jawbone and some teeth of one of these, known as *Parapithecus*, or 'near ape', were discovered in the same fossil locality in Egypt which produced the remains of ancestral elephants. Later, in the Miocene, more advanced apes appeared round the shores of the Mediterranean. One of these from the sea's European shores was *Dryopithecus*, the 'tree ape' which, before Dr Leakey's achievements established East Africa as the cradle of mankind, was regarded as one of our possible direct ancestors. *Dryopithecus* persisted in the Mediterranean and central Europe and even

Hyracotherium, formerly known as *Eohippus*, a horse-ancestor the size of a small modern dog.

extended its range to Asia for at least ten million years, and is still found in the Pliocene Epoch in fossil form. In this Epoch, too, another famous primate made its appearance. This was *Oreopithecus*, found in Italy in an early Pliocene coal seam many decades ago. At first it caused little stir, being dismissed simply as a kind of monkey, but more recent researches on the bones suggested it might have been ancestral to man. A further search was made for fossils of the creature. Much new material was turned up, and the popular press began printing their usual unguarded headlines claiming 'missing link discovered', and so on. Unfortunately the scientists who studied the new finds more soberly came eventually to the conclusion that the animal was a brachiating ape not unlike a chimpanzee. So *Oreopithecus*, after its brief moment of glory as the possible father of us all, sank back into obscurity as a modest, although interesting, sidebranch of primate advance.

The brief survey given in this chapter has been mainly devoted to the life and physical environment existing in the Mediterranean region up to the opening of the Pleistocene Epoch. This Epoch, now regarded as being some two million years old, saw the first establishment of man in the region and his development there before the birth of civilisation. These events, full of interest and wonder to anyone who wishes to understand the historic period and the modern Mediterranean in depth, will be discussed in the next chapter.

Oreopithecus, one of our ape cousins from Italy.

3

Man Comes to the Mediterranean

Mediterranean man, as stated in the previous chapter, did not originate in the region although relatives of our species dwelt there from very early days in the Tertiary Period. Man as we know him was an immigrant to the shores of the sea, and his appearance there formed part of an immense radiation of ape-men and early members of the genus *Homo* from their possible evolutionary centre in East Africa.

The exact starting point of this radiation is still a subject for speculation, but was almost certainly the region now covered by Kenya and Tanzania. From this cradle of mankind, perhaps as long ago as a million or more years, different branches of the prehuman stock were radiating both south and north. They became firmly established in southern Africa, in Asia, and along both the northern and southern shores of the Mediterranean. Later true men even crossed into the New World to settle there as the so-called 'Indians' of Canada, the United States, and South America. These first Americans were able to travel quite easily, for the Old and New Worlds were then joined by dry land at the present Bering Strait. The cast of their features, with their obvious Mongoloid affinities, is evidence of the Asiatic phase of their development.

But these broader aspects of the human story, fascinating as they are, cannot concern us here. We must restrict ourselves to the men who occupied the Mediterranean basin itself, first as hunters and food gatherers, then in fixed settlements of greater or lesser degrees of complexity, and finally in the earliest civilised communities from which all later Mediterranean history has stemmed. These men, it seems likely, did not come direct from Africa but went through the preliminary stages of their

(*Opposite*) A reconstruction of a Neanderthal family group at Gibraltar.

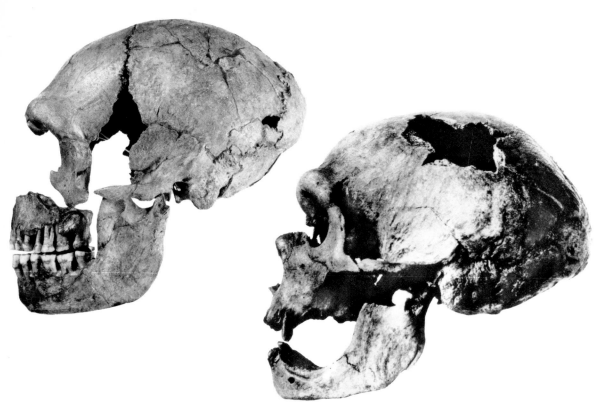

Skulls of two Neander-
thalers. (*Left*) Female skull
from La Quina. (*Right*)
Male skull from La Chapelle-
aux-Saints.

evolutionary development in Asia, whence they re-entered the Mediterranean basin more than a quarter of a million years ago. They were of two
main types. The first arrivals, who were also the less intelligent, were the
Neanderthal Men, who are scientifically referred to as the species *Homo
neanderthalensis*. Their successors, who eventually supplanted them, were
true men of the species *Homo sapiens*.

The Neanderthalers are named after the Neanderthal Valley, near
Düsseldorf in Germany where the first fossil bones of this species were
found in 1856. Since then there have been between seventy and a hundred
further finds on all the shores of the Mediterranean, as well as deep in the
hinterland of Europe and Asia, which shows that Neanderthal Man was a
widespread and highly successful species. All these bones belong to the
Pleistocene Epoch but their exact dating is still to some extent speculative.
Recent advances in geochronology, the science which measures the age of
the Earth, has led to revised views concerning the dating of the Pleistocene. This Epoch was formerly thought to have begun about a million
years ago, but it is now virtually certain that it is twice as old. But a lack
of complete precision here does not affect the main outlines of the story.
It is enough to know that the Neanderthalers were in all probability well-
established in the Mediterranean region by, at latest, 300,000 years ago and
persisted there till 40,000 years ago or maybe even longer.

What, then, did these cousins of modern Mediterranean man look like?
The old picture of Neanderthal Man as a kind of shambling ape, more
animal than human, with little brain and no imaginative capacity has had

to be abandoned as prehistoric archaeologists have discovered more and more evidence of his true nature. Certainly some remains of Neanderthal Man suggest that he was of rather brutal aspect, but this is not the whole truth. More recently-discovered bones give a much more agreeable picture, although they obviously belong to men of the same species. It is not always remembered that individual variation accounts for a wide range of differences in prehistoric man just as it would if one compared a number of individual skeletons of men of contrasted types living today.

The Neanderthalers of the Mediterranean can nevertheless be broadly subdivided into two main physical types, with the intermediate forms inclining more towards one or the other. The more brutish or conservative type is represented by fossils near the coasts of all three continents bordering the sea. The skull is typically large and thick with a much-flattened braincase, protruding jaws, receding chin, and heavy brow ridges whose main evolutionary purpose seems to have been to protect the eyes from attack. The body is stocky and thick-set and the limb-bones generally shorter than in both the more advanced Neanderthalers and in true men. The reduced limbs are the main reason for the short stature of the conservative Neanderthalers, who seldom attained a height of more than 1.68 metres ($5\frac{1}{2}$ feet). But they were not, of course, unique in this. Several races of modern man, such as the African pygmies, are tiny by comparison with the shortest Neanderthalers, and one only has to look at mediaeval armour to see that the comparatively large stature of western man today has by no means always been one of his characteristics.

The more progressive members of the Neanderthal species more closely resembled ourselves. There was much less 'snoutiness' in these creatures, although the brow ridges remained prominent and the jaws massive. Particularly important finds of bones belonging to both Neanderthal types have been found in Israel. One such find was made in some caves in Mount Carmel in the early 1930s by a joint Anglo-American expedition headed by Miss Dorothy Garrod. This was followed by equally significant discoveries in caves in the Jebel Kafzeh near Nazareth. In addition to examples of each type, some skeletons showed a mixture of the characteristics of both. For instance the remains of a woman found in the Tabūn cave at Mount Carmel possessed not only the typical heavy features of the classic Neanderthalers but the more highly vaulted cranium of the progressives. Another skeleton found in the nearby cave of Skuhl, also at Mount Carmel, had a comparatively vertical instead of receding forehead, a pronounced chin, and a cranium as rounded as that of true man. The limb-bones were, moreover, far longer and more slender than those typical of the conservative form, and their owner, when erect, must have stood about 1.80 metres (5 feet 10 inches) tall. These characteristics at first led some authorities to suggest that true man may actually have descended from Neanderthal Man, but there were difficulties in accepting this suggestion. The most important was that, contrary to what one might expect, modern dating techniques revealed that several of the progressive skeletons actually belonged to an older period than the conservative types. It is therefore more likely that *Homo neanderthalensis* and *Homo sapiens* evolved in parallel, with the latter gradually replacing the former as the two species found themselves competing more and more for the available living-space. This does not, however, exclude the possibility that some degree of inter-breeding took place, as shown at Mount Carmel.

The Mediterranean Neanderthalers are not only known by their fossil bones; we have evidence also of their cultural activities. Like their pre-decessors in Africa and the Far East they knew how to make fire, and their hearths are found in association with many Mediterranean sites. And like all the men of the Palaeolithic, or Old Stone Age, they had a flourishing industry of tool-making. This industry is known as the Mousterian, after Le Moustier, in the Dordogne region of France, to which, among many other places in Europe, they also migrated. The most typical products of this industry are hand-axes, points, side-scrapers, and other roughly-fashioned tools made of flint, chert, or similar hard stones. Most of the tools were made of stone flaked off larger pieces of stone, but the residual core was sometimes also fashioned into a utilitarian shape. The aborigines of Australia, who are still in the Palaeolithic stage of cultural evolution, are to this day making tools in the tradition of the first Mediterranean men.

Although primitive by later standards these Mousterian tools were an effective aid to our Mediterranean ancestors in many tasks. With the scrapers they could clean the animal skins they used as clothing, while the points would have been used mainly as weapons, either held in the hand or hafted to a piece of wood to form a javelin or spear, and the hand-axes for cracking bones, both of animals slain for food to extract the marrow, and of the brain-cases of enemies in combat. A more domestic use of the points would have been to make holes in skins so that they could be joined together as tent-covers, or to protect the entrances of the Neanderthalers' more permanent cave homes from the cold winds.

The Mediterranean Neanderthalers are of particular interest in giving us some of our first evidence in human history of the development of man's metaphysical awareness. Once, while I was travelling in North Africa, an eminent archaeologist who specialised in classical antiquities and was rather scornful of my interest in the Palaeolithic remarked to me with lofty finality that 'primitive man had no soul'. This judgement appears nowadays to be generally wide of the mark and certainly, as we shall see, the first men of our own species had begun to develop those spiritual apprehensions, rooted in cosmic fear and hope, that distinguishes man from the apes. But still earlier, in Neanderthal times, these faculties were in the making. At several sites near the European shores of the Medi-terranean animal skulls are arranged in ritualistic patterns. These were usually skulls of the giant cave bear which flourished at that time, and their presence suggests a comparison with the bear cults that undoubtedly existed among the hunting tribes of Europe at a later date. Still more significant has been the discovery of several Neanderthal burials. For instance, at Mount Carmel almost all the skeletons showed clear evidence of burial in ritualistic positions, the legs being drawn tightly up beneath the buttocks. Again, in a cave on the Gulf of Gaeta north of Naples, a Neanderthal skull was discovered in 1939 lying on its side in a small pit

Man Comes to the Mediterranean

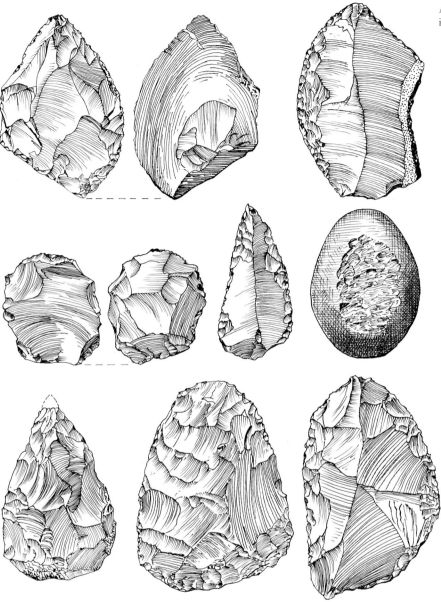

An example of Mousterian implements.

surrounded by a ring of white stones. It is not unreasonable to suggest that this cave was once some kind of sanctuary with the stones representing a magic circle and the skull as its centre-piece.

The Neanderthalers, like the true men of the later Old Stone Age, subsisted in the Mediterranean or elsewhere entirely by hunting and food-gathering. Those who did not establish fairly permanent headquarters in caves were nomadic, following the migrations of the game. They therefore travelled light, carrying with them only their weapons and the skins which gave them shelter in their temporary bivouacs, and seldom pausing for more than a few weeks at a time in one place. However, in recent years

73

evidence has come to light of encampments of a somewhat less primitive type, and one exceptionally interesting discovery deserves singling out as being of the very greatest historical interest.

In the mid 1960s were discovered, a few yards from the present commercial harbour of Nice, the remains of an encampment probably 300,000 years old where there are traces of the very first human architecture. The evidence consists of a series of superimposed living floors which bear the imprint of stakes some $7\frac{1}{2}$ centimetres (3 inches), in diameter and several series of stones arranged in an oval shape. From this data it can be deduced that the stakes formed the supports for huts and that the stones were used to brace their walls. Some of the stones measured as much as a foot across and in several instances they were even piled one on the other. Within the oval outline of the huts, which were between 8 and 15 metres (26 and 49 feet) long and 4 to 6 metres (13 to 20 feet) wide, the living floor itself consisted of a thick bed of organic matter, and ash from the hunters' hearths. The age of the encampment was established by the use of modern scientific dating techniques applied to the many thousands of stone tools revealed by the excavations. These tools were of even earlier age than those of the Mousterian culture described above; and the Neanderthalers may prove to be of even greater antiquity than is thought at present.

This encampment, now of world-wide fame, is known to prehistorians as Terra Amata, 'the beloved land', a romantic name inappropriately borne by an insignificant alleyway in modern Nice. The site was probably used in the summer months only, but the hunters returned to it each year and in the intervals of fishing and the chase relaxed in their huts to enjoy the fruits of their labours. There are also signs that they actually manufactured tools there, and it is most probable that role-specialisation of various kinds saw the beginnings of modern social organisation. For example the élite may well have been the hunters themselves, while other members of the group had special prestige as tool-making artisans. Others again built and repaired the huts, while the women tended the fires, cooked, and prepared skins for tents and clothing.

In these early days, although the broad outlines of the Mediterranean were much as they are now, there were periodic advances and retreats of the sea, and also considerable fluctuations in climate. These were related to the different phases of the Great Ice Age, a time of oscillating heat and cold, which coincides with the geological Pleistocene. There is no space to elaborate on the intricacies of Ice Age chronology here, but briefly the polar ice-caps at this time were alternately advancing and retreating, causing widespread changes in the physical environment. As the cold advanced southwards in Europe, more water was trapped in the glaciers and ice-sheets which covered the land to the north. This caused the sea-level to fall. Conversely, in phases when the ice was melting the water level rose. The geological evidence for these fluctuations is found in traces of raised beaches on all the Mediterranean shores, showing the various points to which the water rose during the warmer phases. It was once believed that in the phases when the water level fell Europe and North Africa were joined by isthmuses of land at Gibraltar and between Sicily and Cap Bon so that the Mediterranean consisted of two gigantic lakes; but although much more land was undoubtedly exposed in those areas than is now the case, most modern geologists would regard the idea of continuous isthmuses with much mistrust.

The fluctuations of the Pleistocene climate led to changes in the animal populations and therefore in the quarry of the early Mediterranean hunter. Typical large game of the colder phases were the woolly mammoth and the woolly rhinoceros. When milder conditions prevailed these animals followed the snows northwards, and the shores of the Mediterranean were inhabited instead by a warm-temperature fauna including such animals as hippopotamuses, lions, and true elephants lacking the typical hairy coats of the mammoths. All these animals are now extinct or found only south of the Sahara, although lions and elephants persisted in North Africa until quite recently in the Christian era.

It is a cause of surprise to many people that men equipped with the comparatively unsophisticated weapons of this time could have success-fully slain animals as formidable as mastodons and mammoths. Neverthe-less a study of the techniques employed by modern hunting tribes shows that such feats lay well within the range of the earliest men of Neanderthal or *sapiens* type. For instance, until quite recently, and perhaps still in some regions of the Congo today, an elephant could be successfully killed by a single man equipped with a heavy-bladed spear. He hunts stark naked, for even a loin cloth might impede him by catching on thorns or other obstruc-tions, and he covers his body with dung to disguise the human scent. By careful stalking, taking advantage of wind and cover, he can approach sufficiently close to plunge his spear into the quarry's throat or bowels. With luck this will lead to the death of the animal after several hours, the hunter following its blood trail and then summoning other members of the tribe to partake of the feast.

Admittedly this means of hunting is greatly simplified by the use of metal spears, and by the forest cover of western Africa, but comparable techniques were doubtless employed by Mediterranean man in the Stone Age. For instance an elephant, mammoth, or mastodon could be easily hamstrung by a practised hunter using a sharp flint blade hafted to a piece of wood. Thus incapacitated, it could be finished off by the combined assault of many hunters using similar weapons. Although there is no certain evidence, we may reasonably assume also that plant poison, placed in the elephant's body by sharp-tipped 'points', was effectively used. Traps were another expedient. When true men replaced the Neanderthalers and began to decorate the walls of their caves with pictures, possible represen-tations of traps of various kinds are found. Camouflaged pitfalls, where the quarry fell on an array of upward-pointing stakes when it stepped on the flimsy roofing, were used in the same way as by primitive tribes of more modern times. Another method of hunting was to drive herds of herbi-vores to death over steep cliffs.

The Mediterranean in the Ice Age, therefore, saw early man practising a typical hunting and food-gathering life. During the latter part of the Age, however, when the Neanderthalers had become extinct, or their remnants

Man Comes to the Mediterranean

assimilated by interbreeding into the ranks of *Homo sapiens*, some particularly exciting events were taking place in man's spiritual development. Aesthetic and religious aspects of culture began to play an increasingly important role in the day-to-day activities of men. We see the first sure signs that the practical, utilitarian aspects of life were going to be enlarged and ennobled by metaphysical values.

These new elements in human evolution, far transcending those already alluded to as characteristic of the Neanderthalers were the creation of men of our own species. The fossil remains of true men are found widely in the Mediterranean, and some of these sites actually overlook the sea itself. A particularly famous one is situated at Grimaldi, a village on the Franco-Italian border just east of Menton. It consists of a number of caves, one of which is called the Grotte des Enfants after two badly-damaged children's skeletons turned up there in 1874 and 1875. These could not be adequately interpreted by the archaeologists of the time. Twenty-five years later, however, the well-preserved skeletons of an old woman and a youth were discovered in the same cave. The skeletons, which were unmistakably those of *Homo sapiens*, were found in a flexed position and partially stained with red ochre, suggesting a ritual burial. This cave can still be easily visited by descending the cliffs below the main road in a lift, and then making the somewhat perilous crossing of the main railway line, along which the express trains linking Rome and Paris now run just past the doorstep of this ancient human habitation.

Although Grimaldi man has left no important evidence of his cultural traditions at the site itself, he was probably at about the same stage of evolution as the other true men of the later Old Stone Age who occupied the hinterland of the Mediterranean coast. The artistic sense of these men was quite remarkable and the new, more refined and often decorated implements they have left behind, as well as the engravings and great polychrome frescoes they scratched or painted on the walls of their caves, bear witness to a rich and diversified cultural complex. Indeed, both in time and space many different 'schools' can be recognised which are as distinct in character as the national arts of different Mediterranean countries at a later stage of history. Examples of the cultural 'schools' of the first true men are usually broadly grouped under five heads, the Chatelperronian, Aurignacian, Gravettian, Solutrean, and Magdalenian, all named after localities in France where the remains of implements and art forms of the time were first discovered. At a later stage, in what is called the Mesolithic, or Middle Stone Age, there was an equally rich diffusion of cultural traditions. Thus the great explosion of mind and sensibility of which the Mediterranean was the most important focus was already well under way even before the complete switch-over had been made from a hunting and food-gathering economy to one based on agriculture and stock-rearing.

Many books on the art and industries of the Upper Palaeolithic and Mesolithic are available in every European language and the reader whose interests are mainly in this aspect of Mediterranean life can follow the matter up from the sources suggested in the *Guide to Further Reading*.

(*Opposite, above*) When the ice sheets descended from the north the woolly mammoth and woolly rhinoceros were common along Mediterranean shores. (*Below*) Early elephants, lion and hippopotamuses lived in the Mediterranean basin in warmer times.

The skeletons of an old woman and a youth were found buried in a flexed position in a cave at Grimaldi.

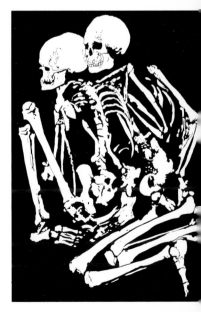

Man Comes to the Mediterranean

He will also find sites of interest in the majority of Mediterranean countries. To visit at least one or two of these will stimulate the imaginative traveller far more effectively than any amount of book-learning on its own. Armed with some simple but accurate background information, he will find that these distant times can be as effectively recreated in his mind as if he himself had been there to watch and participate.

My own most memorable experience of this kind did not occur at one of the better-known sites, but in a comparatively obscure cave on the North African coast. My wife and I were on the same coastal journey along the fringes of the Sahara already mentioned in Chapter 1. Being travellers of omnivorous curiosity we were delighted to hear on our arrival in Benghazi that, quite apart from the main reason for our visit – which was to study the remains of the ancient Greek city of Cyrene – there was an opportunity to visit an Old Stone Age excavation being carried out at that very time by Dr C.B.M. McBurney of Cambridge.

The excavation was taking place almost at sea level near the little Arab village of Apollonia, where great white combers break at the foot of a wild landscape of barren mountains. The cave itself was at the foot of a cliff up a moderately steep slope and was characteristic of the Eocene limestone formations in the district. It was virtually a huge 'bubble' in the rock, the front wall of which had been weathered away, exposing the vaulted interior. It must have measured about $18\frac{1}{2}$ metres (60 feet) high, $18\frac{1}{2}$ metres (60 feet) deep and 37 metres (120 feet) wide. The excavation took the form of a huge rectangular hole which McBurney had sunk into the cave floor. In the walls of this, carefully smoothed flat by the archaeologists, no less than eighty-eight successive strata were exposed like the layers of a gigantic sponge cake. In the lower strata the remains of ancient hearths and the bones of Neanderthalers had been found. Moving upwards, a complete series of prehistoric layers was revealed containing the bones of cave lion and rhinoceros, and the shells of late Pleistocene snails. But the series did not stop at prehistory. At the top evidence of first Greek, then Roman, occupation occurred, and we observed that the refuse above these had recently been added to by contemporary Arab squatters who had obviously used the cave as a rude shelter only a year or two before our visit. It was extremely exciting thus to stand in this wild place on the Mediterranean shore and see with one's own eyes such a vast range of history recorded in the earth.

As revealed at Apollonia and elsewhere, the later phases of man's prehistoric advance in the Mediterranean, which represent the transition to civilisation and written history, are perhaps the most exciting of all. This was the time when man's evolving brain enabled him to refine the pleasures (if such they can be called) of a rough, hunting life and to embark on a new form of existence in permanent settled communities. The most highly evolved prehistoric phase is known as the Neolithic, or New Stone Age, from the more advanced and sophisticated type of stone implements which are found at the sites. As it progressed it merged imperceptibly first into the Bronze Age and then into the Iron Age, the evolution of metal cultures being associated with the dawn of the most ancient civilisations.

Man Comes to the Mediterranean

The dating of these phases of human development does not lend itself to an exact chronology in years. As the late Professor Gordon Childe used to point out, some mystic trumpet did not sound in heaven causing men to drop their stone tools and take up metal ones on an exact date; the process was gradual and took place at different times in different places. But very broadly speaking, the Neolithic Age of the Mediterranean was well established on the eastern shores of the sea by 8000 BC and moved gradually westwards. Between four and five thousand years later metals were already in use in Egypt and civilisation was well under way.

The discoveries that made this new phase of life possible were the seasonal cultivation of crops and the domestication of animals. Even in the early days of the nomadic hunters it must occasionally have been possible to supplement the supply of vegetable food taken from wild plants by a snatch crop. It is also very likely that the dog had been domesticated as a hunting companion by that time by the adoption of wolf-cubs, brought at first into the camp circle as pets. But it was not until the Neolithic phase proper that agriculture and the domestication of edible stock allowed the first settlements to grow up on the Mediterranean shores. Although these settlements were at first very rudimentary and may have needed to be moved a mile or two as the first site became exhausted, they finally marked the end of the days of long seasonal migrations to keep contact with the game. The road to civilisation had been opened.

The first cultivated crops in the Mediterranean region were such plants as wheat, oats, rye, barley, flax, and beans. The cultivated forms of these plants were descended from wild ancestors, native mainly to the hilly country of the Asiatic seaboard. Here, for instance, in what are now Lebanon, Israel, and Iraq, grew the plant known as emmer, and further to the north a related species known as dinkel. These wild grasses had the property of growing and ripening quickly, and their seeds could be stored from one season to the next, making planned sowing possible year after year. The more refined implements of polished stone that had now evolved aided the first Mediterranean farmers to prepare the soil and gradually establish increasingly sophisticated methods of agriculture.

Other plants were used to make baskets and, when interwoven, the walls of huts, which were then rendered weatherproof with clay and thatched with reeds and the stems of grasses. Fire was of course widely used as it had been since man's earliest days, but now its value for firing pots came to be understood. The idea of making the first pot for cooking or storage was possibly the result of the accidental dropping of some clay into the white-hot embers of an ancient hearth. One of our more observant ancestors would have noticed how the clay became hardened into a rigid solid. Thus were the principles of firing first discovered, from which it was but a step to the fashioning of clay objects into various shapes, and treating them deliberately with fire to make them sufficiently durable to hold grain, fluids, and cooked foods.

Alongside the development of material culture and farming, the domestication of animals, leading to controlled stock-rearing was also taking place along the Mediterranean shores. The domestication of such animals

The original wild plants on which Mediterranean man founded his agriculture. (*Left*) wild emmer and emmer; (*Right*) dinkel.

79

as the sheep and the goat is particularly characteristic of the Eastern Basin. The ox and the pig, two other animals basic to a stock-rearing economy, were probably first domesticated not only in the east but along the whole Mediterranean littoral as far west as Spain. There are still differences in the minds of archaeologists concerning exactly which species of wild animal gave rise to the various domestic forms, but these specialist wrangles need not concern us here. To sum up the probabilities, it is likely that the ox is descended from the aurochs, or wild bull, of the late Pleistocene; the pig from the wild boar; the sheep from the wild argali; and the goat from the bezoar. This is, of course, a great over-simplification; the pig, for instance, almost certainly numbers two types of wild boar among its ancestors, and the aurochs gave rise not only to the domestic ox of the fields (which may in some cases have been crossed with the zebu) but to the bulls which inspired such legends as that of the Minotaur, and those which are still bred today to fight in the arenas of Spain.

The stages by which domestication occurred are of course conjectural, but it seems very probable that the instinct to pet young animals may have led partially to their acceptance, or at least tolerance, in the family circle if they strayed into an encampment or were orphaned by the killing of their parents in the hunt. More realistically, young animals were probably kept in wattle-fenced paddocks until they grew to a size large enough for slaughter. But gradually men discovered the advantages of a more elaborate organisation of their domestic stock. Young pigs were not only diverting, and a source of meat when they became adult, but their flesh had a different *quality* if they were eaten young. It was therefore to the advantage of man's palate if some adults were preserved purely for breeding purposes. Thus out of chance happenings, exploited by the more perceptive of our ancestors, Mediterranean gastronomy had its origins. And so it was with many aspects of life in Neolithic times. Quality began to be added to quantity as a yardstick for measuring values.

Archaeological remains from the Neolithic and early Bronze Age of the Mediterranean are widespread and of the very greatest interest. They not only include the skulls of domesticated animals and the pots and implements used by men, but some quite elaborate structures, either of brick or masonry, and evidence of an advanced level of social organisation. Elaborate burials show the increasing complexity of religious beliefs, and the remains of works of pure art and even of musical instruments give proof that man was already well advanced in the use of material means to express metaphysical emotions. These processes, which have manifested themselves in different forms in successive civilisations, were pioneered in the Mediterranean long before a similar stage was reached in the other well-known evolutionary centres of civilisation in the Far East.

Among the Neolithic sites that travellers in the region can most excitingly explore are Jericho, in the Levant, and Çatal Hüyük, in Anatolia. The earliest remains of both date from approximately the same period, that is between 6000 and 8000 BC, but many later phases can be recognised. Jericho, whose later history will be familiar to readers of the Old Testament, lies in a depression below sea level 24 kilometres or 15 miles from Jerusalem in the valley of the Jordan. Its ramparts of brick belong to the Bronze Age, when it dominated some of the chief trade routes from Jerusalem, but the Neolithic pottery and implements found at lower levels show that its antiquity may considerably exceed that of the earliest Neolithic communities in the Nile Valley. Çatal Hüyük was more recently discovered and excavated by Professor James Mellaart of London University. Here again are the remains of a long sequence of habitations, and the finds include whole houses of masonry sufficiently well preserved to show that they were built around courtyards. There were separate living rooms and storage rooms, the first being equipped with raised sleeping platforms, hearths, ovens, and grain bins; the storage rooms were entered by ladders from the roof. The metaphysical culture of early man can also be most interestingly studied here. The bones of ancestors are deposited beneath the sleeping platforms, and skulls have often been restored with plaster and shells inserted in the eye-sockets. There are also the remains of an elaborate bull cult, comparable with, but much older than, the bull cults of Egypt, Crete, and other Mediterranean lands.

In such ancient cities and villages we can relive in our imaginations the triumphant march of early Mediterranean man from savagery to civilisation. They conjure up a stirring picture of the many millions of men long since dead whose growing knowledge, passed from generation to generation, began the shaping of the modern world. The rest of the story belongs to the Age of Civilisation, when written records and a multiplication of art forms provide a fuller picture of the process.

Wild ancestors of the domesticated animals. (*From top left, clockwise*) Aurochs, argali, bezoar, and wild boar.

4

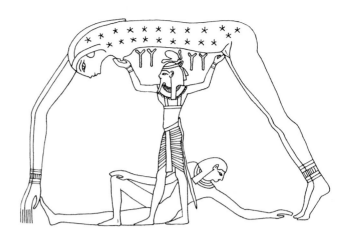

The Dawn of Mediterranean Civilisation: Ancient Egypt

Civilisation on Earth began independently in three river valleys – the Indus, the Euphrates/Tigris, and the Nile – but the civilisation of ancient Egypt on the Nile, although perhaps a little younger than the Sumerian civilisation of the Euphrates and the Tigris, is much the best known. Dating back some six thousand years, it was the starting point of Mediterranean man's first experiment in complex socialisation, and even embodied in its structure institutions such as the calendar, which are an indispensable part of civilisation today.

Why was the Nile valley the site of this first Mediterranean experiment in civilisation? The answer lies in geography, and particularly in that branch of it known as human geography which studies the distribution of man and his works in relation to his environment. As the first farmers grew in number and formed larger agglomerations it was necessary that they should find the answer to two main problems. The first was to devise a means to refertilise the soil on whose richness their crops depended, so that by its exhaustion they were not constantly having to move to new territory. The second was to find the easiest possible means of communication and transport so that their surplus goods could be exchanged with those of others in neighbouring regions.

The Nile was particularly suitable for both these purposes. It has always been a river subject to seasonal floods depending mainly on the seasonal rainfall and thawing of snow in the Ethiopian highlands. These floods were predictable, and their inundation of the river banks provided the rich silt so necessary for rejuvenating the soil. The Nile was also an easily navigable 'moving road', allowing ships and barges to carry goods up and

(*Above*) The goddess Nut whose star-studded body was believed by the ancient Egyptians to span the sky at night. (*Opposite*) The Great Sphinx at Giza.

83

down stream for a distance of nearly 1,600 kilometres (1,000 miles). As man became more adventurous it provided access to the sea for larger ships and a way by which visiting traders could bring their goods inland with a minimum of labour.

The special geography of the lower Nile valley also determined many aspects of ancient Egyptian civilisation. Although when this civilisation was in its early stages the rainfall of north-east Africa was considerably higher than it is today, the climate was becoming continually more arid and the Western and Eastern Deserts were advancing closer and closer to the river banks. Eventually, though quite early in history, the habitable land was reduced to a narrow strip averaging only some 5 to 7 kilometres (3 to 4 miles), in breadth on either side of the river. Even today – apart from the delta and the city of Alexandria – this strip, together with a few small towns on the North African coast and the Red Sea and some still smaller settlements in the oases, constitutes the whole living space of Egypt. It is a phenomenon unique in human geography to find a country with an area of a million square kilometres (386,111 square miles) in which a population of more than 32 million is concentrated in an area of just over 35,000 square kilometres (13,000 square miles).

In ancient Egyptian times there were of course far fewer people in the Nile valley, but its special geography nevertheless had a strong influence on the organisation of its civilisation. The extreme narrowness of the fertile strip from east to west and the easy transport provided by the river between north and south made an homogeneous civilisation comparatively easy to achieve. Where, as in ancient Greece, a country is broken up by mountain barriers, there is an inevitable tendency for society to evolve in small and comparatively isolated groups and unity is very difficult to achieve. In Egypt, however, this was not the case, and at the very dawn of its civilisation it cohered naturally into only two kingdoms. These were the kingdoms of Upper and Lower Egypt respectively, and even they very quickly combined as one. The formation of the valley also played a part in such unexpected aspects of life as religion. The Nile formed a natural barrier between the land of the rising sun to the east and of the setting sun to the west. What more natural than that its right bank should be regarded as the land of the living, the left bank as the land of the dead?

With the growing desiccation of North Africa the amount of water in the Nile valley gradually fell, for from the point some 2,560 kilometres (1,600 miles), from its mouth where its northernmost tributary, the Atbara, joins the main stream, it had to do battle with the desert sands without further contributions of water. It emphasises the immense resources of this river that it actually reaches the Mediterranean at all after traversing such parched and inhospitable country. Yet it does so, and the only evidence of this titanic struggle is provided by the terraces on either side of the lower reaches left, as the amount of water in the river gradually decreased and its bed cut ever deeper and narrower into the north-eastern corner of the African land mass.

It is on these terraces, incidentally, that the earliest phases of the development of Egyptian man can be deciphered. A prehistoric culture sequence, including many beautiful as well as practical objects, gives archaeologists the means to reconstruct something of the lives of the Egyptians before the establishment of the first pharaohonic dynasties.

There are eight terraces in all, beginning just above Cairo and continuing inland to the border of the Sudan, but in the lower four no trace of human habitation can be found. This does not mean that man was unknown in the region at that time, which dates back to the early Pleistocene, for he must already have been travelling down the Nile valley from his evolutionary cradle in East Africa to fan out east and west to Asia, to the European peninsula and along the Mediterranean littoral of Africa. The most likely explanation is either that he did not pause there long enough to make lavish encampments, or, more likely, that the sites of habitations have simply not yet been found. The four upper terraces are, however, rich in remains of artifacts of the Mousterian type used by Neanderthal Man and of a stone culture similar to at least one that was developed by true men in western Europe. Then comes a pause where all traces are obliterated by the Nile mud, after which artifacts, dating back to the Neolithic and the Chalcolithic, or Copper, Age are followed by a comparatively swift transition to civilised life.

What criterion can be applied to define civilisation, a word much abused and misunderstood and susceptible to a vast number of loose interpretations? Such a definition must essentially be subjective, but one criterion of great practical use, which I intend to employ here, is the invention of writing. A secondary consideration of almost equal importance is the discovery of archaeological remains showing beyond any shadow of doubt that men were collecting together into comparatively large agglomerations where there was a distinct specialisation of roles. For example, even in the absence of traces of writing, the ruins of houses, stables, temples, gardens, tombs, granaries, and other characteristic structures of an integrated community would be enough for our purpose to state that we are dealing with 'civilisation'. At different times there have been attempts to complicate these simple criteria by introducing more abstract definitions. For instance in his essay on 'Western Civilisation' in *In Praise of Idleness* even the late Bertrand Russell fell into the trap of defining civilisation as 'a way of life due to the combination of knowledge and forethought' – a definition that is equally applicable to the first tool-making ape-men and even, as has been recently shown by the British scientist Jane Goodall, to wild chimpanzees. Kenneth Clark in his book *Civilisation*, describing himself as contemplating Paris from the Pont des Arts, writes more cautiously than Russell: 'What is civilisation? I don't know. I can't describe it in abstract terms – yet. But I think I can recognise it when I see it; and I am looking at it now.' But perhaps this is too vague and, *faute de mieux*, I still maintain that my simple definitions, conventional as they may seem, are more valuable than a paragraph of abstractions. But perhaps it will always be true that no definition, however simple, however abstract, can put civilisation neatly on the dissecting table. Its essence, as Clark implies, must be felt rather than explained. It is a spiritual as well as an historical phenomenon.

Ancient Egypt

Nevertheless, by our simple criteria, the civilisation of ancient Egypt can be said to have begun during the second half of the fourth millennium BC. The nearest approach we can make to a date for the beginning of a moderately well-established chronology is 3400 BC, when the predynastic Neolithic and Chalcolithic cultures of the Nile matured into the two well-organised monarchies already referred to, one in the delta and the other in the Nile valley proper. Some two centuries later the delta region was subjugated by the south and under King Menes a united Egypt was established. From then until the Persian Conquest in 525 BC was the golden age of the Pharaohs, which saw the dramatic rise, flowering, and slow decline of the Mediterranean's first experiment in civilisation.

I do not intend to give the reader even the briefest record of events in ancient Egyptian history. Compressed to a few paragraphs, all light and shade would be lost and even the best catalogue is a boring companion. The books where this fascinating story is simply and readably told at sufficient length are listed in the Appendix. Here I shall select only some highlights of what can be learnt by tourists and travellers who visit Egypt today with a particular eye for the living story lying behind the archaeological wonders. For to the imaginative person who equips himself with a few facts, an ancient ruin is not just a corpse in stone; it can be filled with the warm, pulsating life of the men and women who laboured and loved and hoped and died within its shadow.

To the ordinary traveller in the Mediterranean, the first archaeological remains to come to mind at the mention of the word 'Egypt' are the pyramids. And this is only natural, for have they not been numbered throughout the centuries as one of the Seven Wonders of the World? In an age that is now felt to be so full of marvels that the imagination can hardly begin to grasp them, it has become fashionable for superior people to regard the pyramids in a somewhat blasé spirit. But this superficial reaction is soon dispelled by maturer reflections. By any standards the building of these great tombs of the Pharaohs remains even in an age of space exploration one of the most daring projects ever to have been conceived and successfully carried through by human endeavour.

All the Egyptian pyramids stand on the left bank of the Nile. That is, they belong to the 'Land of the West', associated in the ancient Egyptian mind with the Kingdom of the Dead where the sun sets daily over the Saharan wastes. The largest is the Great Pyramid of Cheops (the Greek name for the pharaoh Khufu) at Giza, a few minutes drive from the centre of Cairo; the oldest the so-called 'Step Pyramid' of Zoser at Sakkara a few miles to the south. All the great pyramids belong to the Old Kingdom – that is, the period occupied by the Third to Sixth Dynasties which roughly covered the years 2686-2181 BC. The pyramids, of which the great majority are built on the fringe of the Western Desert, number about eighty between Abu Roash in the north and Meidum in the south; but many of these are vestigial, only dust and rubble remaining to mark the site of their former splendour. The great pyramids of the Old Kingdom still in a good state of repair can be numbered on the fingers of two hands.

Aerial view of the Pyramids at Giza, on the edge of the Nile valley.

Ancient Egypt

The Step Pyramid at Sakkara was not intended to have the four smooth surfaces usually associated with pyramids but, as its name suggests, consists of a number of stepped layers of diminishing size built one above the other. It represents the earliest stage in the evolution of pyramid tombs and is nearly five thousand years old. As the Old Kingdom progressed the design of the pyramids was elaborated and the Pyramid of Cheops, the largest of the three still standing at Giza, represents the apotheosis of this trend. The first sight of this mighty structure, raising its vast bulk from the desert was one of my most memorable experiences in a life-time of travel, equalled only by my first sight of the Grand Canyon in Colorado. The effect is of a man-made mountain, and as one later approaches it on foot the sense of immensity and weight is so overwhelming as to inspire a mixture of reverence and terror.

Statistics, often so dull, add an extra dimension to one's appreciation of this extraordinary building. The top $10\frac{1}{2}$ metres (31 feet) of the pyramid are now missing, but originally it rose to a height of 148 metres (481.4 feet). Its base is, within inches, an exact square, each side being some $232\frac{1}{2}$ metres (756 feet) long. The area covered is 5 hectares (13.1 acres). But it is the sheer volume of the stone used in its construction that paralyses and even oppresses the imagination. Making allowance for the comparatively fractional amount of space taken up by passageways and chambers inside the pyramid, the weight of the stone of which it is composed is at least 5,700,000 tons. It is built up of some 2,300,000 individual blocks, some of which weigh over 15 tons.

To make these statistics more comprehensible several comparisons may be used. For example, St Paul's Cathedral, Westminster Abbey, St Peter's at Rome and the cathedrals of Florence and Milan could all be stood in its base-area. If the stone of the pyramid were cut into cubes measuring a foot each way these would, if laid end to end, reach about two-thirds of the distance round the earth at the equator. One particularly graphic illustration was thought up by Napoleon during his Egyptian campaign. Accompanied by some of his generals he visited the pyramid and the generals decided to climb it. Napoleon, being a sensible man, preferred to wait at his ease at the base and while doing so worked out that there was sufficient stone in the pyramid to build a wall ten feet high and one foot thick round the whole of France. This estimate was confirmed, it is said, by the famous mathematician and physicist Gaspard Monge, the inventor of descriptive geometry, who was one of the scientists on the expedition.

It is still possible to climb the Great Pyramid today if one is in good condition and does not suffer from vertigo. The Tura limestone with which it was once faced to give it a smooth surface was plundered long ago except for a few fragments near the base, and the pyramid consists of a number of rough 'steps' taller than a man. However, there are routes known to the guides, or 'dragomans', by which these can be negotiated on foot. The view from the top, stretching across the Nile to the Mokattam Hills in the east, over the green acres of the delta to the north and the wastes of the Sahara to the west, and southwards along the narrow fertile strip bordering the river, is one of the most moving in the world. Espe-

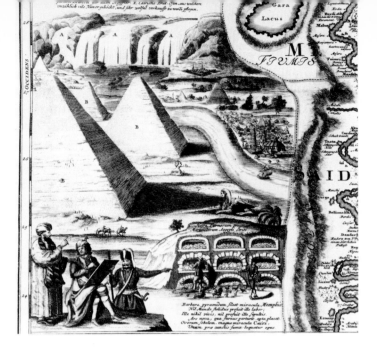

cially as the sun descends as a great red disc to the desert horizon, one can
recapture here the feeling of awe that must have so deeply affected the
ancient Egyptians as they saw this mysterious life-giving fire in the
heavens. They identified it with the great Sun God Ré-Atum of Heliopolis, who they believed either flew in the form of a falcon or was pro-
pelled by a scarab-beetle on a daily journey westward from the land of the
living to the land of the dead. He then returned during the night through
the body of the goddess Nut, which they believed spanned the sky like a
gigantic arch.

The sheer magnitude of the pyramids is a sufficient cause for wonder,
but it is at least equalled by our appreciation of the immense labour and
difficulty of constructing them. They are an achievement that was made
possible only by the existence of a slave society, although it seems that the
ancient Egyptians treated their slaves well and their lot was in general a
happy one. The pyramids, like all ancient Egyptian buildings, were
designed by highly-skilled architects who belonged to a professional élite.
They had to consider a large number of complex problems even before the
first stone was put into place; for instance, they needed a good knowledge
of the geology of the region so that a site could be chosen where the rock
substratum was solid enough to bear the colossal weight without cracking
or subsidence. They then had to see that the surface sand was removed
and the rock of the foundations fully exposed and levelled. The extraordinary accuracy with which this was achieved is demonstrated particularly by the Great Pyramid, where the margin of deviation from an
absolutely level plain throughout the whole vast perimeter is in the region
of half an inch.

Once the site was prepared the tremendous labour of quarrying and
transporting the rock began. The main quarries were on the right bank of
the Nile, so the vast blocks of masonry had to be ferried across on barges
and then transported to Giza on sledges and rollers. The sledge was pulled
along the rollers by gangs of many hundreds of men and raised to the

desired height by ramps which could be built higher and higher as each successive level was reached. Altogether thousands of slaves worked on the construction for periods of many years, and a human touch is to know that these pyramid-builders were divided into gangs with individual names and marked their names on the quarried stones. For example, at the Pyramid of Meidum such inscriptions as 'Vigorous Gang', 'Sceptre Gang' and 'Enduring Gang' have been discovered, while at the Great Pyramid itself a block bears the words: 'Craftsmen Gang: how powerful is the White Crown of Khnum Khufu!'

The archaeological remains in Egypt, even within a day's drive of the twin mouths of the Nile, are so numerous as to give the traveller cultural indigestion. Apart from the pyramids and many smaller tombs, a profusion of temples, shrines, and the remains of houses give the imaginative person exciting clues to the life and beliefs of the men of this earliest Mediterranean civilisation. But it is essential to be selective if one is not to lose one's way in a maze of detail, and all I can do here is to name a few outstanding sites. The visitor to the region should follow two golden rules. The first is to read a few of the books listed in the Appendix at his leisure before setting out. The second is to break off his expedition immediately he begins to feel hot and cross. Part of one site, seen with perception and reflected on in a local café, will be a far more valuable memory than a frantic attempt to see everything, which is anyway impossible even to men who have devoted a life-time to Egyptology.

A few yards from the Great Pyramid stands the Great Sphinx. There are innumerable sphinxes in Egypt, but none as imposing as this huge couchant beast that guards the Pyramids of Giza. The role of sphinxes in Egyptian religion was a protectors of sacred places, and they were usually represented with lion-like bodies and human heads. The Great Sphinx at Giza, probably sculpted in the time of Chephren, the commonly-used Greek name for the Pharaoh Khafre, is said to be an actual portrait of the Pharaoh, not just a formalised representation. Its proportions are on the scale of the pyramids themselves, for it measures some 74 metres (240 feet) long and $20\frac{1}{3}$ metres (66 feet) high. The head alone, at its widest, has a breadth of 4 metres 11 centimetres (13 feet 8 inches).

In spite of its familiarity to tourists and its representation in hundreds of thousands of book illustrations, the Great Sphinx is one of the most evocative statues in Egypt. This is not just due to its extraordinary magnitude – although size alone can have a considerable emotional effect when a conception is as daring as this. It lies rather in the combination of the strength of the recumbent body and the calm expression of the face, which seems rapt in contemplation of some wondrous but infinitely distant vision.

Less well known to most people than the Sphinx at Giza is the so-called 'Solar Boat'; discovered in the early 1950s. This lies in a pit near the Great Pyramid and owes its unique state of preservation to having been sealed beneath a roof of forty-two stone blocks. The interstices of these were filled with gypsum by the ancient Egyptians and the whole was then gradually covered by wind-blown sand. The boat, which is made of wood,

Statue of the sacred bull Apis from the Serapeum at Sakkara.

is nearly 30 metres (100 feet) long with a high prow, oars, fenders, a rudder, and mats made from rushes and leaves. Its exact significance in Egyptian religion is unknown, but it is believed to be associated with Sun worship in some form, perhaps to bear the Pharaoh in his role of Sun God across the sky. Another possible explanation is that it was simply provided for the use or diversion of the Pharaoh in the Land of the Dead.

Not far from Giza is Sakkara, where the Step Pyramid already mentioned is man's earliest spectacular triumph in large-scale architectural construction. But also at this site, and even more evocative than the pyramid, is the Serapeum, the burial place of the sacred bulls. The bull cults of the early civilisations of the Mediterranean have already been noted in passing, and their history and interrelations right down to the ritual of the modern Spanish bull-ring form a fascinating, if complicated, story. In ancient Egypt the worship of sacred bulls was an extremely important part of religious belief and was associated, as are all bull cults, with the attractions of power and potency.

The sacred bulls of ancient Egypt were for the most part identified with the god Apis, and during their lifetime were kept in the Temple of Apis which stood near the Serapeum at Memphis. This great ancient Egyptian city formerly extended for many acres around the Step Pyramid at what is now known as Sakkara. During the long centuries when the bull cult flourished at Memphis there was only one sacred bull in the temple at a time. When this bull died its spirit was supposed to pass into its successor, which had to be a bull peculiarly marked to conform with the Egyptians' idea of their Bull God. If we are to believe Herodotus, not always a very wise thing to do despite his attractive and readable style, a suitable bull must have been very difficult to find. He describes the obligatory characteristics as follows: 'He is black, with a square spot of white upon his forehead, and on his back is the figure of an eagle; the hairs in his tail are doubled, and there is a beetle upon his tongue.' The likelihood of all these characteristics coming up at once or, indeed, of some of them coming up at all, suggests that the priests must have exercised a good deal of licence. However, we do have evidence that those who provided bulls acceptable to replace the living Apis were handsomely rewarded with honour and gifts of land.

The death of a sacred bull was the signal for a ceremonial interment in the Serapeum as well as rejoicings at the advent of its successor. The Serapeum itself is one of the most impressive and evocative of all Egyptian sites. It once formed part of a complex of chapels, temples, and guardian sphinxes, but many of the sphinxes have been buried in the desert sand and only scanty ruins of most of the structures remain. The whole complex properly bears the name Serapeum, but this is now restricted in general usage to the mausoleum of the bulls as being the best preserved remnant. It was discovered by the famous French Egyptologist Auguste Mariette, whose excavation headquarters nearby have since been turned into a rather disheartening refreshment stall. The mausoleum lies entirely below ground level and is approached by a ramp, at the foot of which one turns left into the galleries. Here, in an oven-like temperature, a central aisle is flanked on either side by a series of great side-chambers or chapels measuring about 3 metres (12 feet) wide and 6 metres (20 feet) high, their floors sunk several feet below the level of the aisle. The sarcophagi of the bulls, which are fashioned from red or black granite in a plain rectangular shape, are about $3\frac{1}{2}$ metres (13 feet) long, $2\frac{1}{3}$ metres ($7\frac{1}{2}$ feet) wide and $2\frac{3}{4}$ metres (11 feet) tall. Each weighs about 65 tons.

In his report of the discovery Mariette writes: 'I confess that when I penetrated for the first time on 12 November 1851 into the Apis vaults, I was so profoundly struck with astonishment that the feeling is still fresh in my mind, although five years have elapsed since then.'

When my wife and I repeated Mariette's adventure some hundred years after he had first penetrated the mausoleum, we were affected by similar emotions. These were heightened by a discovery we made on our way back to the daylight by an alternative ramp to the one we had used to descend. Here, about half way up, was jammed one of the sarcophagi which must have been left where it was at the very moment it was on the point of being placed in the vault. The space between the sarcophagus and the walls of the passage-way was so narrow that we could only squeeze through with difficulty. What can have been the reason for this interrupted labour? Had there been war, or pestilence, or had the cult of the sacred bull of Apis suddenly fallen into disrepute? For the aware and curious time-traveller, not only in Egypt but in the whole Mediterranean region, such tantalising enigmas are always presenting themselves.

Before leaving ancient Memphis there is one other site of particular interest because, like so many of the remains further afield in Upper Egypt, it gives us an insight into the daily lives of these first civilised

Mediterraneans. This is the Tomb of Ti. The tomb lies a short distance from Mariette's house and is approached by a track across the hot desert sands. It is built on two levels, the upper one consisting of a small pillared courtyard, two chapels, and a *serdab*, or doorless room, which was the habitation of the spirit of the dead person. Below lies the actual burial chamber containing the tomb. Ti himself was a man of humble birth who reached high office in the early years of the Fifth Dynasty and eventually married a girl named Neferhoteps, a member of the royal family and possibly the grand-daughter of a Pharaoh. But the main interest of the tomb today is that it contains some of the finest representations of visual art to be created in ancient Egypt, many of them depicting scenes of everyday life from which one can reconstruct a vivid picture of the times.

The pictures are in bas-relief, and many of them have still preserved their brilliant coloration. They reveal that Ti must have been a very wealthy man indeed and also an attractive one – if his noble features and good-natured expression are not due to the flattery of sycophantic artists. He seems to have been an enthusiastic and efficient farmer, and some of

Interior of the Serapeum at Sakkara, with the fallen lid of a bull's sarcophagus.

Coloured relief from the tomb of Ti at Sakkara; the figures of slaves and cattle symbolize the extent of the deceased's estates and possessions.

the pictures show him and his wife inspecting their estates with obvious pride. Much can be learnt from the pictures of the agricultural customs of the closing years of the Old Kingdom, more than four thousand years ago. Representations of sowing, tilling, reaping, and winnowing are all to be found, together with pictures of cattle being fed, rams treading in the newly-scattered seed and even of clerks in the estate office completing stock sheets and filling up returns of the different kinds of produce. Although much Egyptian art is rather static and formal, these pictures in the Tomb of Ti are remarkable for their naturalism and vitality. For instance, in one carpentry scene the impression of life and energetic activity would do credit to the most talented artist working on studies of arts and crafts in any Mediterranean country today. Pictures of animals, such as birds calling or taking flight, calves kicking up their heels in the fields, or Ti hunting hippopotamus, are equally lively. The long history – one might almost say the timelessness – of these basic human activities, which have persisted alongside all the refinements of man's most advanced technology, is emphasised at many Mediterranean sites, but nowhere is its enduring quality better revealed than in this early sophisticated example.

I said earlier that one of the definitions I was going to use for civilisation was the development of writing, and this occurred at an early date in ancient Egyptian history. The value of writing in communicating ideas is obvious. It makes it unnecessary for people to be together in the same place at the same time or to depend on oral traditions handed down from

94

generation to generation with all the consequent dangers of distortion or loss.

The characteristic writing of ancient Egypt, at least for formal purposes, was the hieroglyphic script, which evolved from the simple pictograms and ideograms of still earlier times. Pictograms represent writing at its most primitive, the object being simply represented by a crude drawing. Thus such objects as a flower, a horn, the sun, the moon, or an arrow or stone implement, would be expressed by an engraved or other visual representation of the object itself. In ideograms this process was somewhat refined, a key object in some general idea or situation being more or less symbolically employed to represent the whole. Thus the picture of an arrow would not only be used to represent the arrow as such, but, perhaps, a battle or a hunt with arrows. From this point writing became still more elaborate and in the hieroglyphs a whole set of different signs and symbols are employed in various combinations to represent quite subtle sequences of ideas. It would not be relevant here to go into this question in depth, but the hieroglyphic writing of ancient Egypt was obviously of great historical importance in the development of communication as a whole. Even the visitor to Egypt whose interests do not extend to studying hieroglyphs in any detail will find them both intriguing and visually attractive.

One result of the development of writing was that it enables us to learn something of the ideas and legends of early people as expressed in their literature. Some of the most beautiful and evocative legends of the ancient Mediterraneans are, for instance, immortalised either in hieroglyphic writing itself or in the so-called 'hieratic script' which was simplified from the more elaborate hieroglyphs for everyday use. These legends were sometimes recorded on stone, but more often by scribes who wrote them down on scrolls of papyrus. Papyrus, from which the word 'paper' is derived, is a kind of swamp plant which used to exist in profusion along

A single head of papyrus. Apart from the use of papyrus stems for making writing-material, the shape of the plant itself was a constant inspiration to the ancient Egyptian artist and architect.

the banks of the Egyptian Nile and still grows over vast areas in the upper reaches of the White Nile in the Sudan. To make papyrus scrolls the ancient Egyptians used first to cut the stems into lengths about a foot long, which were then flattened and dried. The stems were next placed side by side in a layer, with a second layer above and at right angles to the first. Finally the two layers were coated with an adhesive substance and pressed together. Another material used for writing was a block of wood or flake of limestone coated with plaster. This was used owing to the expense of papyrus, and the plaster was incised with the hieroglyphic or hieratic characters. Sometimes these blocks were fastened together at one side by strings made of palm fibre so that they resembled a cumbersome version of a modern book.

One of the most touching ancient Egyptian legends to be handed down to us is that of the great goddess Isis and her husband Osiris, who was also her brother. Isis personified the seat or throne of Osiris, but when the latter was elevated in Egyptian mythology to the place of chief god she became a goddess of equal importance. Not only was she the consort of Osiris, but also Goddess of the Moon and the Nile. The cow was her sacred animal, its branching horns representing the crescent moon, and her chief temples were at Abydos, Busiris, and Philae. Her temple at Philae, built by Ptolemy II, was the last centre of pagan worship in Egypt, and remained in active operation until it was closed by the Emperor Justinian in the sixth century AD. Isis was the symbol of the mystery of idealised womanhood and of wifely fidelity, and her worship was practised not only in

(*Left*) The goddess Isis, engraved on one of the sides of the granite sarcophagus of Rameses III; 20th Dynasty.

(*Opposite, top*) Relief from the mastaba tomb of Ti, at Sakkara, showing a procession of slave girls carrying sacrificial offerings. (*Bottom*) Wooden model of a bakery and brewery, from Deir-el Bahari. 11th Dynasty.

ancient Egypt but in Greece under the name of Aphrodite and in Rome under the name of Juno. The Greek philosopher Proclus, of the fifth century BC, quotes an inscription on a statue which reveals her identification with the eternal feminine. It reads: 'I am that which is, has been, and shall be. My veil no-one has lifted. The fruit I bore was the sun.' Hence is derived the phrase 'to lift the veil of Isis', meaning to penetrate to the heart of a great mystery; the inscription also reveals certain parallels with the idealised character of the Virgin Mary.

But it is in legend that the more human qualities of Isis are revealed – that is, her capacity for simple wifely care and loyalty and the devotion she showed when disaster overcame her husband. According to the legend, Isis learnt that the brother of Osiris, who was named Set, was jealous of the God-King's popularity and success, and hankered to overthrow him. She warned Osiris of the danger, but the god's character was so pure that he could not allow himself to believe badly of anyone, least of all his own brother. This was his undoing. According to Plutarch, Set 'contrived a proper strategem to execute his base designs'. He invited Osiris and a number of his own henchmen to a great banquet at which was produced a richly-ornamented chest. This was much admired, and Set said he would give it to whichever of his guests would be found to fit it exactly. Many of the guests jokingly lay down in the chest, but by pre-arrangement it was made sure that they were either too short or too tall to fit it; the chest had in fact been especially made to fit the body of Osiris exactly. When the God-King's turn came and he lay down in the chest, the conspirators immediately slammed shut the lid and fastened it down with nails, pouring molten lead over it to seal the cracks. It was then thrown into the Nile and floated away towards the sea.

When Isis heard of her husband's fate, Plutarch records that 'she immediately cut off one of the locks of her hair and put on mourning apparel upon the very spot where she then happened to be. ... After this she wandered everywhere about the country full of disquietude and perplexity in search of the chest, enquiring of every person she met with, even of some children whom she chanced to see, whether they knew what was become of it'.

From one of the children she questioned, Isis learnt that the chest had been thrown into the Nile, and she eventually found it lying in one of the great papyrus swamps of the delta. She bore it away and, Plutarch continues, 'no sooner was she arrived in a desert place, where she imagined herself to be alone, but she presently opened the chest and laying her face upon her dead husband's, embraced his corpse and wept bitterly'. She hid the body in the desert sands, hoping thereby to preserve it and allowing Osiris to take his place in the realms of the dead. But Set had heard of its rescue and went in search of it. Eventually it was found, and in his fury at the discovery that it was still intact, he hacked it into fourteen pieces which were scattered throughout the whole land of Egypt. However, the faithful Isis set out once more in search of the remains, burying each where she found it and consecrating a shrine to immortalise the spot. Eventually the whole body was found except for the penis, which Set had thrown into

(*Opposite*) Unfinished quartzite head of Queen Nefertiti, found in the sculptors' studio at Tell-el-Amarna. 18th Dynasty.

Ancient Egypt

the Nile. It was there eaten by a fish, which was ever afterwards held to be sacred by the followers of Osiris. The God-King was eventually avenged by his son, Horus, who overcame Set in single combat, but Isis remained inconsolable. She became in Egyptian religious tradition the symbol of sorrowing womanhood and it was believed that the annual rising of the Nile was caused by her tears.

Although poetry and literature are among the glories of most Mediterranean countries, artistic expression of this kind is not usually associated with ancient Egypt. Yet Egypt has, for those who know it, a poetic tradition of great beauty, particularly in the field of love poems. Indeed it is not surprising that the beautiful, high-born ladies of the court with their dignified bearing and challenging eyes, and the slim, provocative dancing girls who added to the gaiety of Egyptian feasts, should inspire men to devotion. In the songs dedicated to these sensual and alluring women one can detect also the spirit of romance which characterised the finest poets of later times. Here, for example, is a poem to an unknown queen who lived about 700 BC, from an Egyptian stele now preserved in the Louvre:

(*Above*) Isis is often represented in Egyptian art as Woman herself, without any of the trappings of a goddess, as in this exquisite statue in the Louvre.

The Salt Head, one of the masterpieces of Egyptian sculpture. This painted limestone head was found in the region of Thebes at the beginning of the nineteenth century and is thought to date from the New Kingdom.

'The sweet one, sweet in love; the sweet one, sweet in love in the presence of the king; the sweet one, sweet in love before all men; the beloved before all women; the king's daughter who is sweet in love. The fairest among women, a maid whose like none has seen. Blacker is her hair than the darkness of night, blacker than the berries of the blackberry bush. Harder are her teeth than the flints on a sickle. A wreath of flowers in each of her breasts, close nestling on her arm.'

Painted limestone group of Akhnaton and Nefertiti. Amarna period, end of the 18th Dynasty.

And here is another example from a collection of poems composed about 1200 BC:

'The kisses of my beloved are on the other bank of the river; a branch of the stream floweth between us, a crocodile lurketh on the sand-bank. But I step down into the water and plunge into the flood. My courage is great in the waters, the waves are as solid ground under my feet. Love of her lendeth me strength. Ah! She hath given me a spell for the waters.

'When I kiss her, and her lips are open, then need I not ale to inspire me. When the time is come to make ready the couch, oh servant! then say I unto thee: "Lay fine linen between her limbs, a bed for her of royal linen; give heed to the white embroidered linen, besprinkled with the finest oil." '

In such poems we can catch a glimpse of the essential humanity and passion of this ancient Mediterranean people. They have a timeless quality as old as the mysterious glamour of women in the yearning hearts of men. They help us to see the ancient Egyptians as people of flesh and blood like ourselves, not just as a strange and incomprehensible race.

Ancient Egypt

In searching for an understanding of any ancient people as people, not just as names in history books, even as unpromising an object as a museum catalogue can be of help. Behind the routine listing of objects there can sometimes be detected by the imaginative person a scent of that vitality, that authentic re-creation of the life of the past, which every true historian hopes to reveal. A glance through the catalogue of the Egyptian Museum at Cairo, or of the Louvre, the British Museum, or the Museo Egizio at Turin, will quickly show what I mean. Here are listed, not only stones and statues, but such humanly evocative objects as household utensils, children's toys, musical instruments, beds and tables and other pieces of furniture, and such touching feminine things as perfume bases and little pots of cosmetics and ointments with which the ancient Egyptian women, just like their modern descendants, used to fortify confidence in their allure.

To conclude this chapter we should ask what influence the civilisation of ancient Egypt had on the future of the Mediterranean region as a whole. The answer is that this influence was, on the whole, small. While it is true that the Egyptians did make military and trading expeditions abroad, particularly in the Levant, they did not really leave a permanent mark there. However, Egypt itself was the target of many invasions, notably by the Hyksos, or Shepherd Kings, who swept down on the Nile valley from western Asia in the second millennium BC (incidentally bringing the horse to Africa for the first time), and later by the Assyrians, the Persians, the Greeks, and the Romans. It was Alexander the Great who, in 332 BC,

Painted wooden group of Nubian archers found at Assiut in the tomb of an officer of the 10th Dynasty.

initiated the period of Greek domination marked by the rule of the Ptolemys. From this date onwards, Egypt was for more than 2,000 years continually under foreign rule, and it was not until the withdrawal of British troops from the Canal Zone in 1956 that she regained her independence.

Egypt, therefore, for some twenty-two centuries has been the recipient of foreign influences rather than an influence herself. Her role in the development of Mediterranean history has been a passive one. She has been visited by tourists and travellers for the wonders of her past but has made little contribution to the evolution of the present. One unfortunate result of this long period of subjection has been the creation in Egypt of a national inferiority complex which is now bedevilling the political stability of the eastern Mediterranean. Any visitor to Egypt will quickly find that young educated Egyptians, and even those of maturer years, often seem to feel that 'oppressive imperialist influences' have only to be resisted for the country to enter on the millennium and see a restoration of its ancient glories. This essentially emotional view is, of course, an oversimplification, but, all those who visit Egypt should learn to understand and sympathise with it. The defusing of the Middle East will depend on encouraging such potentially creative people as the modern Egyptians to strive for the achievement of as intelligent an attitude among their politicians as had already been shown by their scholars in the work they are doing on Egypt's past.

The so-called ecclesiastical throne of Tutankhamen, made of partially gold-plated and inlaid wood, was used during religious ceremonies only.

5

The Ancient Greek World

The character of human life in the modern Mediterranean, like that of western civilisation as a whole, is almost entirely due to developments in the Greek peninsula some three thousand years ago. We are, as H. A. L. Fisher says at the opening of his famous *History of Europe*, the children of Hellas. The ancient Greek world was the channel by which all the earlier achievements of man were concentrated, elaborated, and eventually passed on to form the modern world.

The archaeological evidence of the ancient Greek presence in the Mediterranean is found on almost all its shores, and ruins are less dead if looked at with imagination. This evidence is not unique, however, and traces of many other ancient peoples also remain. The ruined buildings of the great civilisation of Rome are, of course, even more widespread than those of the Greeks, and will be discussed in the next chapter. But alongside the remains of these two major civilisations of classical antiquity many other early Mediterranean peoples have left evidence of their lives and achievements. Before considering the ancient Greeks in more detail, therefore, I intend to glance briefly at some of their contemporaries and immediate predecessors in the Mediterranean world.

Piecing together the early history of civilised man in the region is by no means easy. The use of the ancient Egyptian hieroglyphs did not spread far from the Nile valley, and therefore written records are absent until the time of the Homeric poems, composed according to Herodotus during the ninth century BC. While it is true that such early people as the Hittites were literate, and a form of hieroglyphic writing was developed independently of the Egyptian in ancient Crete, it is still to ancient Greece that we

(*Above*) Attic geometric crater from Dipylon cemetery showing a funerary procession. (*Opposite*) Etruscan cinerary urn with the portrait of the deceased on the lid.

must go for the main literary evidence of early Mediterranean life. Apart from writing, the main sources of our knowledge are the discoveries and interpretations of archaeologists during the last 100 to 150 years. What broad picture of the Mediterranean of that time emerges from these twin sources?

It would be impossible at this distance in time to give an accurate picture of the emergence of man in the region from the twilight of pre-history, still less to sort out the complicated story of his numerous conquests, alliances, and migrations, nor even to say with any certainty in what order his various cultural centres evolved. The record of early civilised man cannot be so conveniently docketed for the convenience of historians. But what we can say is that before the first centres had developed there was a constant ebb and flow of peoples, the general tendency being a movement westward from a central pool in Asia to the western extremity of the European peninsula. The first wave of these adventurers probably fought and easily overcame their more savage predecessors who, as at Terra Amata and other northern Mediterranean sites, have left evidence of an occupation to be measured in hundreds of thousands of years. These newcomers brought with them not only superior strength but a superior culture. They came in successive waves during the second and third millennia BC, fighting or mingling by the various processes of conquest or treaty until a comparatively stable pattern began to emerge. But the word 'comparatively' is definitely the one to stress. As we know at the cost of much human misery, the struggle for supremacy among European peoples has continued throughout history, and is only now, at the end of the troubled twentieth century, being extended on a global basis to the struggle between two or three supranational ideologies.

In Homeric times – that is, during the half millennium or so before 850 BC – several characteristic cultural traditions were emerging in addition to those centred on the Greek peninsula and the Aegean. To enumerate them all would take me far beyond the scope of this book. But before coming back to the main theme of ancient Greek civilisation I must just say a few words about the background to some other contemporary cultures which have left archaeological evidence behind them and can be reconstructed by imaginative visitors to actual sites that still exist today. Of these I shall mention only the most important and rewarding, which are without doubt the cultures of the Etruscans, the Phoenicians, and the first civilised inhabitants of Crete.

Although they possessed one of the most advanced and attractive civilisations of the ancient world, the Etruscans have always been an enigma to historians. Their early history, their place of origin, and even their language is shrouded in mystery. According to Herodotus and the classical writers who followed his authority they were immigrants from western Asia, but another school of thought regards them as being descended from earlier indigenous tribes in north-central Italy. The attempt to interpret the Etruscan language, known from a multitude of inscriptions both in Italy itself and elsewhere in the Mediterranean, must be accounted one of the most remarkable failures of scientific scholarship. In spite of a few tenta-

Marble head of an idol from Amorgos. Early Cycladic period.

tive and unconvincing guesses not a word of it can be certainly understood. Except for their splendid visual arts, the Etruscans therefore remain a shadowy people. This is indeed an odd fate for a civilisation that was a forerunner of, and in many ways influenced, the mighty civilisation of Rome itself.

The Etruscans first come into history about the twelfth or thirteenth centuries BC, when they were established in Italy in a fertile region between the Tiber and the Arno and bounded in the east and west respectively by the Appenines and the Tyrrhenian Sea. This region was known in classical times as Etruria, and its inhabitants were known to the ancient Greeks as the Tyrrhenoi or Tyrsenoi, from the first of which the name of the Tyrrhenian Sea derives. The second name is suggestive of their supposed eastern origin, for although Asia Minor is favoured as their point of radiation in several theories, it is at least equally likely that they came from farther south. The name Tyrsenoi may therefore be connected with the ancient seaport of Tyre, which was also one of the headquarters of those famous navigators the Phoenicians.

But we can safely leave the scholars to argue about such details. Here, however, I feel the reader may be better rewarded by taking a look at some Etruscan sites and works of art as they can be seen today. It is in the pouring forth of the spirit as represented by art, rather than in a dated sequence of historical facts, that we may catch a glimpse of the peoples of the past as living beings.

For the modern traveller in the Mediterranean all the Etruscan sites on the mainland of Italy are within easy striking distance of Rome or Pisa. The names of some of the most important ones on the west coast, all fairly easily accessible by train if one lacks a car, will be familiar to readers of D. H. Lawrence's evocative travel book *Etruscan Places*. Examples are Cerveteri, Vulci, Volterra, and of course Tarquinia itself, the former centre of Etruscan civilisation where a splendid series of painted tombs still survives. A few days wandering round this enchanted region in the heat of summer, although perhaps not particularly comfortable, will evoke a far more poignant picture of ancient Etruria than can be gained from a multitude of books. Having thus first soaked in the atmosphere of the sites at first hand, the interested visitor can then enjoy the wonders of Etruscan art to be seen in many museums throughout the world with greatly enhanced pleasure.

The Etruscans made numerous sorties from their central territory, but their homeland corresponded, despite certain variations in the boundaries, with modern Tuscany. The main railway from Paris via Marseilles to Rome lies along the coastal strip of this province and the most interesting of the northernmost sites lies within a short distance of Pisa. This is Volterra, the remains of a great Etruscan city built some 550 metres (1,800 feet) above sea-level and commanding splendid views over the neighbouring hills. Although approached up a romantic valley green with vines and olive trees, the site itself is bleak. It is nevertheless full of atmosphere and as one wanders round the old Etruscan walls which lie close to the rather characterless modern town, one can recapture a little of the

The Ancient Greek World

spirit of the life that was once associated with them. But the main archaeological interest of Volterra today lies in the funerary urns collected in the Etruscan Museum, which show that the Etruscans habitually cremated their dead. There are many hundreds of these, made in the form of small alabaster sarcophagi, not the typical round amphorae, or jars, in which the ashes of the dead are usually stored. Probably because alabaster was readily available locally, these sarcophagi are unique to the Volterra region and are not found at any other Etruscan site.

The sarcophagi are for the most part elaborately and most attractively decorated. It has been fashionable at certain times in the past not to regard them as at the highest level of aesthetic achievement, but in my view D. H. Lawrence was quite correct in thinking them much more attractive than many more allegedly perfect and fashionably acceptable works of art. The decorations have a simplicity and vitality which banish morbid thoughts of death and appeal immediately to our spirit of delight. And it is surely one of the most valuable functions of true art that it should delight us in purely human terms as well as stimulating, as it does in its very highest manifestations, our profoundest moral and spiritual sensibilities. The Etruscan sarcophagi, with their pictures of sea-monsters, mermaids, and winged serpents, their fabulous birds and strange hippocampi, or horses of the sea, radiate an unsophisticated spirit of wonder that must gladden the heart of any romantic zoologist.

Elaborate Etruscan terracotta sarcophagus in the shape of a banqueting couch, found in Cerveteri. 6th century BC.

108

Equally attractive and even more interesting are the decorations showing scenes from everyday life. Carvings of processions, ships, the storming
of cities, circus games, banquets, and boar hunts, give us the same picture
of the Etruscans as human beings as do the murals in the tomb of Ti of
the life of the ancient Egyptians. There are also, as in ancient Egypt,
representations of women and slaves and children, and such touching
scenes as a man bidding a tender farewell to his wife as he embarks on the
adventures awaiting him in the Land of the Dead.

But the richness of Etruscan art is still more vividly displayed at the
best-known of all these sites – Tarquinia. This lies about a two hours'
leisurely drive north-west of Rome, where it stands some 5 kilometres
(3 miles), from the sea on a low hill rising to just 123 metres (400 feet),
above the fertile, wheat-covered plain. There is, as might be expected, a
museum at Tarquinia. Museums, although necessary evils, are usually
qualified disasters, being at worst junk rooms and at best historical filing
systems in which objects of wonder and beauty are displayed, coldly
labelled, in far too great proximity to one another. Of course there are
some honorable exceptions, the Museum at Tarquinia is one, for it has
avoided the usual effect of depressing impersonality, being domestic in
character and containing a comparatively limited collection of objects, all
found within the region itself. The courtyard is filled with sarcophagi,
mostly of the late Etruscan period, surmounted by carved effigies of the
persons whose remains lie within them. Upstairs there is a rich display of
painted bowls, amphoræ, dishes and vases spreading over the thousand or
more years of Etruscan history. It is, in general, an attractive and easily
assimilable display.

But the main glory of Tarquinia is the series of painted tombs which
comprise the City of the Dead. In many civilisations, ancient and modern,
it has been the custom for the dead to be buried in a quarter of their parent
city wholly set aside for the purpose. One example of the custom in
modern times occurs in Cairo, where there is a Moslem City of the Dead,
the streets lined with tombs instead of houses. Here the living come on
Holy Days to commune with the spirits of the departed. The Etruscans in
ancient times followed a similar practice, and a hill near the modern town
of Tarquinia was given up to a vast necropolis. Not that one would now
realise this as one approaches it on foot. The hill appears to be like any
other – wild, windswept, and covered with a growth of short grass and
flowers. Once, many now vanished tombs stood on the hilltop, however,
and others still survive below the level of the ground. These have each
been given individual names, such as the Tomb of the Feast, the Tomb of
Hunting and Fishing, the Tomb of the Leopards, and so on, and are
approached by steep steps leading into the bowels of the earth. To come
on the richness of their mural decorations in such a sombre setting is an
unexpected and exciting revelation.

The names of the tombs derive, of course, from the scenes painted
within them. Thus the Tomb of Hunting and Fishing contains frescos of
birds flying, fishes leaping, and men hunting, fishing, or rowing in boats.
The Tomb of the Leopards, its yellowish walls painted in varying shades

Fishing scene with dolphins and birds, from the Tomb of Hunting and Fishing, Tarquinia. Second half of the 6th century BC.

of blue and green and ochre, derives its name from two leopards in heraldic positions at the top of the end wall. But it is chiefly remarkable for the marvellous vitality of the male figures dancing, running, gesticulating, and playing pipes, on the frieze below. A similar vibrant energy brings all the tombs miraculously to life. This is especially remarkable in the Tomb of the Feast where men and women are shown gaily banqueting in the Land of the Dead just as they would have done in the sunny halls of Tarquinia more than two thousand years ago.

One characteristic of all things Etruscan is that they show the origins of a tradition which still perists in the Mediterranean today. We may be delighted by the intellectual and aesthetic perfection of the Greeks, and admire the stern efficiency of the Roman legions which conquered the then civilised world, but the Etruscans, with their unrepressed enjoyment of natural life, have a simpler, more familiar appeal. One feels that these people did not place the main accent of their ambitions on conquest, domination, or a profound concern with philosophical problems. True, they were good survivors and could look after themselves, but the main motivating force of their lives seems to have been an uncomplicated desire

Fragment of pediment from the Etruscan Temple of Mercury, showing a mythological winged figure playing the double flute.

to express themselves to the full with passion, fun and enjoyment. More than any other people of the ancient Mediterranean, the Etruscans embody the rare and delightful quality of *joie-de-vivre*.

The spirit of gaiety that typifies the Etruscans is underlined by their passion for music. Many of their murals and other works of decorative art show musical scenes, and the playing of instruments, singing and dancing were enthusiastically practised in their everyday lives. According to Greek writers the Etruscans invented the horn and the trumpet and were particularly fond of the music of the double flute. Baking, wrestling matches, and even scourgings were said to be accompanied by the shrill tunes of this instrument. The Roman historian Claudius Aelianus, generally known as Aelian, who was writing in the third century AD, even gives in the twelfth book of his *On the Characteristics of Animals* an account of the use of music by Etruscan hunters to catch deer and boars. Freely translated, it reads:

'This is how they do it. On all sides they set out nets and other hunting equipment to make traps for the animals. A skilful flute player then takes up his station and plays the purest and most harmonious melody, the sweetest airs the

The Ancient Greek World

One of the greatest achievements of the Phoenicians was the establishment of the modern alphabet. Stele from Carthage showing an example of Phoenician writing.

instrument can produce. In the silence and calm the sounds penetrate with ease to the peaks and into the valleys and woods where the lairs of the animals are found. When they hear the sounds they are at first astonished and filled with fear, but then become overcome with pleasure, indeed transported, forgetting their lairs and even their young. Even though they do not care to go far from their homes they are drawn irresistibly to approach the sounds. And thus they are overcome by the power of music, and fall into the nets and are taken.'

This passage may not be as entirely far-fetched as it sounds. The hypnotic power of music on animals, even though denied by some scientific sceptics, is sufficiently well documented not to be dismissed out of hand.

Among other peoples who made their mark on the ancient Greek world, some of the most important were the Phoenicians. Their homeland was the narrow coastal strip along the coast of Syria which included the important ancient seaports of Tyre and Sidon, which they founded. The Greeks, Etruscans, Romans, Cretans – in fact all the peoples of the ancient world – were to some extent seamen and navigators, but all were exceeded in prowess in this field by the Phoenicians. These were the main traders of the ancient world, and, setting sail westwards, not only established commercial centres on all the shores of the Mediterranean, but penetrated beyond the Straits of Gibraltar and as far north as Britain and possibly Scandinavia. There is also a strong probability that some time between 609 BC and 593 BC they sailed in a clockwise direction round the whole continent of Africa, a commission given to them by Pharaoh Necho. They set off from the Red Sea, went ashore on two occasions long enough to plant crops and reap their harvest, and returned through the Straits of Gibraltar some two and a half years later.

As with the Etruscans, the origin of the Phoenicians is obscure, but they were well established on the eastern seaboard of the Mediterranean by the beginning of the first millennium BC. Apart from their adventurousness they were a cultured people, and one of their greatest achievements was the first establishment of the modern alphabet. They took the hieratic script of ancient Egypt and transformed and modified it into a form suited to Semitic languages. From this point the Phoenician alphabet was still further modified by the Greeks, who inserted vowels and made other changes. The role of the Phoenicians in the evolution of writing from the ancient pictograms to the forms practised today cannot therefore be over-emphasised.

The meteoric rise of the Phoenicians in the Mediterranean world began at the opening of the first millennium BC and their influence was only extinguished by the capture of Tyre by Alexander the Great in 332 BC and the sacking of Carthage by the Romans in 146 BC. Carthage was the Phoenicians' most famous colony and the only power in the Mediterranean that almost succeeded in toppling the might of Rome. It lay on the North African coast not far from modern Tunis, but unfortunately it was so completely destroyed by the Romans, such ruins as were left being used as quarries by the later inhabitants of the region, that very little of archaeological interest remains. However, the visitor can see some vestiges of the ancient port and houses and, standing on the hillside which overlooks the

(*Above*) Phoenician terracotta mask found in a
necropolis. 6th century
BC (*Far left*) Necklace of
gold, semi-precious stones
and pottery beads, found in
a grave at Borj-jedid,
Tunisia. (*Left*) Phoenician
female protome found in
Ibiza.

The Ancient Greek World

site of the city can sweep his eyes over the seascape across which Hannibal once sailed in an attempt to conquer the world.

Although the Phoenicians were skilful builders in wood and stone, and of course excelled in the building of ships, the creation of works of art was not their strong point. Stone carvings, pottery vessels, jewellery, figurines, and so on, have come down to us, but they show a solid rather than an exceptional talent and many of the more aesthetically-pleasing objects are obviously derived from contact with the Greeks. Perhaps the most original Phoenician work is in the form of figurines. These were mainly of bronze, a few being in copper, and although mostly primitive in conception they possess an originality and a vitality that is not characteristic of the Phoenicians' more pretentious work. Their jewellery is pleasing but not particularly original in style, and their terracotta masks resemble many hundreds produced by other peoples of the ancient world.

As might be expected in a trading people, Phoenician coinage is elaborate and attractive, often figuring real or mythical animals and scenes from Phoenician life as well as the more conventional profile heads of leaders. One coin is of particular interest to zoologists, for it clearly depicts a domesticated African elephant. There was for many years a controversy as to whether Hannibal in his famous passage of the Alps took with him African elephants, which were once thought too wild to domesticate, or Asiatic elephants imported from the East. This coin proves conclusively that the African elephant was used, the animals being probably captured and trained in the Atlas mountains and the neighbouring plains. At that time these regions were far more fertile than they are today and were the home of a wide range of game now found only south of the Sahara.

Well before the Phoenicians were embarking on their adventurous voyages from the Levant, a glittering civilisation was beginning to develop in the Aegean. Although its manifestations were widespread, its focal point was in Crete where the archaeologist Sir Arthur Evans first revealed its existence by his excavation of the Palace of Minos at Knossos in the first decade of the twentieth century. This civilisation, known as the Minoan, is one of the most ancient in the Mediterranean. In fact it can be correlated in many respects with the civilisation of ancient Egypt, and Evans revealed that it had three main phases. Of these the first was roughly contemporary with the first ten Egyptian dynasties (3400-2100 BC), the second with the 11th to 17th Egyptian dynasties (2100-1600 BC), and the last with the 18th and 19th dynasties (1600-1200 BC).

As with the other Mediterranean civilisations, the origin of the Minoans is speculative. Historians, when in doubt (and historians often are), speak of the arrival of man in the Mediterranean region in a series of waves from some mysterious centre in the east. In fact when scholarship has done its best we can still not get a much more distinct picture of what actually happened. But this is unimportant. What *is* important is to look at a living culture with living eyes irrespective of its exact historical position or chronology. The past is only really valuable to use insofar as it illuminates the present in terms of human values, not a string of dry-as-dust dates. He who reads about ancient Crete or travels in what were formerly the

Carthaginian coin showing a domesticated elephant.

(*Opposite*) Etruscan wall-paintings in Tarquinia: (*Top*) Lyre-player from the Tomb of the Feast. (*Bottom*) Man at a banquet, from the Tomb of the Lionesses.

The Ancient Greek World

domains of the legendary King Minos of Knossos will find himself delighted, intrigued, or moved to the full extent only by regarding the region in this light.

What, then, was the special quality of Minoan civilisation? It seems to have flourished, at least in its opening centuries, in a period of peace; its cities were unfortified and body armour is found only towards the end of the second millennium BC. There were, in fact, no real challengers to Minoan supremacy, and in these auspicious conditions a civilisation of great refinement and luxury had an opportunity to evolve. The life was largely centred on the royal palaces, not only at Knossos but particularly also as Phaestos, where archaeological finds have shown a richness and capacity for *joie-de-vivre* worthy of the Etruscans themselves. The palace of Minos at Knossos was so huge (it covered 5 acres) and had so many rooms that it surely must have played a part in the conception of the legendary Minoan Labyrinth. This, according to tradition, was the home of a savage monster, half man, half bull, called the Minotaur, to whom the Athenians had to send seven of their fairest young men and maidens each year as a tribute. The Minotaur, the legend goes, slew these sacrificial offerings without mercy, but was eventually slain itself by the Athenian hero, Theseus, who volunteered to accompany one of the groups of victims for this very purpose. He was allowed by King Minos to enter the labyrinth because it was believed that he would never find his way out again and would therefore become a sort of bonus victim. However, fate, in the form of a woman, was to take a hand. Ariadne, the daughter of the King, fell in love with Theseus and gave him a thread which he could unwind as

(*Opposite*) Stone altar in the precinct of King Minos' palace at Knossos, representing the Horns of Consecration, symbol of the Minoan Mother Goddess.

Theseus slaying the Minotaur. Painting on an Attic vase.

The Ancient Greek World

he entered the labyrinth and use to find his way out again. In this way Theseus succeeded in his task and sailed away to safety.

Such legends have come down to us through Greek writers, but this is not to say that the Minoans did not have a literary tradition of their own, even though it has not yet been revealed. Certainly they had writing, and numerous inscriptions have survived. Sir Arthur Evans demonstrated that there were three phases in the evolution of Minoan writing. The first consisted of pictograms analogous to the Egyptian hieroglyphs, which was followed by a more cursive or flowing form which he termed Linear A. Finally came Linear B, which seems to have been an early form of Greek. For fifty years none of these scripts was deciphered, but eventually through the patient work of the young British scholars, Michael Ventris and John Chadwick, most of the secrets of Linear B were revealed. It was a great disappointment that the inscriptions deciphered in this language were mostly of inventories. As Leonard Cottrell has aptly said, it is as if the English language were unknown and in seeking a clue to its meaning one had come not on the works of Shakespeare but on a laundry list. Yet the decipherment itself was a tremendous achievement, and it is still possible that new discoveries will open up a richer literary heritage in Crete than has so far come to light.

An example of Linear B script on a fragment of a late Minoan tablet.

Detail of a sarcophagus from Haghia Triada, Crete, representing a procession of women and men bearing gifts and pouring libations. According to a Minoan convention the women are shown with fair skin and the men with dark skin.

The Ancient Greek World

Gold pendant of the early
Minoan period, with
filigree work representing
two hornets. *c.* 2000 BC.

In the absence of literary evidence, wall-paintings and decorated pottery still give a vivid picture of everyday life at the height of Minoan civilisation, and the artistic inspiration of the metal-work is at a particularly high level. We can deduce from such archaeological remains that the Cretans were not only a pleasure-loving people but also, like the ancient Egyptians, ardent devotees of an elaborate bull-cult. Their religion seems to have been pantheistic, and the Mother Goddess of nature was held in particular veneration. The darker side of their beliefs was symbolised by animal-headed demons which evoked the forces of nature inimical to man.

The favoured geographical position of Crete contributed greatly to its affluence. The Cretans even anticipated the Phoenicians in their skill in seafaring and navigation. By 2000 BC their merchant ships were sailing the whole of the eastern Mediterranean, trading with other peoples in the Aegean islands, on the mainland of Greece, and in Cyprus, Asia Minor, and Syria. Like all great civilisations, the Minoan had a period of growth and flowering followed by a decline. By the beginning of the first millennium BC troubled times descended on Crete. During the preceding thousand years, apart from such legendary episodes as that of the Minotaur, the Cretans had on the whole friendly relationships and cultural interchange with the peoples of the mainland. They traded particularly with a people known as the Mycenaeans, who had established themselves (again probably coming from the east) in what is now Salonika. But man, it seems, is never satisfied with friendship and peace; sooner or later he seems driven to prove his superiority over his neighbours by competition or force of arms. Thus there came a time when the Mycenaeans embarked on a career of domination, overcoming many of the surrounding peoples, occupying Athens and eventually sacking Knossos itself. Thus the Minoan civilisation meaninglessly perished at the hands of violent men, and all that is now left of it is the archaeological treasure dug up by Sir Arthur Evans and his successors.

This, then, was roughly the situation in the Greek world at the beginning of the first millennium BC. There followed the rise of Hellas itself, the civilisation that was the wellspring of all later Mediterranean culture and the ancestors of what we now term Western Civilisation. This is the cultural complex that was eventually to spread and dominate the world, but in a simple companion to the Mediterranean I cannot dwell at any length on such a mighty theme. I shall therefore restrict myself to a very summary account of the life and organisation of the first Greek states and a description of some of the oustanding sights that still repay a visit from the archaeological point of view. These, like the Roman sites to be established later, are not restricted to the mainland of Greece but are spread along all the shores of the Mediterranean. To visit only a few of them helps to re-create in one's mind and spirit a moving and often dramatic picture of our cultural origins.

First, the organisation of Greece itself. The country was not a single nation in the modern sense, being divided into a number of autonomous city-states, each with its own laws and its own methods for putting them into effect. This special character of ancient Greece was largely dictated by

120

The Ancient Greek World

the facts of geography. The peninsula consists of a complicated pattern of mountains and valleys, the high ground creating difficult, and at some seasons insuperable, barriers between people living in adjacent regions. It was thus natural that the administration should be conducted from local centres rather than being more centralised, as is the case with communities dwelling in countries where there are no major obstructions to communication.

But although the city-states of ancient Greece retained their autonomy to a large extent, their members had a strong sense of kinship. The 'Greekness' of Greek civilisation was something recognised and respected by all the states and was the main inspiration of their loyalties. It was based according to Herodotus, whose views in this connection deserve every respect, on the deep-seated ties of common descent, a common language, a common religion, and a shared cultural tradition. Friendship and mutual respect between the Greek states was thus normally very strong and stable, and it was only in situations of extreme stress that any conflict of interests or attitudes led to the danger of serious disruption.

The origin of the Greeks, like that of all peoples of the Mediterranean, cannot be decided with certainty. Once again we have to fall back on the time-honoured historical theory that they were immigrants from the east who arrived in successive waves some time before 2000 BC. The first arrivals were probably at the Neolithic stage of development, but later

Neck of a large terracotta vase with an archaic representation of the Trojan Horse. c. 620 BC.

The Ancient Greek World

(*Opposite*) The Calf-Bearer, one of the masterpieces of Archaic Greek sculpture. *c.* 560 BC.

(*Below*) Ancient Greek male types: (*Left*) Archaic head with traces of blue paint on hair and beard, found in the Parthenon. (*Right*) Classical head of the Charioteer at Delphi, a votive bronze sculpture of King Polyzalos of Gela.

immigrants may well have brought with them a copper and bronze culture. The ancestral Greeks were doubtless warrior-farmers who, while capable of exploiting the soil to the full, would also not have been averse to gaining new riches by conquest. Owing to the mountainous nature of Greece they probably occupied the peninsula by slow stages, beginning from the north and consolidating their position in the different sheltered valleys as they advanced slowly southwards.

To what physical type did these first Greek immigrants belong? Though certain representations of the gods and heroes in Greek visual art suggest that they were not of the typical dark-skinned Mediterranean race which is found so commonly in the region today, but had lighter skins, paler eyes, and brown to fairish hair, this physical type was not usual, however. In fact it was probably from its very rareness that it came to be identified with the popular concept of a god or hero. The typical ancient Greek was, as we can tell, very similar to his modern counterpart.

The origins of the Greek language are as impossible to unravel with any certainty as the origins of the Greeks themselves. When the newcomers arrived in the peninsula they would certainly have brought their own language with them; but different dialects distinguished the different waves of immigrants, and their individual characteristics were doubtless further consolidated according to the geographical locations in which they settled.

The Ancient Greek World

Basic Greek was one of the great family of languages known as Indo-European, a linguistic group to which all other Mediterranean languages belong except that of ancient Egypt and, for some still unexplained reason, Etruscan. The five main dialects of ancient Greece were Aeolic, Doric, Ionic, Attic, and Achaean, and all were written down in an alphabet taken over and modified from the Phoenicians between about 900 and 800 BC. Doric, Ionic, and Attic were the main dialects of Greek literature but Attic, which was the language used by the great Athenian writers, surpassed the other two in importance. As Greek influence spread through the Mediterranean world Attic became the *lingua franca* of the whole region, and was adopted by the local inhabitants of most of the Greek colonies particularly during the years of economic dominance by Athens. This situation continued until, through the spread of the power of Rome, Greek was largely superseded by Latin.

The Greeks, like the Romans after them, were justifiably snobbish about the purity and excellence of their language. Both these great civilisations of the ancient world referred to those who did not naturally speak their tongue as 'barbarians'. The Greeks, with their inborn aristocracy, even went so far as to regard those who could not speak their language as in some way inferior by nature as well as in culture – a somewhat arrogant assumption which they applied to the highly civilised Persians and Egyptians as well as to the uncouth barbarian tribes to the north.

Before considering how Greek thought influenced the development of the Mediterranean as a whole and glancing at a few of the archaeological sites which can still be visited today, it will help to bring this remarkable people to life if we see how they went about their day-to-day affairs in the city-states. One of the first things to stress, not often realised, is the extreme smallness of the states both in area and population. In fact the word 'state' in its modern connotation cannot be applied to them at all; they corresponded rather with very small English counties or such vest-pocket countries as Monaco, Liechtenstein, and Andorra. A typical city-state might have an enfranchised population of only ten thousand people and Athens was the only state to have a population of more than twenty thousand. In spite of this, each state had its own administration, its own system of laws, and its own army, even though in several states the regular soldiers could be comfortably transported in six or seven modern double-decker buses; in time of war the armies' numbers would be increased by a voluntary militia.

The small size of the city-states gave them something of the character of a closely-knit family rather than an impersonal community. The leading citizens all knew each other by name and all had a right to play a personal role in the government by appearing and speaking themselves at the assembly where the laws were formulated. This right did not extend, however, to every member of the community. Although the word 'democracy' is of Greek origin, and means 'government by the people', the Greek system did not conform to what we would consider democracy today. The community was divided into a privileged class of rich citizens who controlled the destinies of the state, and a much larger number of people who

The Ancient Greek World

had no say at all, but were, if we are not to mince words, simply slaves. This was not so reprehensible as it sounds, however, for the people without the franchise were in fact very well treated, it being part of the Greek philosophy of government that those who had the advantage of superior wisdom and education, based on a long aristocratic tradition, had a duty and responsibility to regard the welfare of those less privileged than themselves as important as their own. While this provided no scope for the equality of opportunity which is so rightly stressed in the more socialised forms of government in the modern world, in practice at that time in ancient Greece the system worked very well. The numbers of people were manageable and if, as only seldom occurred, abuses did arise, they could be settled informally at the councils of the ruling class. Again the analogy of the family is apposite. The slaves had all the benefits of belonging to a benevolently-administered group within which they could find a satisfying occupation according to their education and talents, as well as security and protection. That the arrangement worked well in practice, however alien it may seem to modern theory, is proved by the devoted loyalty of the slaves in times of crisis. Had it not been satisfactory to them, there would have been many opportunities for the system to be overthrown.

The city, which formed the focal point of the life of each city-state, was built whenever possible on high ground so that it would have a military advantage in times of unrest. The territory of the larger states also included a number of villages, but all the administration was conducted from the city. The most famous of the city-states was of course Athens, which under Pericles in the fifth century BC saw the cultural flowering of one of the greatest civilisations the world has ever known. The main buildings of Athens were concentrated on the high ground known as the 'Acropolis', from the two Greek words *akros* and *polis*, meaning literally 'the high city'. Pericles aimed to build on the Acropolis hill of Athens the finest collection of architectural masterpieces ever assembled – an aim in which he largely succeeded. Behind an imposing entrance gate there stood a picture gallery, several administrative buildings and numerous temples, of which the most famous is the mighty Parthenon. Although severely damaged by an explosion when it was being used as a powder magazine during the siege of Athens by the Venetians in 1687, and further defaced by Lord Elgin who removed most of its famous frieze to the British Museum, the Parthenon remains the most impressive single ruin in the whole of eastern Europe. The greatest architects in Greece, working under the direction of the sculptor Phidias, were employed to build it, and the grace of the enormous structure and the delicate refinement introduced to preserve a perfect impression of physical balance are as miraculous as those displayed in any structure in the world.

Below the Acropolis, on the slopes of the hill and extending onto the surrounding plains, were first the houses of the principal citizens and then those of the artisans and slaves. Although some of the major private houses were large and finely finished, the general layout of this part of ancient Athens was far less orderly than that of the Acropolis itself. Narrow streets twisted and turned in all directions, and in the poorer

(*Opposite*) The colonnade of the Roman forum adjoining the original Greek agora at Cyrene. During the decline of the Empire the forum was used as a fort and suffered accordingly, but it was extensively rebuilt by the Italians this century.

Marble head of Pericles.

General view of the Acropolis at Athens, from the south west. From left to right can be seen the Propylaia, the Erechteum and the Parthenon.

quarters it was customary to get rid of rubbish by the simple expedient of throwing it outside. This happy-go-lucky approach to sanitation strikes us as odd in such a civilised people, but it has been characteristic of many Mediterranean countries right down to the twentieth century. The Greeks, it is true, had a special corps for cleaning the main streets and squares before important processions; but it was really only in the time of the Romans, with their passionate sense of order, that any serious attempt was made at cleaning up the lesser thoroughfares in denser centres.

As in many parts of the Mediterranean today, there were in the cities of ancient Greece a number of streets devoted to the practice of different trades. For example there would be a street of cobblers, a street of metal workers, a street of potters, and so on. But otherwise the streets were not formally named and a visitor to a stranger's house could only find it by asking for him by name. However, with such a small population, where everyone in a neighbourhood was known to everyone else, this presented no problem. When the house was reached it would probably consist of one, or at most two, storeys, and would appear strange to modern eyes by the absence of windows. However, when one went inside the answer to this seeming mystery would quickly be revealed. The typical Greek house was built so that the rooms faced inwards and gave onto a central courtyard open to the sky. This courtyard, known as the *peristylon*, was usually rectangular in shape and surrounded by a collonaded walk. In some houses there was an altar in the middle of the rectangle. Giving off the *peristylon* were a series of sleeping and store rooms and also a number of separate rooms of larger size where the men and women could meet alone with members of their own sex. In the smaller houses rooms for children and household servants would also be placed on the ground floor, but in more elaborate constructions occupied the second floor. One of the rooms leading off the *peristylon* was known as the *triclinion*, or dining-room, where couches were set out beside low tables so that the diners could recline at full length and enjoy the food and drink brought by the slaves.

It was in such settings as these that many of the thoughts which formed the core of the Greek attitude to life were formulated. The Greeks were great talkers and good listeners and the interchange of ideas in the *triclinion*, with a plentiful supply of food and the wine flowing freely, was one of their main delights. The rhetoric and formal intercourse which took place in the great buildings of the Acropolis were here forgotten, and in the relaxed atmosphere of a Greek home the leading thinkers of the day would enjoy the thrust and parry of civilised discussion, or a Socrates discourse about art and beauty and justice and the good life until the sun rose over the Acropolis hill.

I have mentioned that the Greeks, like all the major peoples of the ancient Mediterranean, were great sailors. The Odyssey of Homer, their earliest and greatest epic poem, shows how deeply the spirit of maritime adventure had entered into their lives. But it was not only romantic dreams that set them sailing across the waters of the Mediterranean, even though these probably inspired them as much or more as any seafaring people; there were also the more prosaic but nonetheless vital motivations of trade and commerce, a desire to ease the over-population problems at home. The colonies set up by the Greek states contributed greatly to the prosperity of the homeland as well as playing an important role in the general opening up of the Mediterranean to commercial enterprise. But as I want this to be a companionable book, not an academic history, I do not intend to weary the reader with the names of even the most important trading-posts set up by the Greek voyagers. This sort of detail can be gained from other sources, and is particularly clearly given in a little book entitled *The Greeks Overseas* by John Boardman of Oxford University. It will be more interesting to the reader, I think, if I restrict myself to just one of the sites I have actually visited myself, and for this purpose I have chosen Cyrene in Libya, from which the name of the Libyan province of Cyrenaica derives.

My wife and I first visited Cyrene in a journey we made across the northern Sahara in 1955 and my impression of the place has remained indelibly imprinted on my mind. The site itself is of dazzling magnificence, being set on one of the highest spots of the Djebel el Akdar, or 'green mountains', of north-west Cyrenaica. It is easily reached from Benghazi, the approach being through a forest of pines, cedars, and cypresses planted before the Second World War by the Italians as part of their drive to attract the tourist trade to their then colony. The forest itself, being artificially created, reminded us of many a suburb in southern England or the United States where conifers have been introduced for their decorative effect. But round about all is much wilder, the hillsides being covered with juniper and *Pistacia lentiscus* and even the vineyards and cultivated

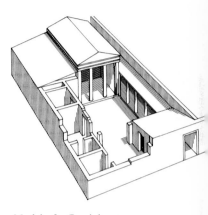

Model of a Greek house, with the central *peristylon*.

plantations of tomatoes, peppers, and pumpkins being well in character with the typically Mediterranean landscape. Beyond the forests and cultivated land, one finds oneself on the northern edge of a mountain plateau which falls away towards the sea in two distinct steps separated by a plain. From this lofty point of vantage there is one of the finest views of the Mediterranean that I have ever seen.

Much of Cyrene, in spite of being largely built on a narrow defile, still commands the same splendid panorama extending to west, north, and east as far as the eye can see. A great many of the surviving ruins are Roman, for the imperial legions often made their centres on or near ancient Greek sites; but a good number of the original Greek structures also survive. The city was built on two main levels and on the upper one there is a tiny but charming Greek theatre and also a Greek *agora*, or market-place, both in a good state of preservation. One of the most evocative monuments is the Temple of Zeus which, although hardly one stone still stands upon another, is in my view more impressive in its authenticity than those buildings which have been extensively re-built and restored. The temple's great stone columns lie on the ground, their capitals radiating outwards from the central plinth where once stood a gigantic statue of Zeus. The destruction of the site, it was formerly believed, was the result of an earthquake, but it is now thought to have occurred during the Jewish revolt in the time of the Emperor Trajan. The pillars at that time were still intact, but the rebels under-cut them and propped them temporarily with wood; they then set fire to the wooden supports and so toppled the whole structure. Other remains of both the Greek and Roman periods exist in profusion on the lower of the two levels referred to above, but to describe them in detail is the province of a guide book, not this companion. The most moving impression of the city can in any case be best obtained by avoiding too much concentration on detail and letting the imagination wander at will. Strolling in solitude through Cyrene's silent but eloquent ruins and contemplating its magnificent geographical setting can give the imaginative visitor a really deep insight into the spirit of the ancient world.

To conclude, how can we best sum up the influence of the ancient Greek world on the later history of the Mediterranean? This is indeed difficult, for it was not only the Greeks themselves but their contemporaries and immediate predecessors whose attitude to life affected the evolution of the region. Yet although the Mycenaeans, the Phoenicians, the Etruscans, and the other early peoples of the eastern Mediterranean all had their contribution to make, it is to the Greeks themselves that we owe the biggest debt. I think this is because, in their art, their literature, their philosophy, and their basic scale of values, they anticipated as a people all that is most noble and enduring in the spirit of man. The Greeks themselves summed this quality up in a single word – 'goodness'. But this word did not mean for them something rigid or narrowly canonical. The good man was for the Greeks (and here I am referring to the educated classes, although the same spirit was passed down to all members of Greek society, including the slaves) one who exemplified the cardinal virtues of physical and moral courage, temperance, justice, and wisdom. These qualities were expressed in such things as tenderness in human relationships, the avoidance of exaggeration and excess, and a sensibility to beauty and balance in both art and conduct. Goodness was for the Greeks what virtue was for the Romans: the quality that raised manhood to its full dignity.

It was the Greeks who first formalised this ennobling concept and injected it into the mainstream of history. It was a concept that, although often temporarily forgotten and obscured in the centuries following the decline of classical civilisation, was never entirely lost. It not only imbued the finest creations of the ancient Mediterranean world but was to become an essential feature of the best of western thought. In this way the Greek ideal spread eventually over the whole surface of the earth, irradiating for those who felt its force the dark places of meanness, cowardice, and selfishness in which men have so often been engulfed.

The Greek ritual baths of Artemis at Cyrene. The baths are cut in the rock, with niches above each for water jars and lamps.

6

Rome and the Roman Empire

Rome was the great unifying force in the ancient Mediterranean. Before her rise to power the various civilised communities that had grown up on the sea's shores, although they interacted with each other by war and trade, never formed a single cohesive unit. The material evidence of their culture is found throughout the length and breadth of the region but there seems to have been no unifying idea to band them together. In the great days of the Roman Empire all this was changed. After pacifying the great rivals of Rome, such as Carthage, the imperial legions had their domination virtually unchallenged. Roman merchants and savants could travel throughout the whole Mediterranean region without danger of molestation. Glittering centres of culture sprang up, not only in Italy and eastern Europe, but much further to the west and along the whole North African coast. On all these centres the spirit and character of Rome was indelibly stamped.

Even today the atmosphere of ancient Rome in the Mediterranean can be powerfully sensed. Everywhere there are Roman remains. The resident or traveller has only to scratch the surface of what he sees around him to feel the Roman presence. The countries of the littoral, and even the sea itself, are peopled with Roman ghosts.

Where and how did this great period in human history originate? The precise origin of the Romans is as shadowy as that of all Mediterranean people, but it seems likely that their ancestors entered the Italian peninsula as warrior-farmers at the same stages as the Greeks were entering their homeland further to the east. But as the Apennines run longitudinally down the country their progress would have been less impeded by physical

(*Above*) Marble group of Amor and Psyche in the courtyard of the House of Amor and Psyche at Ostia. (*Opposite*) Votive altar found at Ostia showing Romulus and Remus fed by the she-wolf and discovered by the shepherds.

Rome and the Roman Empire

(*Opposite*) Courtyard of the House of the Faun at Pompeii.

barriers, and along the Adriatic coast at least their advance may have been quite swift. True, they would have encountered local tribes, but the very fact that they made their enterprising penetration of the peninsula in the first place shows that they were superior in strength and intelligence to the peoples they encountered. These were doubtless swiftly overcome, or assimilated by treaties into a new and larger community. But on the west coast of Italy things would have been more difficult for the newcomers, as the ancient civilisation of Etruria was already established there. The people who eventually founded Rome may therefore have come westwards over the Apennines themselves, by-passing the main centres of Etruscan power. It is really futile to speculate on exactly what happened. The early movement of peoples in the Italian peninsula is shrouded in mystery, and even the founding of Rome itself at the comparatively late date of 753 BC is a matter of legend rather than real historical knowledge.

The legend recounts how Rome was founded by two brothers named Romulus and Remus, who achieved their object only after enduring even more vicissitudes than seem to be normally the lot of any legendary characters who try to do something worthwhile. The brothers, it was believed, were the sons of the god Mars, who seduced one of the famous Vestal Virgins appointed to guard the sacred fire at the pre-Roman settlement. Her name was Rhea Silvia, and her indiscretion so sullied her reputation for virgin purity that she was put to death and her two sons cast into the Tiber. However, they were washed ashore and suckled by a she-wolf which, if we are to seek an anthropological explanation for this zoologically unlikely idea, may have been the totem of one of the local Latin tribes. Be that as it may, Romulus and Remus survived and came to manhood, whereupon they decided to found a city at the place of their deliverance. But, as even brothers will, they quarrelled over the plans and instead of acting together became rivals. Omens were much believed in at that time, being a powerful influence in both Etruscan and Roman metaphysics. The situation between the brothers was therefore not at all improved when Romulus decided that an omen given by a flight of birds showed that he was to be the sole king of the new city, and Remus should be relegated to obscurity. Quite naturally in the circumstances, Remus was highly piqued, and when the foundations of the city began to grow, he showed his contempt for his brother and his work by jumping over a newly-built section of the city wall. Incensed by this insult, Romulus slew his brother and took full credit for the new city, naming it after himself. Thus in a savage legend which may nevertheless enshrine some elements of historical fact, we have the first account of the founding of Rome.

The subsequent history of the city and its achievements belong more to the realms of historical knowledge than fantasy, and the study of Roman literature and the physical remains of her achievements throughout Europe has given us a remarkably full and consistent picture of her development. Within the space of a few centuries this obscure, newly-founded city on the west coast of Italy rose to be mistress of the western world. But the story of its progress from Kingdom to Republic to Empire, and of its eventual decline and fall belongs elsewhere. All I intend to do here is to

Rome and the Roman Empire

sketch in the nature of the Roman character as revealed in the daily life of its citizens, and to comment on some of the structures and works of art and literature they left behind them. By this impressionistic technique I hope to give at least an idea of the special role of Roman civilisation in the past of the Mediterranean as a whole.

Generalisation is always dangerous because of the importance of the many exceptions which can be cited to contradict it. But in the present context, where all I can hope to do is to arouse human interest without falling into the trap of pedantry, generalisation cannot be avoided. First, then, how can we say in the broadest terms what constituted the essential difference between the Romans and the Greeks? To express it most briefly we may not be too far from the truth in saying that whereas the Greeks were undoubtedly a people of genius, the Romans were a people of talent. This is not to say that so great a talent cannot approach genius, but it lacked the inspirational quality that emerged with such force from the Athens of the fifth century BC. The Greeks created a whole new way of looking at the world; they put facts that were already known in a new perspective and added new facts which fitted quite naturally, all with a highly characteristic and essentially spiritual attitude to life.

The Romans, by contrast, were far more practical. Their technical ability, their sense of order, their meticulous attention to detail – in all these things and many more in the field of organisation they rank second to none. They tackled every problem with a Germanic thoroughness, in the best sense of that word. By an energetic adherence to this attitude they not only created a condition of prolonged stability in the ancient world, the so-called *Pax Romana*, but also provided the means by which Greek civilisation was transmitted to future generations. Having said this, it is perhaps ungrateful to feel that, despite all their achievements, they lacked some essential quality. It is a quality almost impossible to define, but some readers will perhaps go along with me if I identify it with what the French call the *feu sacré*, divine fire.

Leaving aside, now, these abstract and risky generalisations for something more concrete, let us look at the lay-out and some of the buildings of the city of Rome and try to reconstruct the everyday life of an average Roman citizen. The period we shall mainly consider is the second century AD, when Roman civilisation had already reached its peak; but the routine of daily life in the city remained much the same for many centuries, so our findings can be taken as typical of a much longer period. The size of Rome and the numbers of its population in the second century have been a subject of much learned argument, but it is now generally agreed that the city covered an area of between 1,536 and 2,048 hectares, (6 and 8 square miles), and that its inhabitants numbered something over half a million. Its main public buildings all stood near the Forum, but around them the residential quarters and the higgledy-piggledy streets occupied by the poorer people and slaves spread out widely over the seven hills on which Rome was built. To the west of these ran the Tiber – the second longest river in Italy after the Po – along whose banks many dances and festivals were held. The Tiber was also an early example of the pollution

(*Opposite*) The Roman Forum looking east, with the Temple of Vespasian in the foreground and the Temples of Castor and Pollux, and Saturn on the right.

The Roman Forum in the present day (*above*), seen from the bell tower of Santa Francesca Romana, and (*right*) as it was in the early Christian era.

of the environment by man, its waters being permanently fouled by the refuse and sewage for which the inhabitants of the Eternal City, as of any other, had to find a means of disposal. Roads radiated in every direction from the city complex, some simply leading to the nearby agricultural land or to local towns and villages, others being the starting points of the great trans-continental thoroughfares of the Roman Empire.

Modern Rome and its immediate neighbourhood are richly endowed with remains of the region's antiquity. Any good guide book will give the basic facts concerning such impressive structures as the Colosseum, the Forum, the Column of Trajan, the Baths of Caracalla, and the hundreds of other antiquities that meet the eye on every side. It will also say something about the private houses, many of whose ruins still exist, of the aqueducts which brought water to the city, of the sewers whose remains can still be seen, and of the docks and shipyards which have been excavated along the banks of the Tiber. But without imagination and some knowledge of the doings of the Roman people such factual descriptions only form an arid catalogue. Ancient ruins are skeletons that need to be clothed with flesh.

The main public buildings, as has been said, were grouped round the Forum, or market-place. They were the inspiration of the Emperor Trajan, who made a creditable attempt to emulate Pericles of Athens in producing an homogeneous group of structures distinguished by their dignity of style, boldness of design, and balanced relationship to each other, to achieve a total effect. Thus the majestic simplicity of the huge esplanade of the Forum itself was augmented by a basilica known as the Basilica Ulpia, two libraries, one devoted to Latin manuscripts and the imperial archives, the other to Greek manuscripts, and the gigantic Column of Trajan itself.

During the period from dawn to midday, when the Romans took an early light lunch, the scene in and around the Forum must have been one of great animation. Before the market was re-sited in a less congested spot, the Forum itself would have been filled with portable stalls from which merchants cried their wares just as they still do in many Mediterranean towns today. Visitors to the city would have been inspecting the Basilica or gaping in amazement at the huge Column of Trajan just like their modern counterparts. Scholars and public officials would have been climbing the steps to the libraries, and those who were strolling through the city with nothing special to do would have chatted and interchanged news and gossip while sipping a drink at one of the refreshment stalls. A reflective half-hour spent in this central quarter of modern Rome will soon people the cold stones with living beings, and cause the visitor to realise that in many respects Mediterranean life continues today much as it did two thousand years ago.

A similar imaginative exercise can be performed in the nearby Colosseum. This was the site of many of the major spectacles of ancient Rome, including wild animal shows and contests, and the gladiatorial exhibitions in which two men fought each other to the death, and which have rightly cast a stain on our picture of the Roman character. The Colosseum, which is still in a magnificent state of preservation, was started in the time of

Relief showing the collection of taxes.

Vespasian, completed by Titus, and decorated during the reign of Diocletian. It was built of travertine stone from quarries near the modern town of Tivoli, which was transported to Rome along a specially-constructed road. The huge oval amphitheatre which measures 188 by 156 metres (620 by 514 feet) is enclosed by four-storeyed walls rising to a height of 57 metres (188 feet).

In this setting scenes of unspeakable carnage used to take place. Africa was ransacked for animals which were either pitted against one another in the arena or taught to perform extraordinary tricks; the spectators could watch while elephants traced Latin mottoes in the sand with their trunks or teams of cheetahs pulled carts and chariots. Sometimes men were pitted against the animals and the combats evoked the same kind of sadistic excitement among the onlookers as can be seen to this day in a Spanish bull-ring. But even more degrading were the gladiatorial combats between two men. The contestants were either slaves or men of better class who had fallen on bad times and were forced by financial necessity to adopt this terrible means of livelihood. They were housed in luxurious barracks and given the finest foods so that they would be at the peak of their condition when they had to face their ordeal.

The combats were of many different kinds. In some, two fully-armed men would simply be put to fight one another until one was at the other's mercy. A 'thumbs up' or 'thumbs down' sign from the Emperor or presiding magistrate was then sufficient to determine whether or not the victor should put the vanquished to death. In others, a fully-armed man was pitted against another who carried only a net and a trident. The latter tried to ensnare his opponent with the net so that he might stab him to death before he himself was cut up by the fully-armed man's sword. Far more savage spectacles than these, involving torture and every kind of degrada-

tion, were thought up to satisfy the blood lust of the populace. By their barbarity these performances bear witness to the progressive decadence that was in the end to bring about the downfall of Imperial Rome.

A poultry shop sign from Via della Foce. 2nd century BC.

The Colosseum was only one of the places of entertainment in ancient Rome. There were numerous theatres, including the famous Theatre of Marcellus, and particularly popular was the Circus Maximus, a huge open-air stadium with straight sides and semicircular ends. It measured some 549 metres (600 yards) long, and 183 metres (200 yards) wide; surrounding it were tiers of seats that could hold nearly half the population of the city. This was the scene of the chariot races which the Romans followed with the same enthusiasm as some people follow horse-racing or motor-racing today. The charioteers were usually slaves, but some of them by their immense courage and skill rose to be public idols. These, like modern bull-fighters, could command such high wages that they often retired as millionaires after only five or ten years' racing. The races worked the crowd up to a fever of excitement which reached its peak at the turning posts where the more skilful charioteers, by taking a riskily close turn, could often gain the advantage. The slightest misjudgement could lead to a fatal crash, and if the charioteer took the post too wide he might easily lose position or be fouled by the chariot behind as it swung inwards to take the straight. Nearly all the charioteers were young when they started their careers and many were killed in their early twenties. We have records of one Fuscus who was killed at the age of 24 after fifty-seven victories and of another called Crescens who only survived until he was 22, but in his short life earned vastly greater sums than many of his older rivals. The veteran charioteers might compete during their working life in many thousands of races. Thus the doyen of them all, named Diocles, competed in 4,257 races and carried off first prize 1,462 times.

In the Colosseum (*right*)
there took place contests of
different kinds for the entertainment of the people.
(*Below*) A boxer in repose.
(*Bottom*) Gladiatorial combats and combats with wild
beasts. The gladiators are
all identified by name.
4th-century mosaics.

(*Above*) Remains of the
Circus Maximus.

(*Right*) Chariot race in the
Circus Maximus. The turning
post is marked by three
conical columns. Marble
relief of the 1st century A.D.

Rome and the Roman Empire

The spectacles at both the Colosseum and the Circus Maximus were extremely colourful and were preceded by processions led by the magistrate in charge of the entertainment who had often paid for the whole show to curry favour with the populus. He was usually dressed in the style of a general in triumph and wore an embroidered white toga over a scarlet tunic. In his hand he brandished an ivory baton surmounted by the eagle of Imperial Rome. The charioteers' horses, which were specially bred on stud farms in Italy, Greece, Africa, and Spain, wore harnesses and breast-plates studded with pearls; while the charioteers themselves, with their glittering metallic helmets and arrogant expressions, could easily claim by their appearance alone the hysterical adulation which today is reserved for pop singers.

But life in Imperial Rome was not all circuses. For most of the time the day-to-day routine of work and home life went on just as it does now. The typical Roman house belonging to a member of the middle or upper classes was grander than its ancient Greek equivalent, but was built on roughly the same plan. That is, the rooms faced inwards towards an open courtyard surrounded in Greek style by a colonnade. In fine weather most of the social life of the householder was conducted in this open-air setting, but in winter the family and their visitors adjourned to the *atrium*, a large room with a hole in the middle of the roof designed to admit light and allow the smoke from a central fire to escape. However, as might be expected of such a rough and ready chimney, not all the smoke found its way outside the house. The roof of the atrium was often covered in soot and the very name of this room may come from the latin word *ater* meaning 'black' or 'filthy'.

From Roman writers we can reconstruct a very good picture of how these comparatively wealthy citizens spent their day. The master of the house would rise early, normally just before dawn, for in an age when artificial lighting was poor he would wish to make the best use of the hours of daylight. Moreover his bed would not have encouraged him to lie in, for although Roman beds were often ornate, the mattress was hard and was supported only by a lattice of webbing straps stretched across a wooden frame. He would have slept naked or clad only in a loin cloth known as a *licium*, warmth in winter being provided in the cold bedroom by three bed-covers. The under-blanket on which the sleeper actually lay was known as the *stragulum*, while immediately above him was a second cover known as the *operimentum*. Over all was placed a coloured quilt called the *polymitum* which not only provided additional warmth but gave the bed a more attractive appearance when it was unoccupied in the day time. The bedroom furniture was normally very sparse and simple, but an indispensable article was the chamber-pot. This was either a simple earthenware receptacle or, in the more pretentious homes, a vessel of fine silver encrusted with precious stones.

Dressing in the large semicircular drapery known as the *toga*, the citizen would have a frugal breakfast of bread and wine. This simple but satisfying 'Roman breakfast' is still commonly eaten by peasant families in the Mediterranean today. Very probably after breakfast the householder, if he

(*Overleaf*) The great peristyle of the Villa of Diomede, outside the Herculaneum Gate at Pompeii.

Rome and the Roman Empire

were at all rich or influential, would receive a number of 'clients' who had come to pay their respects or ask a favour. Clients were comparatively poor citizens who had sought the patronage of one of their wealthy neighbours and sought to enjoy his protection by a little discreet boot-licking. On their visits they had to observe a strict etiquette, putting on their best clothes and addressing their patron as 'My Lord'. Failure to observe these niceties led to their going away empty-handed, but if they stuck to the unwritten rules the patron was obligated to welcome them to his house for occasional meals and to assist them with generous presents in money and kind.

Having escaped from these chores and left the house, the citizen's first visit would in all probability be to the barber. Whereas Roman women had their hair done by servants at home, the men used to treat the barber's shop as a kind of male club where they could chat with their friends before getting down to work. This visit to the barber was a daily ritual, not of course because the men needed their hair cut so often but because they were very conscious of their personal appearance and liked to be immaculately coiffed in the style of the day. Many of the less dandified Romans frowned on this custom, however, regarding it as a sign of effeminacy, if not of outright decadence. For example, the poet Marcus Valerius Martialis, commonly known as Martial, who was of Spanish origin and in his youth lived in very humble circumstances, remarked to one man: 'There is always about you some foreign odour', and referred to another 'whose greasy hair is smelt all over the Theatre of Marcellus'.

Patrician Roman types:
(*Left*) Bust of Julius Caesar.
(*Right*) Agrippina as a young woman.

Rome and the Roman Empire

One of the functions of the barber was to give his customers their daily shave. The ancient Greeks frequently went bearded and for a time the Romans followed their example. Eventually, however, to be clean-shaven became the fashion and beards were worn only by philosophers. The best barbers were almost as highly paid as the charioteers and after a decade or so of practice could retire to large houses in the country and enjoy a life of leisure. We may be pretty sure that it was not only their artistry that brought them these rewards, however. One of the indispensable requirements of a good barber, in Roman times as now, was his complete discretion. Many a cat could have been put among the pigeons by a barber who had not learned to hold his tongue.

Now fully accoutred and groomed for the day's affairs the citizen would set out on his rounds. According to his business he would head for one of the public buildings, courts, or libraries, or simply to the Forum where he could discuss the state of the world or his personal projects with friends, partners, and counsellors over a glass of wine. Things are little changed in the Mediterranean in this respect to this day. He would then return home for a light lunch, usually followed by a short nap. The afternoon would be spent relaxing at the baths or going to one of the public spectacles. In the evening, the citizen would come home once more for the main meal of the day, to which guests were often invited, or he would go out to friends as a guest himself. In these activities the wives of married citizens were usually included, for women in ancient Rome enjoyed a large amount of emancipation. They were regarded with

Roman attire: (*Left*) Statue of Junius Brutus carrying the busts of his ancestors. (*Right*) A Roman matron, possibly Agrippina.

A 17th-century painting
by Jean Lemaire showing
Roman senators on their
way to the Forum, with
parts of the Colosseum in
the background.

great respect and, although different from men in mental make-up as well
as in body, as their equals. Women were even allowed to hold jobs,
sometimes quite unpretentious ones such as that of scribe or hairdresser,
but sometimes also positions of considerable responsibility. For instance,
the names of several women doctors have come down to us.

So far I have spoken only of Rome itself, but the same description
could be applied to any Roman city wherever it was built. The Romans
had a unique capacity for establishing centres in their colonies that were
replicas of Rome itself. Some of these were of great size and magnificence,
but even the smaller ones had the same, essentially Roman character. The
hub of the town was always the forum which, even when it was
surrounded by imposing public buildings, often preserved the character
of a general market, at least in the mornings. Peasants would sell their
produce there, fishmongers and bakers would set up their stalls, and
money-changers and bankers transact financial business across their
tables. There would also be a theatre, and sometimes in the larger cities a
great arena nearby. The lay-out of the homes of the citizens would also
follow the Roman plan, the richer men having individual houses of the
kind described above situated fairly close to the forum, the poorer people
living in a less formal agglomeration of narrow, twisting streets, and even
sometimes in tenement blocks several storeys high, at a greater distance
from the centre. If the town or city were built on a river as was often the

Rome and the Roman Empire

case, the watercourse would be spanned by a bridge, and if it were near the sea there might be ship-building yards and warehouses similar to those on the Tiber. The remains of dozens of such colonial centres can be seen on every coast of the Mediterranean today from the Straits of Gibraltar to the Levant.

The Romanisation of the entire Mediterranean on the grand scale eventually achieved was made possible not only by colonial ambition backed by exceptional military skill, but by a special talent for developing and maintaining a system of physical communications which enabled the outposts of the Empire to be in speedy and efficient touch with the centre of government in Rome. Although ships played an important part in this system it was in the construction of roads that the Romans' imaginative daring was most dramatically expressed. They in fact created a finer system of land communications than any to be developed before the invention of the macadamised road in the nineteenth century. As recently as fifty years ago the actual landscaping of roads was often greatly inferior to that employed by the Romans, who would never have built a road with the tortuous twists and turns still so characteristic of main roads in many parts of Europe. It is only since Germany embarked on her programme of autobahns during the 1930s, later adopted by many other European countries, that road construction could in any way compare with the achievements of the Romans at the beginning of our era.

Instead of weaving its way drunkenly across the countryside the typical Roman road struck across all places where there was comparatively level ground in a straight line from A to B. In more mountainous country the

The Via Appia near Terracina. This road was constructed to join Rome to Capua and was later extended to the port of Brindisi.

roads were adapted to the contours of the land with the same skill that they are in the more advanced modern roads, and they were carried across rivers or deep ravines by magnificently-constructed bridges and viaducts. The most elaborate Roman highways were known as *viae munitae*, or 'strengthened roads', which had five layers, or courses. Above a basal layer of compacted earth there were two layers of large and small stones respectively, the small stones being mixed with lime to bind them together. The fourth layer consisted of fine cement and above this, was a paving of hard stone in the form of closely fitting polygonal blocks.

Distances were measured from the famous *miliarium aureum*, or 'golden milestone', which stood in the Forum at Rome. The distances were marked on numbered milestones which stood at the side of each main road. Roadside inns where travellers could obtain a bed, food, and, if necessary, a change of horses, were a feature of the principal highways, and it is interesting to find that these hostelries were called by such names as the Cock, the Wheel, or the Dragon, reminiscent of the names given in later ages to wayside inns. These hostelries were erected mainly for the benefit of the poorer class of traveller, however, as more exalted personages preferred when possible to stay at the houses of friends or important local officials who offered them hospitality. Many remains of the Roman highway network can still be seen along the shores of the Mediterranean, including sometimes parts of the original surfacing and the ruins of inns. Modern roads in the Mediterranean region, as elsewhere in western Europe, often follow exactly the routes of the old Roman highways, and several bridges, such as the famous example at Alcantara in Spain, also survive virtually intact.

The roads were not only used by civilian officials and merchants, but served for the rapid transportation of the legions when permanent garrisons had to be relieved, or in time of war. The immense efficiency of the army was, with the advanced system of communication made possible by the roads, the twin key to the successful establishment and maintenance of the Empire.

At first the Roman army bore little resemblance to a modern army in its organisation. There were no paid soldiers, and the fighting was done mainly by wealthy members of the upper classes, known as 'patricians'. These men were proud to serve in the army as a patriotic duty, and often claimed that they could trace back their ancestry to the founding fathers of the city. Later, members of the lower classes, or 'plebeians', were admitted to the ranks but these again were not paid, their service being regarded as one of the obligations of citizenship. As time went on, however, and the Empire's frontiers were continually enlarged, it became obvious that such a tribal organisation of military duties was no longer possible. As early as the fourth century BC there was a system for introducing mercenaries into the army, and two centuries later the great general Gaius Marius established the principle of long-service commissions for up to twenty years.

I have no space, nor would it be appropriate, to give here a detailed description of the way the Roman army was organised. I will, however,

(*Opposite*) Roman dramatic masks made of stiffened linen were often copied in marble (as shown here) for decorative purposes.

say a word or two about Roman camps, as the remains of these can still be seen in many parts of the Mediterranean region. The siting and building of camps was regarded by the Romans as extremely important, and even if the army were only to pause in its march for one night, elaborate fortifications were erected to protect the troops and their commissariat. The camps were always built on the same plan whether they were to be occupied for a day or two or many months. In this way each individual soldier knew exactly what the lay-out was if he were summoned to his post in case of emergency. In the centre of the camp was placed the general's tent, with another for the officers adjacent to it. Blocks of tents for other ranks were placed in rectangular formation all around, while in front of the western gates was an open space known, in the camps as in the cities, as the forum; this corresponded to the modern barrack square. The camp was bisected by a main thoroughfare, the *via principalis*, and smaller roads running parallel or at right angles to it divided the soldiers' tents into groups. The completed camp was in the form of a square and it was surrounded on all four sides at a distance of about 66 metres (200 feet) from the tents by a rampart of earth surmounted by a palisade of wooden stakes. The earth was dug from a ditch on the outside of the rampart to give it greater height. The immense discipline and endurance of the legionaries was shown by the fact that even after a hard day's march they would construct such an elaborate camp for use only on a single night.

By the first year of the Empire the Roman army had grown from a few legions to at least 25, and numbered about 150,000 men. The legionaries wore a simple uniform consisting of a leather doublet over a woollen tunic; for warmth they had a brown-coloured cloak which also served as a blanket. They went bare-legged when fighting in the Mediterranean region, although legionaries sent to the far north were equipped with breeches or puttees. Hob-nailed sandals were the usual footgear. In battle

Rome and the Roman Empire

the soldiers' armament and weapons were equally simple and effective. The higher-ranking soldiers wore interlocking metal strips, although the heavy armour of high mediaeval Europe was not carried by the Romans. The officers wore plumed metal helmets; the rank and file had less elaborate – but equally protective – helmets of leather. All the foot soldiers carried in their left hand a *scutum*, or shield, and began the engagement by hurling two javelins at the enemy to bring down two men if possible. They then followed up their attack in hand-to-hand fighting with a two-edged sword, carrying with them a dagger as a reserve weapon if the sword should be dropped or broken.

The army deployed itself in a block-like formation, six ranks deep with a frontage of 500 men. On the wings of the phalanx were small parties of cavalry and also of infantry for scouting, skirmishing, and making sudden forays. It was always the infantry who bore the brunt of the fighting for the Romans were never exceptionally skilled in the saddle. This system of deploying troops, which provided for a great concentration of manpower in one place, was extremely successful, but it also had its disadvantages. In particular it was rather inflexible, and when Hannibal surprised the Romans by introducing so strange an antagonist as the armoured elephant, he succeeded in throwing their ranks into confusion. But the Romans were quick to counter this, introducing a more open deployment known as the *quincinx*, in which the lines of battle were deliberately broken at intervals. This allowed the leading soldiers to fall back behind their reserves if they were suddenly surprised by an elephant charge. The object of this arrangement was to hold up Hannibal's foot-soldiery while allowing the elephants themselves, already started on their charge towards the enemy, to pass through the Romans' ranks to the rear of the field where, being unsupervised, they fell into confusion and could be hamstrung and killed.

Reliefs of Roman soldiers showing their uniforms and weapons, including the *scutum* in the right-hand photograph.

We arrived at this digression on the Roman army by way of the roads they built, and no picture of the Romans in the Mediterranean would be complete without some further reference to their prowess in civil engineering. This took many forms, and the Roman sewers, canals, and aqueducts were in their own way quite as impressive as their roads. The sewers of ancient Rome, many of which are still in existence, were begun long before the time of the Empire; in fact work had begun on them in the sixth century BC, rather less than two hundred years after the founding of the city. They were constantly developed and improved, and were conceived on such a gigantic scale that a fully laden wagon could be easily driven down some of the larger conduits. Throughout the length and breadth of subterranean Rome a whole maze of these conduits converged on a central sewer, which was also the oldest of them all, the Cloaca Maxima. This huge channel collected the sewage and waste brought down to it by the lesser conduits and transported it from a spot just below the Forum to the Tiber, into which it was discharged. The exit from the Cloca Maxima, a semicircular arch 5 metres ($16\frac{1}{2}$ feet) in diameter, is still in a perfect state of preservation and can be seen today.

Exit of the Cloaca Maxima into the Tiber.

Remains of aqueducts
built by the Emperor
Claudius near Rome.

But although the Roman sewers made a great contribution to the cleanliness of the city, they do not seem to have been as effectively used as they could have been. The value of sanitation in preserving health is not easily recognised by uneducated people, who tend to take the easy way out by depositing their filth in the streets. Unfortunately Rome, even at its greatest, could not entirely eliminate these abuses, and many contemporary writers referred to the appalling condition of the streets in the poorer districts. It was not entirely due to the apathy of the people that this state of affairs came about. Although the authorities constructed public latrines in the streets which were connected with the main sewers, in private houses the arrangements for the removal of sewage seem to have left much to be desired. Aqueducts brought water to many houses, especially those of the better class citizens, but even in these the private latrines were not connected directly with the main network of city sewers. The very rich could overcome these disadvantages by building their own latrines on the ground floor in a position where they could be regularly flushed by water from the aqueduct or, if for any reason this was not forthcoming in sufficient quantities, a trench would be built to receive the sewage. This was then probably treated with deodorants and in due course removed from the trench and carted away.

Rome and the Roman Empire

One of the few disadvantages of life in some parts of the Mediterranean today is a shortage of fresh water. This is due in some cases to an exceptionally limited rainfall, but more often to the strongly seasonal flow of the rivers and the direction of the drainage in a particular region. The Romans were constantly faced with this problem, and although they normally established their main centres on rivers with a reliable flow, sometimes the water supply had to be supplemented by the construction of large aqueducts, often many miles in length, from better watered regions. These aqueducts were carried across the countryside with the same daring, imagination, and intelligence that characterised the building of the main Roman roads. They occur in all parts of the Mediterranean, but it will be sufficient here to describe only one, the famous aqueduct of Nîmes in western Provence. This was originally some 50 kilometres (31 miles) long and conveyed water from the vicinity of the modern town of Uzès to the great Roman centre of Nîmes, famous among other things for its exceptionally well-preserved amphitheatre.

Although the route of the aqueduct is known, little of it remains intact. Like all Roman aqueducts, it was lined and roofed with stone slabs which were inevitably pillaged from the original structure and used for building operations by later generations. But it has a very special interest because of the magnificent bridge known as the Pont du Gard, which carried the aqueduct over the river Gard in the French *département* of the same name. Except for a few stones of the bridge and some missing roofing slabs on the aqueduct itself, it is in an almost perfect state of preservation. To carry the aqueduct over the river at the required height of 49 metres (162 feet) it was necessary to employ three superimposed tiers of arches, six on the level of the river itself, eleven above, and thirty-five smaller arches on the top level to support the conduit. The huge blocks used in the construction, some of which weighed six tons, were lifted by a system of derricks and pulleys attached to a windlass, or winding-drum. This last was powered by a number of men in the interior who kept it revolving rather like mice on a treadmill. As the structure rose, scaffolding was erected to permit gangs of men to lever the stones into their appointed positions at the higher levels. Stones of bigger than usual length were left projecting at intervals from the sides of the bridge to provide points of support and attachment for this scaffolding, and can still be seen today.

For my wife and myself this corner of the Roman Mediterranean, hidden in a remote Provençal valley, has always had special associations. The valley of the Gard at this point is of surpassing beauty. The river flows musically along a stony bed lying between tree-covered hillsides where in spring and early summer the nightingales sing their nostalgic song. In the daytime during the season the site is often crowded, but in the evening the crowds depart, leaving only those who intend to pass the night in the riverside hotel, formerly a mill, to saturate themselves in the peaceful wonder of the scene. In the morning, when the bridge glows with the rosy light of sunrise, majestically grand and seemingly indestructible, one feels that it would be as easy to walk or ride into the old Roman

(*Above*) The magnificently preserved amphitheatre at Nimes, in Provence.

(*Right*) The Pont du Gard, spanning the river Gard, in Provence.

town of Nîmes as to start off along the hot, petrol-polluted highways that today seem always to lure the traveller to do too much too quickly in too short a space of time.

The unspoiled quality of the Pont du Gard makes it one of the most attractive Roman sites in Europe. But there are of course whole cities that stand in isolation with no modern buildings in the vicinity to spoil the effect. Pompeii is an obvious example, but has been so much written about that I would prefer to take the reader on a brief excursion to North Africa or, more specifically, Libya, to visit two Roman cities that are among the finest in the whole Mediterranean. These are Sabratha and Leptis Magna, both within a few hours drive along the coastal road from Tripoli. The full Roman colonisation of the North African coast was begun after the Punic wars, and by the first centuries of the Empire the civilised centres of Africa Nova, as the Province was called, rivalled in splendour and importance those of Italy itself. The Roman cities, not only in Libya but in what are now Tunisia and Algeria, were laid out with theatres, temples, baths, and dwelling-houses that exemplified all the magnificence and refinement of the best imperial architecture. Around them farms sprang up which provided grain for Europe, and even today it is possible to see Roman wells and cisterns working as effectively in North Africa as they did nearly two millennia ago.

Sabratha is the most westerly of the 'three cities' from which the name Tripolitania is derived, the others being Oea (where modern Tripoli now stands) and Leptis Magna itself. When my wife and I first went there in the mid-1950s Sabratha had the great attraction, selfish as the thought is, of being virtually unvisited by tourists. This situation has now changed, and Sabratha is much visited by the new generation of tourists who spend their holidays at Tripoli, but it is nevertheless far less spoiled than the Roman cities of Europe and their counterparts in the Middle East. The site lies on the sea-shore, and it adds to the pleasure of one's visit to find these evocative ruins in the midst of a splendid natural setting with the untamed breakers of the Mediterranean thundering in from the north, while to the south the vast sandy plain of the Sahara stretches away unbroken hundreds of miles to the threshold of the very different world of black Africa.

The city, which is approached down an avenue of cypresses from the main desert road leading from Tunis to Cairo, was most imaginatively excavated by the Italians before the Second World War. Not only were the excavations themselves conducted with proper scientific precision, but the site was laid out with beautiful gardens and groves of cypresses, and the white stone museum built to contain the famous Sabrathan mosaics is in perfect harmony with the landscape. Of the various ancient buildings at Sabratha by far the most impressive is the Roman theatre, which held about five thousand people and is complete except for the upper row of arches. The theatre lies only a few paces from the sea, and between it and the beach is a most delightful garden surrounded by a portico of Corinthian columns where the spectators doubtless strolled and chatted between the acts of the drama.

Rome and the Roman Empire

Circular painting of the emperor Septimius Severus with his wife and son. Septimius was born in Leptis Magna and the city reached its golden age under his reign.

The public buildings, temples, and private houses of Sabratha lie westwards from the centre, and in one of the dwellings was born Flavia Domitilla, who was to become the wife of the Emperor Vespasian. There are also the ruins of the Justinian Basilica from which one of the most famous mosaics of the Roman world was excavated and can now be seen in the nearby museum. This museum has, like the other small museums I mentioned earlier in this book, a very special charm. The thick walls make it deliciously cool – a very great attraction after the merciless assault of the desert sun which blasts down with such white intensity outside. The exhibits are exquisitely arranged to give each its full value without overwhelming the imagination and glutting the visitor with too rich an aesthetic orgy. The swallows that flit in and out and circle the roof with a velvety-soft flight like bats at twilight add a feeling of life which only enhances the atmosphere of tranquillity. The famous mosaic from the Basilica covers most of the floor of the main room. It depicts the calyx of an acanthus and two grape-laden vines. In the branches of these, birds are feasting and a fine-looking peacock and a phoenix, symbolising the idea of resurrection, can easily be singled out.

Compared with Sabratha, Leptis Magna is even more evocative and impressive. It was obviously a richer city, built on a more grandiose scale. It reached the height of its splendour under the Emperor Septimius Severus who was born within its walls and died at York in England in AD 211. At its greatest extent, at the end of the second and beginning of the third century AD, its population numbered over eighty thousand, but at this time the desiccation of North Africa was proceeding very fast and Leptis Magna diminished rapidly in importance. Evidence of the desperate effort made by its inhabitants to check the encroaching sand can still be seen in the city. For instance, in the peripheral buildings, many of which still stand, the doorways are blocked up with stone. Clearly these houses had been abandoned by their owners, and the authorities had attempted to keep the roads open by making the houses a bastion against the desert. The filling-in of the doorways was part of this defence, as at least for a time it prevented the sand from blowing in through the back and choking the thoroughfare.

All attempts to preserve Leptis Magna as an effective centre came to nothing, however. The desert was too much for it, and with the fall of the Empire there was not even any effective authority to keep the city alive at all. The population died out or dispersed and this once-splendid centre of Roman culture and civilisation was almost completely immersed in the Saharan sand. When those well-known British travellers F.W. and H.W. Beechey were exploring the northern coast of Africa in 1821 and 1822, they remarked with disappointment that Leptis Magna was so deeply buried under the sand that no proper idea could be obtained of its lay-out or character. Yet the very fact that the city was engulfed proved in the end to be a blessing to modern students of the Mediterranean. It was thereby protected from the depredations of later dwellers in North Africa who might have used its stones in constructing their own buildings, and the only real damage it suffered was the removal of about six hundred

(Opposite) The orchestra, stage and scaena frons – the elaborately colonnaded back-screen – of the Roman theatre at Sabratha. 2nd century AD.

(Overleaf) The Roman forum, Sabratha, at sunset. The columns are those of the Temple of Liber Pater.

164

of its best columns, commandeered by Louis XIV for use in the construction of the palace at Versailles, and of some additional examples that were later sent to England to make the phoney 'ruins' that can still be seen at Virginia Water in Surrey. Thus when the protective blanket of sand was eventually removed and the monuments restored by twentieth-century archaeologists, an historic city was revealed that at least equalled Pompeii in its completeness and evocative power.

In all our many travels, which have taken us to countries in all parts of the world, my wife and I have seldom been so deeply moved by any sight. True, we saw Leptis Magna in exceptionally favourable circumstances, for when we were there in 1955 we were again – as at Sabratha – entirely alone except for our kindly Arab host. We therefore had the privilege of wandering about the ruins without distraction. I doubt that even today, however, when more tourists visit the site, any imaginative traveller could find the moving effect much diminished. The city, like Sabratha, stood right at the edge of the sea and in the usual Roman style was laid out with its main public buildings adjacent to one of two impressive forums, with many houses all around. At Leptis Magna these were all laid out in a grid-like arrangement divided by narrow but straight streets. Owing to the flat nature of the terrain the winding streets so typical of the outskirts of Roman towns built in more hilly regions were entirely absent; it was possible at Leptis Magna for expansion to be made by a simple extension of the basic formal plan.

Verbal descriptions of archaeological sites are inclined to be dull to those who have not visited them, so I will not gush about the noble theatre, the magnificently colonnaded main street, the vast central forum, or the more humanly interesting swimming-pool, gymnasium, public baths, and public lavatories. But if one feature of Leptis Magna is to be singled out for its special interest, it would surely be the permanent market. The city, it seems, was sufficiently large and important for the main forum to be kept entirely as an imposing public square and the general market was sited in a different position some hundreds of yards away. This market had permanent features which show that it was dedicated entirely to its purpose and was in continual daily use. For instance, you can see here the stone counters where the Roman merchants sold their meat and fish and vegetables. Some of them are still deeply incised with the marks of the hatchet used by the butcher to chop up his carcases. Other counters, obviously for the sale of materials, are inscribed with a scale like the scales fixed to the counters in modern department stores to enable the assistant to measure out lengths of cloth. At the grain stalls you can still see the stone receptacles used for determining different quantities of barley and wheat, and at some points holes in the stone floor suggest that more temporary stalls erected by the peasants of the surrounding countryside were covered by awnings supported on poles as a protection against the sun. To walk round this market in a reflective mood is to hear the shrill cries of the merchants, the chit-chat passing between the butcher or the grocer and his customers, the angry complaints of dissatisfied clients, the barking of dogs, and the squeals and laughter

(*Opposite*) The Roman theatre at Leptis Magna, showing the beautifully restored auditorium from the north end of the stage. The auditorium was originally surmounted by a portico, parts of which remain.

of children playing around the feet of their gossiping elders. *Plus ça change . . . !*

Finally a few words concerning what I have called elsewhere* the 'metaphysical culture' of ancient Rome, and the role it played in the history of the Mediterranean. By metaphysical culture I mean the general character of a civilisation as evidenced by its arts, literature, music, and religious beliefs – complex topics that lie beyond the range of this companion. But to return rashly for a moment to broad generalisations, we can say, I think, that the metaphysical culture of the Romans never rivalled that of the Greeks, nor was even to be compared with the Romans' own more practical achievements in the field of architecture, engineering, or law-making. The best Roman sculptures were often copies of Greek originals, and even their splendid mosaics were more triumphant feats of decoration than aesthetic innovations. Roman writers and orators were more remarkable for their skill in chronicling events or exhorting their fellows to action than in the subtler, more fragile, world of pure literature. Until the Christianisation of the Empire the religious beliefs of the Romans, although to some extent based on Greek tradition, had far greater affinities with the superstitions of a savager people. Whereas one feels that the Greek gods, despite their supernatural powers, were essentially humane and approachable personages like 'men writ large', the Roman gods seem either a little remote and austere or so disagreeably coarse and unprincipled as to lack any god-like qualities at all.

Yet despite these limitations, it would be a great mistake to underestimate the Roman contribution to man's advance. If many of their statues copied Greek originals it is often only by these copies that we know what the originals were like. If the Romans put their main emphasis on order and stability rather than an apocalyptic vision of the universe, it is only through this very order and stability that the Mediterranean, and with it the rest of the world, could become the testing ground for the most adventurous human ideas. But to proceed further into these deep and dangerous waters of generalisation would lay me open to many justifiable criticisms of ignorance, prejudice, superficiality, or just simple bad judgement. Although this would be an entertaining exercise it could hardly be called constructive, so in the next chapter I will simply conclude this summary account of the Mediterranean in the past by tracing a few lines through the maze of events which took place between the fall of Rome and the present day.

* *A Million Years of Man*, Weidenfeld and Nicolson, 1965.

The basilica built by Septimius Severus at Leptis Magna, seen from the north-western corner.

7

From Rome to the Renaissance

An attempt to give any picture of the story of the Mediterranean for as long a period as fifteen hundred years in one chapter may seem presumptuous, and indeed it is. But no companion to the region could aim to be truly companionable unless it gave perspective to at least some of the major events of this last period of Mediterranean history and mentioned a few of the outstanding monuments dating from the period. I must therefore ask the reader to give this chapter his special indulgence and not to be too irate if I cannot tell him many things that he might want to know.

The story begins with the break-up of the Roman Empire, of which the immediate cause was the pressure exerted upon its European frontiers by the barbarian tribes of the north. During the period of its greatness the Empire could easily have dealt with this threat, but ironically it was its very success as a unifying force that eventually caused the fragmentation of its territories. The point is that the little replicas of Rome which sprang up all over the Empire gradually acquired an autonomous life, and through the long years of peace and prosperity their link with the mother city became ever more tenuous. It was just as much fun to live in Massilia (the modern Marseilles), Leptis Magna, or Carthago Nova, as it was in Rome itself, and each of these major cities of the Empire, as well as many others, basked in their sense of security and independence. It seemed as if the *Pax Romana* would never end. The colonists, like the dwellers in the capital, became progressively more hedonistic and self-satisfied, and the ideals of the Stoics and others who believed in a simple, self-disciplined life, were swamped by the accelerating trend to decadence.

(*Above*) A medieval Islamic astrolabe.
(*Opposite*) The interior of St Sophia, Istanbul.

From Rome to the Renaissance

Coin of Constantine.

Coin of Justinian.

The real crisis came at the beginning of the fourth century AD when the Emperor Constantine was compelled to move the capital of the Empire to Byzantium, the city on the Bosphorus which became known first as Constantinople, after the Emperor himself, and then as the modern Istanbul. The Empire was therefore divided into an eastern and western part with the main centre of power in the east. The western part, which still retained Rome as its nominal capital, struggled on for another century, but constant harassment by the barbarian invaders eventually brought its glories to an end. It was left to Byzantium to be the custodian of classical civilisation and pass on its ideals and achievements to future generations.

The story of the next fifteen centuries is intensely complicated and it would be impossible for any one mind to unravel the mass of detail and draw a coherent picture. The broad lines of development in the Mediterranean region are, however, clear. Three main influences were at work. The first of these was Byzantium itself, a centre that gave the lie, as it has often been given since, to Kipling's statement that 'East is East and West is West and never the twain shall meet'. Byzantium, as we shall see, was a meeting-place and melting-pot for culture influences from both Europe and Asia.

The second force that was to shape the latter history of the Mediterranean was the Christian religion. This religion found the terms of its appeal in its very simplicity and its reliance on the basic principle of universal love. It maintained that the real victories in life do not go to the ruthless, the greedy, the power-seekers, or to those who are simply physically strong. It insisted courageously that all life is a unity, and that aggressive behaviour always loses out in the end when faced with charitable but firm gentleness. The success of this philosophy of loving-kindness is proved by the fact that it permeated the greater part of the Mediterranean in an astonishingly short space of time. A third, and admittedly more militant, influence was that of Mohammedanism. After about AD 570, the approximate date of the birth of the prophet Mohammed at Mecca, this religion quickly became the unifying force of the Arab world. As the whole culture and thinking of the modern Mediterranean, and therefore the rest of the civilised world, depends on the evolving interplay of these three influences I must now go into a little more detail concerning their respective roles. This is not only necessary to help us understand the culture and character of the Mediterranean today, but also to add interest to the still-existing physical works of man constructed since classical times.

Byzantium, we must remember, was officially a Christian centre, for the movement of the capital there had coincided with Constantine's Christianisation of the Empire. The old gods gave place to the One True God whom Christ insisted controlled the destinies of men. The stabilising force of Byzantium, inspired by the Christian faith, endured for a thousand years after its foundation, and during this millennium it was the only continuously-functioning empire in the world. Unlike its western counterpart, it successfully withstood the barbarian hordes that attempted to

disrupt it from the north and east, and although it was often in danger from these threats it never actually succumbed.

Much of the credit for the strength and stability of Byzantium must go to the Emperors who ruled it in the first two or three centuries of its existence. There was an intensive revision of the administrative system, a tauter and more serviceable codification of laws and, above all, great emphasis on the re-organisation of the army. The Empire was divided into seven districts known as *themes*, each having a military governor with the rank of general and a corps of ten thousand men under his command. The corps in each district was divided into two brigades, each commanded by a brigadier, and these were in turn subdivided into regiments under colonels, companies under captains, and squads of ten men under corporals. In the Byzantine army we can therefore see the organisation of the modern army foreshadowed; its hierarchy, except for some differences in the naming of the ranks of the officers in charge, was virtually the same as is found in the armies of today.

The theory and practice of warfare was also studied in great depth at this time by the generals, and instruction was given to junior officers in military schools. Many manuals of strategy and tactics were written, and some of these have come down to us. It is possible to learn from such sources a great number of interesting facts – for instance, that although the importance of the infantrymen continued to be recognised, there was

Medieval plan of Constantinople. The large domed structure on the right is St Sophia. Across the Golden Horn can be seen the Genoese-built tower of Galata.

From Rome to the Renaissance

a much greater emphasis on the role of the more swiftly-moving cavalry, the potentialities of which had been much neglected by the Romans of Italy.

The heavy cavalry of the Byzantine Empire represented the first use of the heavily-armoured rider who was to play such a spectacular and effective role in the wars of the Middle Ages throughout Europe. Although the Byzantine cavalryman was not, like the late medieval knight, as fully encased in metal as a sardine in a tin, he nevertheless wore a formidable defensive armament consisting of a steel cap, a long mail shirt, steel shoes, and metal-covered gauntlets; his weapons consisted of a broadsword, a dagger, a lance, and a short bow, although not each soldier carried all four. The horses, too, had some protection, those in the front ranks wearing steel breast-protectors and frontlets or metal head coverings.

The light cavalry relied more on swift and unencumbered movement both for attack and escape. Nevertheless the riders wore chain mail which protected them from the worst effects of blows received in skirmishes. Other features of the Byzantine armies were improvements in both medical aid for the wounded and in the engineering services. A special corps carried wounded men to the rear on horseback where they were tended by doctors at pre-established posts. A corps of engineers was also formed which did not play an active part in the fighting except in dire emergency. Their main job was to construct fortified camps and to carry

The Byzantine walls of Constantinople with the remains of watch towers. The walls surrounded the city as can be seen in the medieval plan on p. 175.

pontoons on the backs of oxen and other beasts of burden so that they would be ready to throw bridges across any watercourses that impeded the army's advance.

Apart from a military headquarters there was also in each province a civil and ecclesiastical authority, although the military governor outranked everyone else. The job of the civil governor was to oversee the whole of the administrative structure of the province and to carry out such directives as were transmitted from Constantinople. Each province also had its bishop with his hierarchy of lesser ecclesiastics. These, like the civil governor and his staff, enjoyed a certain amount of local autonomy, but the main cohesive force that caused the Byzantine Empire to hold together came, as it did in the early days of Rome, from the capital.

Constantinople was an extremely well-organised city, a city where, in an atmosphere of opulent splendour created by the mingling of the cultures of east and west, a highly evolved social machine made itself responsible for the day-to-day running of the Empire. At the peak of the social structure stood, of course, the Emperor, who was ultimately responsible for every major decision. After him the most important post was that of the Master of Offices, who was Prime Minister, Foreign Secretary, Minister of Posts and Head of the Civil Service all at the same time. He also had under his control the Imperial Treasury, which was divided into two sections. The first of these, known as the Count of the Sacred Largesses, was the main source of the money needed to fulfil the financial obligations of the Empire. The second, known as the Count of

In the heyday of the Byzantine empire Constantinople was the artistic centre of the world, and famous in particular for its mosaics. Detail of a 6th-century mosaic from the Great Palace.

From Rome to the Renaissance

Private Estate, simply managed the land that earlier Emperors had confiscated.

The money that flowed into the coffers from taxes was assigned to different budgets, the two most important being that of the army, on which the security of the Empire depended, and that of the court. The court spent vast sums on elaborate ceremonies, state journeys, and other displays of grandeur, as well as dispensing alms to the poor of the city and giving help to citizens distressed by such natural disasters as floods and earthquakes. The taxes came from much the same sources as modern taxes and were varied from time to time for reasons of domestic expediency. The running fight between the tax collector and the reluctant taxpayer was thus as much a feature of Byzantine life as it is of ours.

Also centralised under the Emperor was the administration of justice, and it was at Constantinople that the laws of ancient Rome were further evolved and recodified into something like the legal code we still have in force in the west today. All ordinary crimes and disputes were settled by the civil judicary, but more personal matters concerning human relations and behaviour, such as divorce and offences against Christian morality, were referred to the ecclesiastical courts. These also tried civil offences if both parties to the action agreed that an ecclesiastical judgement would be preferable.

So much for the general picture. Now what is the main legacy of the Byzantine world to those who visit the Mediterranean today and wish to re-create in their imagination something of the spirit that infused the Empire at that time? Here without doubt the answer lies in its art, and especially its architecture. Despite the wars that the Empire had to conduct against the barbarians and other hostile forces on its northern and eastern frontiers, its riches were so great that it could provide in good measure the atmosphere of security and certainty which produces the most highly sophisticated art. While it is true that many artists have reached the zenith of their achievement through a constant struggle with external circumstances, these are exceptions rather than the rule and their masterpieces usually represent the intense personal struggle of the artist himself in his attempt to adjust to life. Byzantine art was essentially that of a stable society, secure in its own strength, sustained by the certainties of the Christian faith, and quite sure where it was going. It represented the flowering tradition of a whole people, not the agonised struggle of the individual.

The churches or basilicas of Constantinople and the Grecian provinces are an outstanding expression of this artistic certainty. The basilica was derived from a standard Roman public hall with three aisles divided by interior colonnades. Examples of its use in Byzantine times occur not only at Constantinople itself, where St Sophia is one of the great ecclesiastical buildings of the world, but in Salonica and other provincial cities. As the form evolved, its principal feature became a round dome balanced over a square, a type of construction posing complicated engineering problems that were, however, triumphantly solved. In time, both for engineering and religious reasons, the Greek cross was widely adopted as the basic

The Byzantine style, as used in Western churches. 13th-century cloister at San Paolo fuori le Mura, Rome.

plan for the basilicas, the dome being mounted on the square where the arms crossed. In the Greek cross the arms are of equal length, but during the Middle Ages one of them was elongated to make the more typical cruciform pattern. This was equally effective for supporting the dome as is shown by many thousands of churches in the Mediterranean region and elsewhere which derive from Byzantine models.

The interiors of the churches were decorated with the finest examples of Byzantine pictorial art, much of the adornment in the richer examples taking the form of mosaics. In churches less lavishly endowed, the place of the mosaics was taken by frescoes, but the style of the decoration remained similar. Byzantine art was dedicated to the glory of God and the instruction of the worshipper. It broke new ground in moving away from naturalism and adopting a more abstract means of expression based on the interplay of form and colour. By belittling it as naïve, some critics have only betrayed their own naïvety, for all Byzantine art is in fact highly sophisticated. It foreshadows the work of such artists as El Greco, and almost any twentieth-century painter would find himself more at home with it than with most of the art of the preceding five or six centuries.

179

From Rome to the Renaissance

Remains of Byzantine churches with their magnificent mosaics are common still in Turkey and Greece, but splendid examples can also be seen by the curious traveller in Italy and France. One of the most ravishing is the church of San Vitale at Ravenna, which so impressed Charlemagne when he visited the city that he determined to have a replica erected at his residence at Aix-la-Chapelle. He had settled there because he liked swimming in the hot springs, and felt that a copy of San Vitale as his palace chapel would be an additional aid to contemplation and repose. The replica, built by Charlemagne's architect Odo of Metz, still exists, and although it lacks some of the refinements of the original structure it is nevertheless an architectural miracle. Like its model, and hundreds of other churches of the earlier Byzantine period, this church built at the dawn of the ninth century was at least three hundred years ahead of its time both in its intricacy of design and the artistic excellence of its decoration.

The later story of the Byzantine Empire, and the stages by which a new Christianised empire, known as the Holy Roman Empire, evolved in the west, are far too complex to lie within the scope of this companion. These matters belong to the history books and are sorted out with tremendous verve and imagination in H. A. L. Fisher's classic *History of Europe*. It is, however, necessary to say something, even if only in general terms, about the growth in the Mediterranean region of those two great manifestations of the human spirit, Christianity and Mohammedanism.

Christianity, as we have seen, was one of the major influences in maintaining the stability of the Byzantine Empire. But it was not only at Constantinople that the influence of this outstandingly successful religion was felt. The spirit of Christianity, radiating from its starting point in the eastern Mediterranean, was not only to imbue the Mediterranean itself, or at least its northern shores, with an entirely new set of personal values, but in an astonishingly short space of time to conquer the whole of the western world. When we consider that the Christian era has even now lasted only two millennia, and when we contemplate the vast number of works of art and architecture it has inspired, not to mention the contributions it has made to western morals and western thought, we cannot but be amazed at its spiritual power.

With the growing conflict that arose through the centuries between Jew and Gentile, it has sometimes been forgotten that Christ himself was a Jewish prophet. He was constantly quoting the Old Testament, and it was only through the revolutionary nature of some of his ideas that he became an outcast from Jewry. Persecuted not only by the Roman authorities, but even by members of his own religion, he nevertheless spoke words and propagated a new attitude to life based on a simple goodness and integrity that must have appealed to some deep inner need of mankind at that time. And not at that time only, for in the centuries that have followed almost all the great cultural achievements of western man have been inspired by what is basically a Christian attitude, whether this has been openly recognised or not.

In the Mediterranean region it is mostly in the design and decoration

St Peter's, Rome.

of the churches that the imaginative visitor can see the full range and quality of the Christian spirit. These churches show an astonishing variety. They range from the mighty St Peter's at Rome to the humblest chapel in a hilltop village in Provence. There are also many striking modern churches, such as the Chapelle du Rosaire by Matisse at Vence, and the imaginative little church at St Martin-de-Peille where two picture windows, one each side of the altar, seem to bring the very mountains into touch with the congregation and to augment the inspirational effect of the service with an awareness of natural wonders.

All of these churches have their own character, but all are imbued with that particular brand of Roman Catholicism which is so typical of the Mediterranean atmosphere. This is difficult to define exactly, but briefly the Catholics of the Mediterranean seem possessed of a simplicity and tolerance that cannot be so easily found in the harsher conditions of the north. To me, at any rate, the Catholic spirit of the Mediterranean, based on the cohesion of the family and the love its members bear one another, is a refreshing and cleansing faith.

Compared with Christianity the spread of the Moslem religion, or Mohammedanism if we prefer, was an altogether more militant affair. When Mohammed was born at the end of the sixth century Arabia showed no signs of unity. Its desert wastes were inhabited by a number of primitive nomadic tribes who were constantly bickering and raiding each other's encampments. They had no common language and each spoke a dialect which was largely incomprehensible to neighbouring tribes. They had no common religion, and a complete lack of cohesion as a social group.

182

From Rome to the Renaissance

The gods of the various religions that existed there were largely nature-gods associated with springs, wells, trees, and other phenomena that relieved the arid loneliness of the desert. The young prophet of Mecca was soon stirred to action by this unhappy state of affairs. He became fanatically religious, with a passionate desire to unite all the peoples of Arabia in a single faith. In everything except humility he strongly resembled Christ. For instance, he preached an uncompromising monotheism, insisting that instead of a bewildering array of local gods there was only One True God, named Allah. This god was omnipotent, omniscient, and omnipresent, the sole ruler of the world and the sole arbiter of human affairs. And just as Christ claimed to be the Son of God in the context of Christianity, so Mohammed claimed to be the only authentic prophet of Allah.

With two religious systems claiming the same thing, it was obvious that the Middle East was heading for trouble. There would, however, have been no serious challenge to Christianity had it not been for Mohammed's extraordinary abilities as a preacher, organiser, and soldier. Whereas a bunch of ragged and disorganised desert tribes, even if not torn by inner dissensions, would certainly have failed to disrupt the fabric of Christianity, the threat from the community of highly-disciplined and fanatical Moslems that Mohammed succeeded in establishing was quite a different matter. In a remarkably short space of time Mohammed's inspiration drew the Moslems together into a close-knit brotherhood and they began to emerge from their Arabian homeland to embark on the spread of their faith and philosophical ideas by force of arms.

The crusading zeal with which the early Moslems sought to propagate their gospel through the Mediterranean world, and even into the recesses of Asia, knows no parallel. Compared with the vast sweep of their military plans the Christian Crusades of the Middle Ages seem little more impressive than local forays. Under Mohammed's immediate successor, Abu Bekr, the Arabs became masters of the whole eastern Mediterranean as far as the frontiers of Byzantium, the whole North African coast, and even advanced into western and southern France by way of the Straits of Gibraltar and Spain. The Byzantine Emperors had to abandon the lands they had conquered in Syria and draw a new frontier in the mountains of Anatolia. The Arabs also advanced relentlessly into Asia, invading Persia and Afghanistan and carrying their religion by armed might beyond the Indus and the Oxus and the lands far into the Indian peninsula.

The effect of these Arab conquests on the Mediterranean was twofold. First, they established a number of important colonial centres distinguished by a characteristic architectural style. The whole of the eastern and southern shores of the Mediterranean are given a special character by the splendid mosques and other ecclesiastical and public buildings put up by the Arabs during the early centuries of their period of domination. Their architecture is also a feature of several regions in southern Spain, many of the buildings both there and in other lands being of great age and a distinctive oriental beauty. The second effect of the Arab conquests was more intangible. It was to do with the quality of their intelligence and

Christ in majesty; detail of the portal of the Romanesque church at Vézelay.

183

وكـاد ينزع الجـمـال الـشّـر وانـشـد

مـا الحـج سهـل ثـا وبّـا واد لا جـا ولا لغـيـا اثـل اجـمـا لا واجـد لـا

(*Opposite*) Stained-glass window in the Chapelle du Rosaire, Vence, designed and decorated by Matisse.

(*Above*) The conquering Moslem army marching. From a medieval Arab manuscript.

thought which, contrary to some unfounded prejudices, was of a very high order. While it is true that the native culture of the Arabs was comparatively limited, they proved themselves to be adept at transmitting the cultural heritage of other eastern peoples and in assimilating into their own traditions the more advanced ideas of the lands they overran. The result of these new contacts was to make the more intelligent Arabs, of which there were many, question the purely dogmatic aspect of their faith and to widen their range of interests. Thus from an elaborate military operation, inspired by a fanatical faith, Arab savants built up an intellectual brotherhood which in the Middle Ages was to be the main custodian of intellectual ideas until the time of the Renaissance.

Of the many contributions which the Arabs made to the Mediterranean world, perhaps the most important was the introduction of Arabic numerals instead of the cumbersome Roman numerals previously used. They also developed many of the ideas which they read about in Syrian translations of Greek books, and the Mediterranean, like the rest of the world, owes especially to the Arabs the development of mathematics. The very word 'algebra' comes from the arabic *al-jebr*. They also pioneered the science of chemistry, which derives its name from the arabic *al-kimia*, meaning 'the art of pouring', and they applied scientific principles to such varied subjects as dentistry, sanitation, cartography, and the design of lenses.

Moslem architecture varies a great deal in style from place to place. This is because the original Moslem hordes who swept along the North African coast and penetrated the heart of Asia were, as we have seen, nomadic tribes with a very rudimentary culture of their own. In consequence they were much influenced by local practices. Originally they had no dwellings except camel-hair tents, similar to those used by the modern

184

(*Opposite*) Painting of a bull-fight in St Mark's Square, Venice, by P. P. Pannini, showing part of the façade of the Byzantine basilica of St Mark's.

A legacy of the Moslem invasion of Spain: a Moorish patio in the convent of Santa Clara at Tordesillas, near Valladolid.

Bedouin, and their first mosques were simply crude enclosures for communal worship. However, in the various countries they conquered, the Moslems were quick to take advantage of the services of trained craftsmen to make their mosques more elaborate. With their growing prosperity they began to adopt the same practice in the building of palaces and houses. The Moslem world is therefore remarkable for the various schools it produced in architecture and also in art. Five of these are generally recognised: the school of Syria and Egypt; the Turkish school; the North African or 'Moorish' school; the Persian school; and the Indian school.

Many of the finest Arab mosques were built in Cairo, and I have been privileged to visit several of these personally. They are characterised by slim, graceful minarets and imposing domes, and the horseshoe arch is a common feature of many Moslem structures both here and elsewhere in the Arab world. The interiors of the mosques are usually decorated with ornamental screens of wood or marble, and stone latticing is often used to cover windows to protect the interior from the glare of the sun. Marble inlay and paving are other common features of most mosques.

Unfortunately, in modern times the rather blatant taste of the Arab people has led to a deterioration in the decor of the mosques. When my wife and I made a memorable stay in Cairo in 1955 we visited a large number of Moslem buildings and were disappointed by the crudeness and vulgarity of much of the more recent decor which often quite destroyed the simple dignity of the original structures. In the Mohammed Ali mosque at the Citadel in Cairo, for instance, the floor was entirely covered

187

A 13th-century Arabic map of the world drawn by the geographer Ibn Said.

with a flashy red pile carpet similar to those found in the foyers of western cinemas. An enormous chandelier was surrounded by a circle of electric lamps, dusty and flickering alarmingly through faulty wiring, which resembled nothing so much as a number of unwashed goldfish bowls. The pulpit was approached by a staircase, shaped rather like the mobile stairways that give access to airliners, painted in the most lurid shades of gold, green, and blue. Too often, also, the modern Arabs have succumbed to the lure of gadgetry. It is now quite rare in the Moslem world to hear the romantic cry of the *muezzin*, or priest, who in the old days used to climb one of the main minarets of the mosque to summon the faithful to prayer. His voice is now recorded – and often very badly recorded – on a scratched disc. This is switched on at the appointed hour and the weirdest noises accompanied by the hiss of the needle assail the listener's ear. It is also not uncommon for the record to be put on in the wrong place, or the wrong call to be transmitted, whereupon there is a hasty fumble with the disc often accompanied by a hideous rasping noise as the needle skids across several grooves at once.

Such disasters scarcely add to the dignity of the mosques or enable one to savour in the right spirit their holy character. However, there are exceptions, and few buildings are more attractive in their own style than

188

the mosques of Sultan Hassan and Ibn Tulun in Cairo, and the little El Giyushi mosque on the heights of the neighbouring Mokattam Hills which fringe the Nile valley to the east of the city. These mosques, as do many others in the Arab world, have a deeply moving religious character and are largely free of eye-sores and distractions. The services in all the mosques are given to segregated congregations. The men occupy the front of the mosque and the women, still heavily veiled in spite of the Egyptian modernisation programme, are placed behind them concealed by one of the wooden latticed screens mentioned above. Christian visitors are not always allowed into the mosques, but sometimes if they remove their shoes in conformity with Moslem custom, they may stand at the back and appreciate the exotic character of the service.

Although the religious ceremonies of the Arabs are greatly different from those of the Christians, despite the fact that the two religions have the same basic idea, the influence of Arab architecture on the ecclesiastical architecture of the west has been considerable. Through contacts with the Arab world during the Middle Ages, and especially in the Crusades, educated observers brought back many ideas that were later incorporated into the history of European gothic. Sir Christopher Wren even went so far as to call western gothic architecture 'Saracenic', the name Saracen being of course synonymous with Moslem or Mohammedan. As an architectural term the word Saracenic is now obsolete, but its use by Wren shows how this master architect recognised the affinities between the two styles. The borrowings in the other direction were less marked, in fact scarcely existent, although many mosques incorporate actual building materials taken from Christian buildings. The habit of quarrying stone from pre-existing structures has been common throughout the history of all forms of building, and the visitor to mosques constructed during the last few centuries should not be surprised to find that they often incorporate Roman and Greek columns and capitals. One interesting influence of Christianity on Mohammedanism which is not generally known is that the very earliest mosques, or rather the rude places of worship that were ancestral to the mosques, were all orientated to face Jerusalem. This was quickly changed, however, and all later mosques are orientated towards Mecca, facing generally east in the Mediterranean world and west on the mainland of Asia.

Arab art is as distinctive as its architecture. Traditionally the faith forbade the representation of the human figure or even of animal or plant life. This taboo can still be traced in the immense reluctance of the less sophisticated Arabs even to have their photographs taken. But already in earlier times some Moslem artists were breaking with tradition – at least as far as the representation of plants was concerned. Leaves and flowers are incorporated in many of their pictures and, later, animals and even human forms were added. This mainly occurred in the Moslem countries of western Asia, however, and even there living things were never represented with the same freedom as they were, for instance, in China. The word 'arabesque' is of obvious derivation and delicate arabesque designs were commonly used in Moslem ceramics, which are equally remarkable

(*Above*) an example of Fatimid impost block from the 12th-century mosque of Vizier Saleh Tala'i, Cairo.

(*Below*) A verset from the Koran used as wall decoration in the Great Mosque at Bursa.

for the harmonious character of their colours and the refinement of their glaze. Moslem art was even applied to the accoutrements of war and, especially in Turkey, cone-shaped helmets were made with beautiful arabesque engravings and decorations of gold and silver. Another expression of the Arabs' artistic sense is found in their calligraphy which reveals a subtlety and refinement equal, if not superior, to that of any other people's in the world.

Summing up the role of the three influences we have discussed on the course of Mediterranean history again involves generalisations with all their dubious over-simplifications. Briefly, however, I do not think we shall be too far off the mark if we regard the moral influence of Christianity as the main stabiliser of Mediterranean society after the collapse of the western Roman Empire. It was not only a force in its own right, but also gave moral authority to Byzantium, where the organising ability of ancient Rome found expression in a still more tautly-knit society which for a thousand years provided a reasonably effective bulwark between east and west. Byzantium, backed by the moral authority of Christianity, in fact provided a kind of blueprint for an orderly and well-administered world. It carried forward the Roman concept of law and government in a highly organised form, and also made an important contribution to the history of Christian art.

The influence of the Arabs was less in the field of order, for they were inexperienced in the arts of government and, vast as their empire was, it

(*Above*) Courtyard of the mosque of Ibn Tulun, Cairo. Built in 876–9, this magnificent building, covering $6\frac{1}{2}$ acres, contains the third earliest example of the pointed arch, two centuries before the establishment of the Gothic pointed arch.

(*Opposite*) Grand entrance to the mosque of Sultan Hassan, Cairo. Lithograph by David Roberts from his book, *Egypt and Nubia*.

From Rome to the Renaissance

tended to fragment with its geographical extensions. Its main value historically proved to be the new stream of ideas it produced, which were integrated into the cultures of the lands it conquered and were in turn influenced by local attitudes. Apart from introducing their system of numerals to the western world, perhaps the most important single contribution made by the Arabs was their effectiveness in transmitting, and also originating, scientific ideas. This even exceeded their contributions in the fields of art and architecture, great as these were. The Christian faith, as it manifested itself in the Mediterranean at that time, whether in Byzantium or elsewhere, was distinctly hostile to science, so in this field the Arabs stood alone. In fact, had it not been for Arab scholars and philosphers, the hostility of Christianity to science might well have led to this particular road to knowledge being greatly retarded. As it was, by a fortunate historical accident, the varying attitudes of the three major influences were able eventually to survive and cross-fertilise each other in that remarkable explosion of human cultural progress known as the Renaissance.

The Renaissance began, like many episodes in history that have proved to have the highest human value, in the Mediterranean region and spread from there to the countries of the north. It was a time of intellectual and spiritual ferment, when a new sense of wonder was returning to the world and men were beginning to reassess their views concerning nature as a whole and the very meaning of human life. No longer could the manifold facts revealed in ancient records or expressed in the art of previous generations be comfortably fitted into a dogmatic frame. Matters that were formerly regarded as incontrovertibly established for all time began to be called in question. Man began to make new voyages not only in space and

16th-century Turkish dish painted in grey-green, blue and turquoise with black outline.

time through geographical exploration and historical research, but also in the analysis of the workings of his own mind and spirit. The masterpieces of Renaissance art and literature that have come down to us bear witness to the profundity of this new stir of evolutionary energy in the Mediterranean region.

The adventures of Mediterranean man from the Renaissance to today are fully documented and set out in a vast array of history books. Having already had the effrontery in my previous book, *A Million Years of Man*, to point the significance of this story in part of a single chapter, I do not propose to try my luck again at an even shorter length. Every traveller in the Mediterranean can use other sources of information to delve more deeply into such aspects of this intricate but wonderful story as particularly intrigue him.

My treatment of this historical outline of Mediterranean culture has of necessity been very brief and sketchy, but for this I make no apology. A companion should not be a bore. It is not its role to make a pretentious display of scholarship, nor to baffle the person who may consult it with a mass of detailed facts. A companion should try above all to be companionable, and if in the course of a few hours chat a curious fact or two should emerge that could be worth further thought, or give a pointer to a line of enquiry that may prove to be of interest, then this is a bonus, not the main object. I nevertheless dare to hope that by now the reader may perhaps at least feel armed with some sort of time-map which, however roughly drawn, will enable him to place some of the things he sees in the Mediterranean in historical perspective. He may in any case care to try using it in an experimental spirit as he joins me in the next Part in looking at some aspects of the Mediterranean today.

15th-century Mamluk helmet engraved with versets from the Koran and damascened in gold and silver.

PART III

ASPECTS OF THE
MODERN MEDITERRANEAN

8

The Green Mantle

I explained in Chapter 1 that the most convenient way of defining the Mediterranean region was the land lying within the olive line. This olive zone, which extends along the sea's shores to varying depths everywhere except to the north of the Libyan and Western Deserts may be likened to a vast botanical garden enclosing a salt-water lake. Not only do such typical Mediterranean trees as olives, pines, and holm oaks grow there, but a rich flora, wild and cultivated, native and exotic, utilitarian and ornamental, which exceeds in variety, interest, and sheer voluptuousness any to be found in a similarly limited and well-defined area in any other part of the world. To take only two examples, in south-eastern France an area no bigger than Rhode Island provides suitable conditions for at least 80 per cent of the world's temperate and subtropical plants, many of which are actually grown there, and the tiny French *département* of Var, which can be driven across in an hour, contains more wild plant species than the whole of the British Isles.

With such a wealth of riches to choose from it is clearly impossible to give more than an extremely generalised picture of plant life within the olive line. I shall therefore begin by defining the principal vegetal zones and then make some reference to the cultivation of Mediterranean plants, both indigenous and introduced, and to some of the more typical, beautiful, or curious species that the visitor can easily see.

Six main kinds of wild and indigenous flora are recognised, all lying broadly within the olive zone although some occur in such high or arid regions that olives do not flourish with them in all parts of their range. Like all such divisions they are largely arbitrary, for vegetation in com-

(Opposite) A maritime pine (*Pinus pinaster*) near the windmill where Alphonse Daudet wrote his *Lettres de mon moulin*, at Fontvielle in Provence. (*Above*) An olive tree in Provence.

The stone or umbrella pine (*Pinus pinea*) is found all over the northern shores of the Mediterranean.

mon with the whole of nature is a continuum with infinite gradations, but as convenient labels to help us sort out the complexities of the subject they will serve well enough.

The first two divisions, consisting of typical Mediterranean forest and mixed evergreen and deciduous forest, lie entirely within the zone of olive cultivation. The most characteristic tree of the typical forest is the holm oak (*Quercus ilex*) which as I stated in Chapter 1 is also a candidate for defining the limits of the Mediterranean natural region. Its range is more extensive in the west and more limited in the east than the olive's, however, so it does not provide so satisfactory an indicator. It is a handsome tree with small, shiny, dark green leaves, gnarled into dramatic shapes in the drier parts of its range (it will tolerate prolonged periods of drought and an annual rainfall as low as 38 centimetres, or 15 inches), but growing in damper spots to huge and elegant proportions. In the Western Basin, particularly on the west side of peninsulas, it is found in association with the cork oak (*Quercus suber*) and is often replaced by it. This tree is well-known to tourists visiting the French Riviera, where it occurs in large numbers on the low coastal mountains. The bark peeled from its trunk is the source of the cork which gives it its name and plays a role in the economy of several western Mediterranean countries. In the east, conditions are not sufficiently humid for its survival and it is not widely found.

Apart from these oaks the most typical remnants of the original wild forest of the Mediterranean are the conifers, especially the pines. The stone or umbrella pine (*Pinus pinea*), with its characteristic parasol-like shape, has an enormous range on the sea's European shores and occurs as high as 914 metres (3,000 feet) in some regions. The maritime pine (*Pinus pinaster*) is often found in association with it, but not at such comparatively high altitudes, while the Aleppo pine (*Pinus halapenis*) is particularly typical of arid regions such as the *garrigue*, or hot heathlands. The smell of the resin oozing from the superheated pines on a July day, combined with the regular throbbing of the cicadas which live on their trunks, is for me, and doubtless for many others, one of the most evocative aspects of the Mediterranean environment. It is full of passion and sensuality and sun magic – a unique experience to anyone imaginatively receptive to the power of smells and sounds.

The olive itself is now almost entirely a cultivated tree, growing in terraced rows on the hillsides or in vast orchards where the individual trees seem to emerge from the ground, in Henry James's phrase, 'like little puffs of grey smoke'. But the wild olive is still found, and is especially common in Greece in the low scrubby vegetation known as the *maquis*. The maquis as a whole is another characteristic feature of Mediterranean vegetation, extending for hundreds of square miles over the wild hillsides where it forms the home of the wild boar, one of the most magnificent game animals to survive in modern Europe. The maquis, like the artificially-created arable land, has largely replaced the original virgin forests of oak and pine which once covered the shores of the Mediterranean on all sides. In botanical terms, it is mostly a degenerate form of the wild

Henry James described the olive trees as 'little puffs of grey smoke'. A view of the valley of the Durance.

The Green Mantle

forests of former times. It is truly wild, however, whereas much of the oak and pine still growing is the result of the artificial reintroduction of trees in man-managed plantations created to fill specific needs.

Typical maquis plant assemblages vary from place to place, and the plant cover has a different appearance in each. In some regions it is continuous, in others patchy; it may consist of exceptionally low woodland about shoulder high, relieved by occasional clumps of conifers and oaks; or elsewhere of shrubs so densely intertwined that they form an impenetrable thicket. There is a great range of maquis plants, including lentisk, oleander, laurel, strawberry trees, privet, broom, gorse, erica, dwarf palms, and many others. The general colour is a dark grey-green, suggesting heat and aridity. In the maquis there is a wilder form of beauty than in the forests of oak and pine for those who can see it. It is uncompromising and slightly sinister, and it is not surprising that the men who have taken to the maquis as resistance workers or revolutionaries during the Mediterranean's stormy history have a special character. Their independent bearing and firmness of thought make them members of a club which is as distinctive in its own way as the brotherhood of true mariners who have sailed distant seas.

A still wilder variant of the typical Mediterranean forest is represented by the *garrigue*. Again using botanical terms, this is yet another stage of degeneration of the virgin forest, sharing the wild character of the maquis, but covering the land more sparsely and being able to adapt to even more inhospitable conditions. Garrigue is found mostly in rocky areas where the soil is thin and poor and the rainfall very restricted. It consists of an incomplete covering of very low bushy plants, often spiny and highly aromatic. It can endure searingly hot winds, long saturation in the blazing sun, and high concentrations of rainfall followed by many months of unrelieved drought. Herbs flourish in the garrigue, as do the euphorbias and asphodels of the steppes. It can live on what appears to be simply bare rock but where in reality the thinnest filling of sandy soil in cracks and crevices suffices for its subsistence. It is typical of such arid zones as southern Spain and southern Italy, where it covers vast areas, but occurs also in sizable patches in southern France, Yugoslavia and the Levant. The typical Mediterranean forest, whether at its climax or in the degenerate forms of maquis and garrigue, in fact occurs on almost all the shores of the sea except where the Saharan sands of Egypt and Libya extend right down to the coast.

The mixed evergreen and deciduous forest, although likewise lying within the area of olive cultivation, differs from the typical regional forest in being unable to sustain such long periods of drought. The Mediterranean conifers are all present but the flora is enriched by increased rainfall to include a range of deciduous trees, especially deciduous oaks. Such trees are at home in the comparatively cool winters of the mixed forest zone, which is especially characteristic of the lower slopes of coastal mountains in Spain, France, Italy, Yugoslavia, and Albania and the plains and hilly country of the northern Aegean. Like the typical forest, the truly wild mixed forest now occupies much reduced areas and has

often degenerated into a covering of stunted coniferous and deciduous plants waist high, or at most shoulder high, to a man. This 'maquis' stage of the mixed forest is known by special names in different regions – for example, the *sibljak* of the Balkans and the *bosco* of Italy.

The transitional zone represented by this vegetation is succeeded at high altitudes by the true deciduous forest which lies above the olive zone. Conifers persist, being adaptable to almost any climate where there is sufficient seasonal warmth and rainfall, but the deciduous trees appear in much richer variety and determine the special character of the vegetation. Here, apart from deciduous oaks, there appear first chestnuts

An example of maquis vegetation in the Valley of the Dead, near Kato Zakros, Crete.

The Cedars of Lebanon.
Watercolour by Edward
Lear.

and then beeches, among many other temperate trees, often associated
with a lush undergrowth of bracken. Cypresses give way to poplars and
the vegetation begins to take on the character of lands lying far north of
the Mediterranean. In the hot dry summers when the blazing sun of the
coast begins to pall, there is no more refreshing experience than to drive
often only a few miles inland to the gentler environment where the
constantly shifting pattern of slow-moving clouds makes a soothing
change from the oppressive heat at lower altitudes.

At still greater heights the conifers again assume their dominant role.
Here there is another zone of mixed forest, but the deciduous trees
gradually diminish in numbers and variety. The typical conifers are the
black pine (*Pinus nigra*) and its near relations in Greece, Asia Minor,
Crete, Corsica, Sicily, and many other regions where the land rises to sufficient height. Cedars also flourish, including that most magnificent of trees,
the cedar of Lebanon (*Cedrus lebani*) mentioned in the Bible.

This high coniferous zone is interspersed with pastures, but these are
never of the highest quality. They are more suited to goats than sheep or
cattle, their vegetation being of steppe origin and lacking the sustained
lushness of the high pastures of, say, Switzerland or Savoie. This poverty
is largely the result of the wide range of temperature and humidity
between winter and summer. For several months of the year the pastures
are at a very low temperature and often covered with snow; there is then
an abrupt change to sustained sunshine and drought, producing very arid
conditions. The only pastures which develop sufficiently to produce hay
require a reasonable supply of summer rain and this is a rare commodity
on the Mediterranean littoral. In fact, as I write these very words in a
Provençal café in late July there has only been one thunderstorm (lasting
under two hours) and one shower (lasting a quarter of an hour) in the
ninety days. The temperature, however, has never dropped below 33°C
(60°F) and has often climbed into the low forties, or high seventies. That
pasture land occurs at all in such conditions is a matter for surprise.

The sixth and last division of the wild Mediterranean vegetation is
almost entirely confined to North Africa. This is the arid zone which is
represented by several different assemblages of plants – and in its extreme
form by almost lifeless desert. Even in North Africa, especially at higher

(*Opposite*) Mosaics and
intricate woodwork on the
ceiling of the dome of Kait
Bey's Madrassa, Cairo, near
Kait Bey's mausoleum.
Built in 1472–4, it is one of
the most impressive sights
of Cairo.

The Green Mantle

altitudes, there are forests, including holm oaks, wild olives, and lentisks, but these do not spread over wide areas as they do elsewhere around the Mediterranean. The typical wild vegetation consists of arid patchy steppe in which such grasses as alfa occur in clumps, separated by patches of barren soil. This is quite different from the continuous grass cover of the American prairies and the northern Eurasian steppes. Some of these grasses are nevertheless commercially exploited and alfa itself, otherwise known as esparto, is exported in vast quantities from Libya for the manufacture of high-grade paper.

The harvesting of esparto in such places as Tripolitania, where it spreads over many hundreds of square miles, is still carried out in a very primitive way. When I visited the esparto areas here and elsewhere in North Africa I found that manpower and the camel were widely used in preference to complicated machines, being cheaper and just as reliable. The grass is first cut and collected in large mounds from which it is carried to a wooden box-like structure for making the bales. The sides of the box will move in or out, the power being provided by a capstan turned by a camel. The grass is placed in the box by the workers when the sides are pushed back to their fullest extent, and then compressed as the turning of the capstan moves them inwards. The compressed bales are next wired up and restacked ready for transportation to the base depots at Tripoli and other ports by lorries. The whole operation is most picturesque, the cut grass being carried to the compressor by camels so heavily laden that they look like walking haystacks. The silence of the desert is broken not only by the creaking of the capstan but by shrill cries of the workers as everyone encourages everyone else and shouts incomprehensible oaths at the long-suffering camels.

Those who may think of the Sahara as completely barren may be surprised to find if they visit the coastal regions that this is far from being the case. It is true, of course, of the areas covered by the great shifting dunes but where the ground is more stable there is everywhere a covering of scrubby vegetation, even though in places this may be so sparse as to be almost undetectable. The desert plants that exist in these inhospitable regions often have very interesting biological adaptations. They can rely hardly at all on rainfall, for even the lightest showers may occur at intervals measurable in years rather than months, so the moisture necessary for their survival is derived almost entirely from the supply they can draw up from the water table. A plant under 5 centimetres only (1 inch) high, may therefore have roots running straight down into the earth for 6-10 metres (20-30 feet). Professor Émile Gautier, one of France's leading authorities on deserts, has described how an Arab out in these barren regions will often pause to brew his tea near one of these plants. (Every desert Arab seems to be even more addicted to tea-drinking than the British). He knows that although the plant projects only fractionally above the surface the roots will provide him with ample fuel to boil the little blue teapot in which the tea is traditionally made.

The plants just described usually grow in complete isolation, but in regions where there is an occasional shower there is a denser – if still

205

sparse – covering of rather larger plants a foot or more in height. This poor fodder is nevertheless sufficient to support the herds of goats that accompany the desert nomads and is the main diet of the camel – a fact that may partially account for this animal's disgruntled expression.

After the rare showers the scrubby covering is enriched for a few days by an assemblage of plants that grow up temporarily between the permanent growth. This is known to the Arabs as *asheb*. Many of these plants belong to the mustard family and they are remarkable for the ability of their seeds to lie dormant for as long as ten years. However, when the shower comes the seeds quickly germinate and new seeds are formed by the purple flowers they throw out within a few hours. The plants then disappear as quickly as they came, leaving the camels still more disgruntled by the disillusionment of a shattered vision of paradise. Few botanical phenomena exemplify as well as the *asheb* the extraordinary tenacity of living things in an exceptionally hostile environment.

Quite apart from their practical usefulness in defining the Mediterranean climatic range and their commercial value, the olives are for me the most evocative of all Mediterranean trees. As A. N. Brangham has said in his splendid book *The Naturalist's Riviera*, 'no scene of powerful grace, of harmony and light, can bring the onlooker closer to reverence than an olive grove or a hillside terraced with orchards of these ancient trees'. They are not only the typical trees of the modern Mediterranean but were as common, or perhaps commoner, there in classical times. The sacred olive groves of Delphi are mentioned in many classical works, and Virgil writes in the second *Georgic*, 'stubborn land and ungracious hills, fields of lean marl and pebbly brushwood welcome the long-lived groves of Pallas Athene'. Pliny enumerates in his *Natural History* no less than fifteen kinds of olives with a range extending from Syria to south-west and central Spain and from the Alps to Africa. A similar variety can be observed today, each differing slightly from the other according to its geographical location and the climatic environment.

The main use of the fruit of the olive is, of course, for food and as a source of the oil extracted from it. The fruit varies greatly in size, ranging from the large Spanish variety to the delicious little olives of Provence. Italy now, as in Pliny's time, is reputed to produce the finest fruit and olive oil, but in my opinion it is exceeded in quality and character by the fruit and oil produced in the south of France, where the main centre is Nice. The large Spanish olives are altogether coarser and produce an oil with a less refined taste. In North Africa in classical times olive production was on a comparatively small scale as the climate and soil were better adapted to the production of grain. Today, however, skilful cultivation has led to vast areas in Tunisia and elsewhere being covered with olive orchards. When my wife and I were in Sfax in 1955 we drove out to a raised promontory from the summit of which we both expected to obtain only a view of the desert. Much to our astonishment we saw instead what must surely have been one of the largest olive plantations in the world. The ground was level and the trees extended in military order from just below our vantage point to the western horizon and to

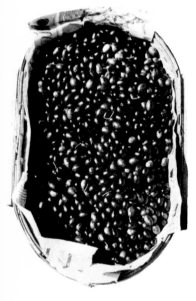

A basket of small Provençal olives before pressing.

our left and right as far as we could see. To judge from the oil that one ate in restaurants in Tunisian towns the quality of the fruit must have been very high indeed. We learnt later that the orchards we saw represented only a minute fraction of the olive plantations that exist in Tunisia. More than twenty million trees were planted there by the French colonists and remain as a legacy, well appreciated by all enlightened Tunisians, of the better aspects of the colonial administration in their country.

In many parts of the Mediterranean olive oil is still extracted from the fruit by very primitive means. Until recently, even within a few miles of such a sophisticated centre as Nice, it was possible to see great boulders

An ancient olive plantation at Itea, possibly the site of the sacred olive grove of Delphi.

207

raised by man-powered winches and lowered into large stone receptacles to crush the juice from the fruit.

In North Africa we saw a somewhat more elaborate device. I had been out in the desert visiting the cave dwellers of Matmata where a neighbour of my Arab host had an olive press of which he was particularly proud. It consisted of a huge stone roller measuring about 60 centimetres (2 feet) across, mounted vertically and attached by a wooden beam to a central pivot. The roller ran in a receptacle of stone which formed a circular trough running round the pivot. The motive power was provided by a camel which was harnessed to the beam between the pivot and the roller. With that aloof and somewhat supercilious patience that has given the camel the reputation of being the only animal to know the hundredth name for Allah, the animal would trudge forward on an endless circular course, thereby pulling the roller round the circular trough. The freshly-picked olives had previously been deposited in the trough where the action of the roller reduced them to pulp. This was then placed into a number of fine-meshed rope baskets of the same design but larger than the metal containers used for swinging salads. As they were filled the containers were placed one on top of another and the juice was then extracted by lowering on to the pile a large stone balanced by a counter-poise. To be able to see these primitive methods of exploiting the vegetation, methods that must have been practised in the Mediterranean for many thousands of years, is one of the pleasures that reward the enterprising visitor who is prepared to seek out the unusual.

Apart from the uses of the olive fruit, many small villages possess craftsmen who make the most attractive and useful objects out of the olive wood. This is hard to work but extremely decorative, and the intricately convoluted grain makes it an ideal material for the enterprising wood carver who can integrate its natural pattern into the design of his product. Such creations range from pure art in the form of statuettes and figurines to objects of more practical use such as cheese boards, pepper pots, fruit and salad bowls, and other containers for food. The fantastic shapes of many of the trees also make them good material for unusually-designed rustic furniture such as small tables, stands for plants, and wooden candelabras. To those who like the simple beauty of natural objects rather than the ornate elaboration of more sophisticated products, olive wood ranks as one of the finest materials in the world.

The harvesting of the olives is still carried out in many parts of the Mediterranean in a very primitive manner. When the fruit is ripe the peasants go out and strike the branches of the trees with long wands so that it falls on to canvas sheets placed on the ground. It is a crude method, as Pliny pointed out nearly two thousand years ago, but effective if care is taken not to damage the fruit or the stems of the branches. Wands wielded indiscriminately or with too much enthusiasm will not only harm the crop being harvested, but make the trees unsuitable for bearing a crop the following season.

Vines are another crop associated in many people's minds with the sunny atmosphere of the Mediterranean. Although the grapes producing

A typically Provençal landscape; the Var vineyards,
with palm-trees and olives.

the finest wine in the world lie to the north of the olive line, those in the
Mediterranean region produce far better wine than is generally believed.
The fruit itself is also eaten widely in the region and forms one of the
Mediterranean's most important food exports. In recent years there has
been a drive, especially in south-western France in the region known as
the Languedoc, to improve the quality of wine that was at one time
regarded as good pool 'plonk' but undrinkable by the connoisseur.
Especially in the smaller vineyards where the grapes are grown with
loving care by individual proprietors, Mediterranean wine can now bear
comparison with many vintages usually thought to be of higher quality.
This is especially true of the *rosés* and the whites.

In north-west Africa, however, a strong and beautifully-flavoured red
wine is produced from the grapes of Algeria and, to a lesser extent, of
Tunisia. Here careful cultivation has made the apparently inhospitable
land very suitable for viniculture. This is unfortunately not the case,
however, further to the east.

The common vine of the Mediterranean, *Vitis vinifera*, is indigenous
and can even be found growing wild. But of course by far the greater
number of plants are under cultivation and I have spent many happy
hours comparing the vintages of France, Italy, and north-west Africa. The
cultivation normally takes place on terraces or in comparatively small
plantations, but sometimes, as in the Languedoc already mentioned,

209

The Green Mantle

hundreds of square miles of flat and rolling country are given up to the vineyards. The roads run for mile after mile through an ocean of vines that can be numbered in millions, their green leaves and large bunches of grapes hanging heavily from each plant giving infinite promise of Bacchanalian delights. In autumn after the *vendange* the vines are cut back and the little leafless plants, their branches thrusting upwards towards the sky like groping black fingers, give another characteristic impression of the Mediterranean landscape.

In some parts of the world, and even in some parts of the Mediterranean, the vines are trained up trellises, but the typical Mediterranean vineyards consist of ground-grown plants which seldom attain a height of little over 1 metre (3 to 4 feet). Some damage is done to these by foxes which, in spite of being largely carnivorous animals, have acquired in some areas a taste for grapes. 'The little foxes that spoil the vines' are mentioned in the Song of Solomon, and Æsop in his fable of the sour grapes, describes the disappointment of a fox living in Phrygia who was obviously expecting to carry out his marauding in a vineyard where the plants grew comparatively low. He found to his chagrin that instead he was in a trellised vineyard with the best of the fruit out of reach. Foxes takes the grapes less to satisfy their hunger than their thirst, and their depredations are therefore particularly common in very arid regions.

Two exotic imports from the New World which have become acclimatised to Mediterranean conditions are the barbary fig and the American agave. Although it can be seen widely in the coastal regions of Spain, France, and further east, the main home of the barbary fig is, as its names

The prickly pear, or barbary fig, in the botanical gardens at Èze, on the French Riviera.

suggests, the Barbary Coast of north-west Africa. It is also commonly known as the 'prickly pear' and the Moroccans call it the 'Christian fig'. When my wife and I were in Tunisia we saw it growing over large areas and it was even used to form a kind of rough hedge – a purpose for which it is well suited as its spines are sufficient to deter any intruder. It consists of flat fleshy lobes which are about the size of a man's hand, or a little larger. The 'figs' which give it its name are egg-shaped growths which obtrude from the edges of the lobes. These are edible, although they contain large, hard, indigestible pips and the taste of the fleshy part, although quite innocuous, is dull and unattractive.

The other import from the New World – Central America to be precise – is familiar to all visitors to the French Riviera and is also found widely on other Mediterranean shores. This is the agave, *Opuntia americana*, which is shown on page 214. A large specimen may measure more than 4 metres (12 feet) from the tips of the opposing leaves, which are broad and fleshy and edged with vicious spines. The central rod-like stem with its odd top which looks like one of those little brushes for cleaning the spouts of teapots, but many times magnified, is not present in all the plants at the same time, being thrown up about once every seven years. In its homeland in Central America the core of the plant from which this rod springs is extracted and used in the manufacture of a particularly potent liquor. Strength is its only virtue however, for it lacks refinement and tends to make those who consume it fighting drunk within a very short time.

A profusion of palms and their allies are among the most attractive imported trees on the European coasts of the Mediterranean. The climate is not sufficiently warm all the year round for them to survive everywhere, but they are particularly characteristic of southern France east of St Raphael, and are also found in sheltered spots between St Raphael and Marseilles. Sheltered pockets on the southern slopes of the Alpes Maritimes also allow them to grow in many places quite a distance inland where they are an exotic and attractive feature of the landscape in some of the hill villages around Grasse. Among them is one of the best known of all palms, the date palm, *Phoenix dactylifera*. This tree actually produces dates in the south of France but unfortunately even that favoured climate is insufficiently warm all the year round for them to ripen and be eaten except in one or two exceptionally hot corners behind Menton. In North Africa, however, the date palm is one of the most important plants not only because of the use of its fruit for local consumption but as an important commodity for export. The boxes of dried dates with their characteristic rounded ends are as much a part of Christmas in Britain and other northern countries as is the turkey and plum pudding. The exported dates originate mainly in Morocco, Algeria, and Tunisia and in their dried form are even more tasty than the fresh fruit from the tree.

One interesting botanical fact about date palms is that they are unisexual – that is, the tree has both male and female flowers. This was known to Pliny, and many travellers in Africa and the Middle East have remarked that the female palm needs fertilisation by the male before it will produce

Date palms in a Tunisian oasis.

(*Opposite*) An olive tree in Sicily.

fruit that is at all palatable. In the words of the sixteenth-century Arab traveller Leo Africanus, as translated by Pory in 1600: 'if they be not joined, the dates will prove starke naught and containe great stones.' This characteristic of the date palm led the more romantic commentators to suspect the existence of botanical love affairs. One of the most delightful references to this fancy occurs in a book by Captain F. W. Beechey, RN FRS and H. W. Beechey, FSA, published in 1828. Despite its rather forbidding titles, *Proceedings of the Expedition to explore the Northern Coast of Africa, from Tripoli eastwards in MDCCCXXI, and MDCCCXXII*, the book's style shows that sentimental yearnings as well as humour lurk even behind the stern façades of nineteenth-century naval officers and members of learned societies. The Beecheys quote a Persian anecdote which, they allege, originated with an inhabitant of the Yemen. It reads as follows:

'I was possessor of a garden in which was a palm-tree, which had every year produced me abundance of fruit; but two seasons having passed away, without its affording any, I sent for a person well acquainted with the culture of palms, to discover for me the reason of this failure. "An unhappy attachment", observed the man, after a moment's inspection, "is the sole cause why this palm-tree produces no fruit!". He then climbed up the trunk, and, looking round on all sides, discovered a male palm at no great distance, which he recognised as the object of my unlucky tree's affection; and advised me to procure some of the powder from its blossoms, and to scatter it over her branches. This I did, and the consequence was, that my date-tree, whom unrequited love had kept barren, now bore me a most abundant harvest!'

The Green Mantle

Of course, in the state of nature the female palms are pollinated by the wind or by the movement of insects, but artificial means are also widely used in North Africa and the Middle East. The male flower is cut off the tree just before the stamens ripen and then suspended among the flowers of the female, thus assuring fertilisation. Apart from the fresh fruit with its refreshing and nourishing quality when eaten directly off the tree, dates are also prepared in other forms, and produce a number of bi-products. I have already referred to the export trade in dried whole dates, but the fruit is also more roughly packaged in dry blocks which form the staple food of the Saharan caravans. Date honey can be extracted from the fresh dates and when fermented produces a mildly alcoholic wine. But this wine can then be distilled into a strong spirit and it is possible that it may be the lotus referred to in old writings. The sap of the date palm likewise produces an alcoholic spirit of a quite different kind. Both drinks are widely produced in the oases and along the banks of the Nile, where they are a popular if religiously illicit component in Moslem festivals.

But we are still not at the end of the catalogue of the date palm's uses. The buds and undeveloped panicles of the flowers are used as a vegetable food known as palm cabbage. The fibre is twisted into rope, the wood of the trunk is used to make furniture and the framework of buildings, and the leaf stalks make good basket frames, walking sticks, and the ribs of fans. The leaves themselves are interlaced to make bags and mats, and even the stones of the fruit have their uses. They can be roasted and ground to form a crude substitute for coffee; they can also be pressed for oil and the residue fed to cattle.

One of the most successful introductions of a food plant to the Mediterranean has been rice. This is generally associated in most people's minds with much hotter regions than the Mediterranean, where there is an exceptionally high seasonal rainfall such as tropical south-east Asia. Yet rice will grow almost anywhere where there is a reasonable degree of warmth and the possibility of permanent irrigation. Its introduction into the Mediterranean region has proved extremely successful, and it is now an important item in the economy of many southern European countries. In France particularly, where the stresses of war caused it to be introduced into the Rhône delta in 1942, rice cultivation has flourished to an astonishing degree. At first the experiment was on a very small scale but the success of the crop astonished even its sponsors and as the years passed many square miles of this region of France were put under cultivation. The bright green rice fields and the numerous refineries dotted about the landscape are now one of its most characteristic features, and although foreign rice is still imported from the Far East, France has if necessary the capacity to be entirely self-supporting in the production of this commodity. In recent years it has also become an item in the country's export trade.

Rice is probably the staple diet of more people in the world than any other food product, and is consumed in smaller or larger quantities by practically every human being. Another plant of equally wide distribution which grows, among other places, on some of the shores of the

(*Opposite*) The agave (*Opuntia americana*), an import from the New World, grows freely on Mediterranean shores. Here it is seen in the botanical gardens at Èze, on the French Riviera.

(*Above left*) Aerial view of
the rice fields in the Rhône
delta. (*Right*) Fellahin
workers cleaning cotton
in a village in the Nile delta.

Mediterranean is used not for food but for clothing; this, of course, is cotton. Cotton (*Gossypium*) is a fibre-bearing shrub which is indigenous to nearly all tropical and sub-tropical countries. In the Mediterranean its main centre of production is Egypt, where the finest cotton in the world is grown. Some 137 varieties of the cotton plant are recognised, but the best Egyptian cotton is the product of one species, *Gossypium barbadense*. When the cotton plant reaches maturity its ripened pods or capsules burst open to display the fleecy product within. In its natural state this fleece is none other than unrefined cotton wool, and the likeness to the cotton wool obtainable at the chemist can be immediately recognised. For the making of fabric the natural cotton is picked and refined and then spun by a variety of processes, some of great sophistication and complexity.

One of the sights of Egypt is to see the vast expanse of the cotton fields with the sweating, half-naked labourers working in rows to bring in the crop. In the mid-1950s, when I was last in Egypt, it was still the custom to have this labour force supervised by brutal-looking overseers who actually carried whips and cracked them over the heads of the pickers if they seemed to be making insufficient effort. The scene was astonishingly primitive – the oven-hot air under a blazing sun, the stooping forms of the pickers, their faces as expressionless as those of dumb animals, and the ever-watchful overseers striding up and down behind them shouting exhortations and flourishing their whips. I had a feeling of shame to see this sight from the air-conditioned comfort of a huge American car placed at my disposal by my Egyptian host, who apart from being one of the fattest men I have ever seen was also extraordinarily civilised and gentle.

216

The Green Mantle

It just seemed that his mind quite failed to connect the immense wealth which he enjoyed with the means by which it was being obtained. This episode brought home to me more dramatically than any other experience I had in North Africa the absolute necessity for the social changes pioneered, with whatever temporary excesses and human mistakes, by the Egyptian revolution.

Apart from the indigenous plants and those, whether indigenous or imported, that are used like rice and cotton for their commercial value, no description of the flora of the Mediterranean would be complete without some reference to the vegetation's aesthetic aspects. To appreciate these the best of all regions is the French Riviera, where a microclimate enables an enormous range of plants – ornamental as well as valuable for food and other purposes – to be grown in a comparatively limited area. Quite often commercial value and beauty are combined, as with the vast forests of mimosa which adorn the hillsides west of Nice. The beautiful yellow blossoms are exported to all the major cities of Europe, and in my native city of London my heart used to be gladdened in winter by the sprigs of mimosa, sold at an exhorbitant price on street barrows, by nostalgic memories of the sun-drenched splendours of the French mimosa forests. One of the main centres of mimosa production is at Mandelieu, near Cannes, where in February it is possible to pick an armful of blossoms in less time than it takes to read this paragraph.

A rich variety of cut flowers are also exported from the Riviera. Some of these are grown under glass, but many in the open. The plantations include such homely flowers as the marigold as well as the magnificently martial arum lilies and carnations of every conceivable colour. The blossom of the fruit trees is also spectacular, as is the fruit itself when, for example, cherries and lush purple plums weigh down the branches to the point where they sometimes even break under the strain.

A more humorous appeal is provided by the fields of lavender which are dotted about the foothills of the Maritime Alps and cover many acres on the high plateaux. The plants are arranged in evenly spaced ranks and are irresistibly reminiscent of an army of purple hedgehogs on parade. The scented flowers of the lavender, like many other blooms, are widely used for the manufacture of perfume, of which Grasse is the leading centre. Apart from such cultivated plants a more delicate charm is provided by the wild flowers that grow not only in the alpine meadows but extend right down to the sea on suitable terrain.

Although the coast here is now largely built-up, there is much compensation for the intrusion of man in his creation of some of the finest gardens in the world. Many of the great villas of the Riviera have gardens that far exceed in beauty, and must even equal in the range of species represented, some of the world's major botanical gardens. Bougainvillea often climbs the surrounding walls like sheets of purple flame, the seductively-named jacaranda grows among palms and other exotic trees, while over all tower the mighty eucalyptuses, with their strap-like leaves and smooth trunks, which were originally imported from Australia but are now a feature of every Mediterranean land.

'An army of purple hedgehogs': a lavender plantation at Bonnieux, in the Vaucluse.

The Green Mantle

The green mantle of the Mediterranean is thus seen to be composed of many facets. There is the original indigenous forest, grassland, and desert. There are the imports, some dating from classical times or even before, others made within the last few decades. There are representatives of both these types cultivated for food, clothing, or other commercial purposes; and finally there are the ornamental plants of all kinds that have been nurtured and developed solely to delight the eye of man. The presence of all these forms of plants in one comparatively small region gives the Meditterranean an historical, intellectual, and aesthetic interest, quite apart from its appeal to the academic botanist, which can be matched nowhere in the world.

An avenue of eucalyptuses, near Sapone in Corsica. These trees were originally imported from Australia, but are now a characteristic feature of the Mediterranean.

9

Land Animals of the Mediterranean

To sort out the living land animals of the Mediterranean in any logical way is an almost impossible task. At least two hundred species are represented. Some are indigenous, some are introductions, some are wild, some are domesticated, and some are feral populations of formerly domesticated animals that have taken again to life in the wild. Moreover, for many thousands of years the distribution of Mediterranean land animals has been enormously affected by the habits and movements of man. Often their natural habitat has been destroyed, or they have been forced to retreat into isolated regions with a new set of conditions so that new physical and behavioural adaptations have had to be made. This chapter, therefore, is more of a 'lucky dip' than a systematic presentation of the subject. I have thought it best to concentrate on a few selected animals which have either specially interested me or are comparatively easily seen by the visitor. Nevertheless I have tried to include at least a few of the better-known representatives of the three major classes of land vertebrates – the mammals, the birds, and the reptiles – and to say just a few words about the amphibians and the invertebrates, which are represented in vast numbers.

The history of land mammals in the Mediterranean goes back some seventy million years to the dawn of the Age of Mammals. In those days, long before man had evolved, strange beasts roamed the Mediterranean coasts, flourished for a while and then became extinct. Man himself, as we have seen in Part II of this book, began his evolution some two million years ago in Africa and probably reached the Mediterranean about a million years later. At first he was a simple competitor with the

(*Above*) The European wolf (*Canis lupus*) is now found mainly in Spain, Italy and the Balkans. (*Opposite*) A black bull of the Camargue.

Land Animals of the Mediterranean

other mammals of the region, which held their own quite satisfactorily against this new predacious ape-like creature that had invaded their environment. But as time went on and man's brain developed precociously to make him the most intelligent organism on earth, his dominance became assured and, even more than such natural processes as climatic change, he was responsible for the extinction or at least the retreat of many mammals from the Mediterranean zone.

Today the mammals exist in the region by courtesy of man alone; he has preserved them for sport, for commercial exploitation, as beasts of burden, or because he has recognised the essential value of certain species in maintaining the balance of nature. In recent years it is gratifying to see that he is also beginning to recognise more widely their aesthetic quality and scientific interest instead of thinking only of his material advantage. Were it not for these factors the survival of animal life on the shores of the Mediterranean would be precarious indeed.

Two of the large mammals that were common in the region even in historic times but are now rare or almost extinct are the wolf and the bear. The European wolf (*Canis lupus*) has now vanished from France except possibly for a few specimens remaining in the wilder parts of the Pyrenees, and its main range is restricted to north-eastern Spain, Italy, and the Balkans. In the Balkans particularly it remains fairly plentiful and a recent report estimates the population in this part of the world as running into several thousands. The wolf, of course, even when common, did not make a permanent home in that part of the Mediterranean strictly contained within the olive line. It can, however, be legitimately regarded as part of the Mediterranean fauna because of the forays it frequently made from the mountains and forests of the interior to the coastal villages to kill domestic animals. Right down to the beginning of the nineteenth century whenever a particularly cold winter created especially hard conditions, packs of wolves would habitually invade the coastal lowlands, where they were a major danger to the domestic herds.

The brown bear of Europe (*Ursus arctus*) has survived rather better than the wolf. It still exists in Spain, France, Italy, Yugoslavia, Albania, Greece, Bulgaria, Roumania, Czechoslovakia, Hungary, and Turkey, as well as countries further to the north and east. According to a recent survey the estimated population of bears in Mediterranean countries is as follows: France, 70; Spain, 40; Italy, 200; Yugoslavia, more than 700; Albania, numerous, but an exact count has not been attempted; Greece, 100; Turkey, numerous, but again there is no exact estimate of numbers. Like the wolf, the bear is normally an inhabitant of wild country, mostly on the lower slopes of mountains or in dense forest. However, it has on the whole been less persecuted than the wolf and is now strictly protected in every Mediterranean country where it still lives. There is a good chance that the present number of bears will be maintained and even increased under properly-controlled conditions.

It is unlikely that the ordinary traveller or tourist in the Mediterranean will nowadays encounter a bear, but if they are patiently sought out it is not impossible to see them. Several naturalists have recorded encounters with them, and the peasants living in bear country are sufficiently accustomed to their presence for it not to be especially remarkable. Unless a bear is persecuted or unduly disturbed it is not a dangerous animal, and although it eats small mammals, fish, birds' eggs, carrion, and occasionally domestic animals or even young deer and wild boar, it is in general a harmless vegetarian. The normal diet of bears includes roots, berries, fruit, nuts (especially acorns), fungi, and grain. They will also sell their souls for honey. But with the exception of domestic animals, which anyway are only very rarely taken, and the honey, the damage done by bears to the peasant's livelihood is minimal, so their protection fortunately involves little or no hardship to man.

For people like the British it is always exciting to travel in a region where one feels one is sharing the environments with such truly wild animals as the wolf and the bear. For me at least, two other animal species found in the Mediterranean evoke the same excitement, the wild cat and the lynx. Few people other than expert naturalists realise that there is a considerable population of wild cats in the Mediterranean region and that the lynx likewise exists in reasonably large numbers in more isolated but not inaccessible places.

The wild cat (*Felis silvestris*) resembles a large domestic tabby. At least, this is true of the typical form, although in North Africa there is a variant of the coat, which is more uniform and lacks distinct stripes. This at one time led zoologists to believe that the North African wild cat was a distinct species, and it was given the scientific name of *Felis libyca*. However, the difference in coat pattern is not now regarded as of taxonomic importance, and the wild cats of the Mediterranean are all considered to belong to one species.

Wild cats are solitary animals with clearly defined territories which they mark out by depositing their urine and droppings at the boundaries and reinforcing this claim to the title deeds by use of the scent glands on their feet. Although primarily ground dwellers, they can climb trees and are commonly found in dense woodland. They are active mainly at twilight and at night, hunting by stealth and surprise rather than by running down their prey. Their hunting technique is therefore similar to that used by a domestic cat when stalking a bird on the garden lawn – that is, cautious advance followed by freezing, the process being repeated until the range is sufficiently short for a sudden pounce to be made.

There are also some unexpected differences between the wild cat and its domestic cousin, one being that it does not bury its droppings like the latter. The reason for this is difficult to state, especially as both kinds of cat certainly shared a common ancestor in the not-too-remote past. Perhaps, as has been suggested, the two contrasted habits are the result of historical factors. Whereas the habit of depositing droppings to define territory remains useful to the animal living in the wild, the cats that allowed themselves to be adopted by man became more conscious of the merits of sanitation. But to me this seems rather a far-fetched speculation which the reader would be well-advised to take with a pinch of salt.

The lynx (*Felis lynx*) is the largest member of the cat family to be found

The lynx (*Felis lynx*); one of the main habitats of this beautiful animal is the Coto Donana in southern Spain.

in Europe. With its tufted ears, its beautiful spotted coat, and the expression of dignified *hauteur* on its face, it is one of the most handsome of all carnivores. Formerly widespread throughout the whole of Europe it now occurs only in isolated pockets. At one time it was thought to be restricted mainly to mountainous regions, but this is not the case. One of the strongholds of the lynx in western Europe is the estuary of the Guadalquiver in southern Spain. Through the generosity of the World Wildlife Fund this region, known as the Coto Donana, has been presented to the Spanish government as a national park. In addition to being a stronghold of the lynx it is also an ornithologist's paradise, nearly half of all the species of European birds being observable there in the course of a single year and one of its star attractions being a breeding population of flamingoes.

The lynx, like the wild cat, is a territorial animal. It also resembles its smaller relation in coming out mainly at dusk and being most active during the night. In May the female gives birth to two or three kittens which stay with her for almost two years, gradually learning to hunt under the tutelage of both parents. In the second year of their lives they reach sexual maturity and often produce kittens of their own. Lynxs, as might be expected, habitually take larger prey than wild cats, which subsist mainly on small mammals, insects, and birds. To the lynx, deer and quite large domestic animals such as calves are manageable prey if available, but fortunately the animal can also subsist quite happily on rabbits, rodents, and ground birds, so that being so limited in numbers it is not a serious nuisance to man.

224

Land Animals of the Mediterranean

There is no reason why the visitor to the Coto Donana or other places where the lynx survives should not see a specimen. Except for keeping a specially good look out at dusk, however, this is more a matter of luck than planning. I have personally seen only one, which passed in front of my car a hundred yards or so away, and disappeared in a dense thicket of reeds. It was, however, an unforgettable experience, as exciting in its own way as my first sight of a wild lion in Africa.

Another truly wild mammal which is found along the European shores of the Mediterranean, and also in those parts of North Africa which are not entirely given up to desert, is the wild boar (*Sus scrofa*). This magnificent game animal may well exceed 2 metres (6 feet) from the tip of its snout to the tip of its tail and stand 1 metre (3 feet) at the shoulder. Although the largest examples are found in the Carpathians, where weights of 300-350 kilograms (about 700 lbs) are not uncommon, the wild boar found in France and south-eastern Europe are impressive enough. The maximum weight recorded for a French boar is about 170 kilograms (about 400 lbs) but anything over 100 kilograms is regarded as large.

Throughout their range the number of wild boars is now much reduced, but even in the sophisticated south of France they still exist in the maquis and garrigue, and in hard winters come down into the delta of the Rhône. One of the favourite sports of the Provençal villagers is to hunt the wild boar with dogs, and this activity tempts many of the more active men away from early morning service on Sundays. It is a splendid

The wild boar (*Sus scrofa*) is a solitary animal, living alone, except during the mating period.

Land Animals of the Mediterranean

sight to see the hunters returning with their quarry slung from a pole, to display it proudly at the local café while quenching their thirst and recounting the story of the chase to an admiring audience. In order to preserve the pleasures derived from the chase a reasonable population of animals must, of course, be preserved too.

Although the atavistic joy found by men in the hunt itself is probably the main reason for the boar's preservation, the animal also makes excellent eating. In the winter in Provence the freshly-killed carcasses can be seen hanging outside the butchers' shops and boar steak is served on the menus of many country inns. The meat is also turned into a magnificent pâté which is available in tinned form in the cities. But the country is the proper place to enjoy these delicacies, as it is for eating all the products of the chase. The sunshine, crisp air, and country smells give not only boar meat but the flesh of deer and game birds a special savour that can never be enjoyed in a crowded city restaurant.

Like the wild cat and the lynx, the wild boar is a solitary species, the males living alone except for a period of rut when they pair up with the females for breeding. They also resemble these two members of the cat family in being mainly nocturnal. It is possible to see wild boar at nightfall, and it is indeed a stirring experience if one should happen to observe a boar moving about in the open near the dense vegetation or forest where they normally make their homes. But by dawn the boars will all be lying up in the dens they make for themselves on rocky hillsides or beneath fallen trees or in other secluded spots, and no further sign of them will be seen until dusk.

The mating season is in winter, usually between November and February, and the young are born in the spring after a gestation period of about four months. Litters may be quite large, especially those of older mothers, and ten or more youngsters have been observed with one parent. Whereas the adult boars are of a single dark colour, the young have bold longitudinal stripes of yellowish-brown and chestnut. They are amusing little creatures, running hither and thither and sticking their long snouts into anything that arouses their curiosity. The mother is entirely responsible for rearing the family, the male retiring after mating to his previous lonely existence. The young often stay with the mother for over a year, so when mating times comes round again they may still be in her care. In fact it is not unusual to see a female boar accompanied by two litters from succeeding years.

The nearest relation to man to inhabit the Mediterranean is the barbary ape (*Macaca sylvana*). This animal is not, however, an ape at all in the strict zoological sense but a cercopithecoid monkey. This rather forbidding word need not alarm the layman; it simply means that the barbary ape belongs to the scientific group of monkeys known as the Cercopithecoidea which are characteristic of the Old World. Its range is extremely limited. In Europe it is found only on the Rock of Gibraltar, to which it may be indigenous. It is more likely, however, that it was artificially introduced there by man from North Africa, where it exists in a limited area but in a truly wild state.

Land Animals of the Mediterranean

In appearance the barbary ape is stocky and thick-set with shaggy fur. There is no externally visible tail. It is of a moderate size, approximately equivalent to that of a golden retriever, and it weighs about 10 kilograms (20 lbs). In Africa it lives in the wooded mountains of the Atlas and can also be seen on rocky terrain. The colony on the Rock of Gibraltar, whatever it may have been originally, is now obviously semi-domestic; the monkeys wander about fearlessly and are ready to solicit titbits from tourists and to grimace at them disrespectfully with the same aplomb as monkeys in a zoo. As monkeys go the barbary ape is not particularly noisy, but from time to time it will break out into a kind of harsh yapping and when particularly excited will scream loudly. The barbary ape is one of the animals which adds a touch of tropical exoticism to the Mediterranean scene. Also, if we know a little evolutionary history, we cannot but look at it with some fellow feeling as an animal that shared a common ancestor with ourselves between thirty and forty million years ago.

Deer are associated in many people's minds exclusively with northern forests, but, in fact, their range for the greater part of their history has been much wider. Several species of deer are still characteristic of the Mediterranean, notably the red deer (*Cervus elephas*), the roe-deer (*Capreolus capreolus*), and the fallow deer (*Cervus dama*). The first two species, although less common than they were, are still widely distributed in the hinterland of the European Mediterranean, where they are both favourite game animals. The range of the fallow deer has been greatly influenced by man, with temporary local extinctions and reintroductions, so it is difficult to determine where the original wild population lived. It is now found in every European country except Norway and Finland, and also in Asiatic Turkey, Persia, and other Middle Eastern countries.

The largest of the three deer is the red deer, which in northern countries has been the model of a large number of bad paintings of *The Monarch of the Glen* type. It is a social animal, the size of the herd depending particularly on the resources of the local habitat. The herds have a well-defined social structure with the usual 'peck order', the larger stags monopolising the best females until they are successfully challenged by a younger and more aggressive male. The venison of the red deer is rich and succulent when well cooked; during the winter it appears on many menus in southern Europe, being a much-prized main dish at the traditional Mediterranean Sunday lunch.

Compared with the large red deer, which can reach a height of more that $1\frac{1}{2}$ metres (nearly 5 feet) at the shoulder, the roe-deer is tiny. It is, in fact, the smallest of all the indigenous deer of Europe. Its shoulder height is usually just over half a metre, or perhaps three-quarters of a metre in large specimens. Roe-deer are very widespread along the European coasts of the Mediterranean, being considerably more common than red deer in this region. They are likewise hunted for sport and for the excellent quality of the venison. Served roasted, with pineapple and *pommes rissolées*, few dishes can taste more delicious.

The fallow deer is about midway in size between the roe-deer and the red deer. It is one of the most attractive of all deer to look at, with its spotted coat and classically simple antlers. Although, as stated above, its range as a truly wild species is difficult to determine and there are reports of diminished numbers and even extinction in some regions, the species is in no real danger. There are many breeding populations maintained under artificial conditions and there is always the possibility of re-stocking whole districts from these sources in case of need. Like the other two deer, the fallow deer is hunted for sport wherever it is found. Its meat is excellent, being better than that of the red deer and even regarded by some (although not by me) as equalling that of the roe-deer in tenderness and flavour.

The Mediterranean mammals associated with high ground are the ibex and the chamois. Their normal range is not contained by the olive line, but the land lying within this is characterised by so much vertical zonation that where mountains come down to within a short distance of the sea both animals can be seen on their slopes. The chamois (*Rupicapra rupicapra*) is found throughout almost the whole of Austria, Switzerland, and Savoie and the Dauphiné in France, but its range on the Mediterranean proper is more limited. It occurs in the mountains south-east of Rome and also extensively on the Adriatic coast of Yugoslavia. It is a neat little animal, standing about three-quarters of a metre ($2\frac{1}{2}$ feet) at the shoulder with conspicuous head markings and short, slender, curving horns. Its small, delicate hooves are well-designed for getting a grip on narrow rock ledges, and it is notable for the wide range of sounds it can produce. These vary from a querulous sheep-like bleating to hisses and whistles when danger threatens. The males utter a deep guttural cough in the mating season.

The ibex or wild goat (*Capra hircus*) is a good deal larger than the chamois and is distinguished by its magnificent backward-curving horns. Both sexes have these, although the female's are smaller. The range of the ibex is much more broken than that of the chamois but it can be encountered in pockets in southern and south-eastern Spain, in the south of France in the massifs of the Maures and the Estérel, and in numerous places along the coasts of Yugoslavia and western Greece. One of the largest concentrations of population is in the Gran Paradiso National Park in northern Italy where there are estimated to be at least three thousand ibex. In fact the numbers there are sufficiently large for them to be culled by sportsmen, who shoot under licence and the supervision of a warden, thereby earning funds for the maintenance of Italy's national parks. The chamois is also found in this park in large numbers, and a similar control method is permitted. The licences are extremely expensive (£800 for an ibex, £90 for a chamois) but nevertheless about fourteen ibex and forty-five chamois are shot each year.

The beaver (*Castor fiber*) is usually thought of as a northern animal and it comes as a surprise to many people to know that it still survives in the Rhône valley. This is its last Mediterranean stronghold, however, and it is now rare. It is a very shy animal, mainly nocturnal, and spends most of its time in the water; when it emerges it waddles along rather slowly and clumsily, but it is an extremely powerful swimmer and diver, with the

ability to stay under water for as much as fifteen minutes without breath-
ing. I have spent many hours at dusk on the Rhône hoping to see beavers
in their natural environment, but have never so far been lucky. Those
who have say it is a most exciting experience.

The animals cruise about the river near the shore, occasionally diving
and remaining out of sight for several minutes. They live in small colonies
and if they are suddenly disturbed all the members of the colony will
disappear below the surface at once, slapping the water with their broad
tails as they do so. The object of this is probably to warn any beaver
that has not noticed the impending danger to take immediate cover. In
the northern part of the beaver's range – that is in Norway, Sweden,
Finland, and Poland – it is famous for building dams and lodges, but this
habit is not practised on the Rhône. This is probably due in part to the
swift-flowing character of the river, but also because the presence of the
structures would give too easy a clue to the beaver's whereabouts in such
a densely-populated region.

Whole books have been written about some of the Mediterranean
mammals so far mentioned and there are many others of great interest.

The ibex is found mainly in
France, Spain and the
Balkans.

Land Animals of the Mediterranean

Some of the species represented are a cause of surprise to the layman. For instance, how many travellers in southern Europe know that the crested porcupine has a wide range in Italy, Sicily, Yugoslavia, and northern Greece, or that the mongoose can be found over large tracts of southern Spain? Both these animals are well known to visitors to zoos, but one has quite a different feeling when one realises that, with luck, one may see a wild specimen on a country stroll. Smaller and less spectacular species such as mice, voles, hedgehogs, and the familiar rabbit and hare are also very common and each has its own interest if some of its less obvious characteristics are studied. However, as this is a book for the general reader the temptation to enlarge on these subjects must be resisted. Instead it may be of more interest to say a few words about some of the animals commonly found under domestication.

The four most obvious examples of domestic animals in the Mediterranean region are the goat, the sheep, the donkey, and of course the one-humped camel of North Africa – an animal so grotesque in appearance, structure, and demeanour that it is a cause of wonder that it exists at all. Owing to the generally poor pastures to be found on Mediterranean shores goats, which are less demanding in this respect than sheep, are by far the more common of these two animals. Poor pasturage is also the reason why cattle, except the oxen still used in some areas for drawing carts, are comparatively rare. The donkey is one of the toughest of all the hoofed mammals and is widely used in parts of Europe as well as in Africa to transport both goods and men.

The ancestor of the domestic sheep is generally thought to be the wild sheep, or mouflon (*Ovis ammon*). The original indigenous Mediterranean population was confined to the islands of Corsica and Sardinia and to Asia Minor, although the range of this third pocket of wild sheep extended eastwards right across Asia into Mongolia. From these centres the mouflon was introduced into many other parts of Europe, where selective breeding has produced the many different kinds of domestic sheep existing today. The original wild animal was rather smaller in size than most of these. The mouflon is nevertheless extremely handsome, with a brown coat and distinctive white patches on the flanks and a white underbelly. The male has great curving horns which may complete a full circle so that the points come forward again level with the eyes. The female also has horns, but these are much smaller, and the light patches on the flank are less distinct.

The ancestry of the domestic goat is more difficult to determine. Wild goats certainly exist in many parts of Europe and the Middle East, but it is almost impossible to say whether they are of pure stock – that is, truly wild indigenous species – or whether they have interbred with domestic goats that have run wild after a period of human influence. Be that as it may, the goat is an exceptionally useful animal in the primitive economy of the Mediterranean. In barren regions which would be incapable of supporting any other large animal it seems to flourish. If there is the slightest trace of vegetation, however dry, prickly, or otherwise unappetising, the goat will eat it. Its body then acts as a kind of

(*Opposite*) The most familiar sound in the Mediterranean region is produced by the cicada by means of a vibrating tymbal in the abdomen which is magnified by cavities in its body.

Land Animals of the Mediterranean

factory to transform this unpromising material into the milk which forms such an important part of the diet of the poorer Mediterranean peasants.

This milk itself is also used to make cheese, which when processed by advanced techniques is delicious to the taste, and considered by some superior to the cheese made from cow's milk.

In North Africa the most obvious and useful domestic animal is the camel. For many reasons it is ideally adapted to the harsh desert conditions found there. To take some examples: it seems to be virtually tireless and can march along all day in temperatures and conditions that would reduce any other animal to a state of exhaustion in an hour or so; in the structure of its feet, with their broad pads, it is excellently adapted to locomotion on the soft desert sand; finally, and most important of all, it has the ability to store water in its tissues so that it need not drink for periods as long as two or three weeks.

There was once a popular belief that the camel stored water in a special compartment in its stomach, or even that the hump was a kind of gigantic reservoir. This is quite untrue. The camel's stomach is comparable to that of any other ruminant, and the hump, which consists mainly of fat, is of more use for storing the energy provided by food than for storing water. Several experiments have emphasised the camel's extraordinary ability to withstand high temperatures and long periods of drought. In one of these a camel was tethered in the sun for seventeen days with hay and dates to eat, but no water. The shade temperature was 45°C (100°F). At

(Opposite) A hermit crab in a whelk shell with three commensal anemones.

(Left) A camel fight in a ruined amphitheatre in Tunisia.

(Overleaf) A herd of wild horses in the Camargue.

the end of the period it showed no signs of distress and had quite enough spirit to reprove the scientists who were indulging in this apparently inane task with a condescending stare and a sad shake of its head. Nevertheless when, on the seventeenth day, water was provided, it did take in 20 gallons without a break – a performance that would surely have done credit to a whole rugger team in the pub after a thirsty match.

Although these four domesticated animals are the most common in the Mediterranean region today, a word or two must be said about the semi-wild bulls and horses that can still be seen in such regions as the Camargue. The black bulls of the Camargue are of a different stock from the cattle that were the immediate ancestors of the domestic oxen. It is generally believed that they contain a great deal of the blood of the magnificent wild cattle, or aurochs (*Bos primigenius*), of the Pleistocene. They are not, of course, of pure aurochs stock, having been much adulterated by man, but the similarities can be clearly seen. They are also very closely related to the bulls of the Spanish bullring, although the cult of bull-fighting in Spain has led in that country to the creation of many subtly-varying strains based on the skill of the particular ranchers in artificial selection.

As recently as twenty years ago a visit to the bulls of the Camargue was an enthralling experience. One went out into the unspoilt country with the *gardian* or 'cowboy', and saw the herds of noble animals strung out across the plain. Afterwards one could go into Les Saintes-Maries-de-la-Mer and take an aperitif with one's companion in an atmosphere of early frontier days in North America. On fête days the cowboys would put on their finest clothes and broad-rimmed hats and swagger through the streets to the admiration of the pretty Provençal girls who used to vie for their attentions. But, sadly, nowadays the development of the Camargue for rice growing and the enormous increase in industrial building in the surrounding countryside has rendered such occasions rather an anachronism. They still happen, but one feels the taint of sophistication and commercialism which here, as elsewhere, is ruining so many simple pleasures.

For me at any rate, who am not ashamed of perennial nostalgia when I visit this region where I spent my honeymoon, the spectacle of the horses is also somewhat devitalised. Whereas in formers days all of them used to run wild like the bulls, now a number of them have been coralled on poor imitations of what the Americans call 'dude ranches'. The simple cafés with their zinc-topped counters at Les Saintes-Maries have been replaced by Coca-Cola stalls, and ultra modern petrol stations obliterate the wistful timelessness of the Provençal *mas*. However, the individual horses which still exist in wild country are as beautiful as ever, with their flying manes and long unclipped tails. Forcing the disagreeable visions of the towns from one's mind one can, with an effort, transport oneself in imagination to the days when horses very like these roamed in vast herds over the steppes of Eurasia and were captured and tamed by Scythian tribesmen to make their forays into the cradles of civilisation.

Turning to the birds of the Mediterranean, we find ourselves confronted with an even greater problem than in dealing with the mammals. Many hundreds of species live in the region and the selection of which to mention must be very largely arbitrary. There is, however, one criterion that should obviously be used. Many species of Mediterranean birds are also found in the rest of Europe; in fact the great majority of all continental birds found west of Russia can also be seen in Britain. So it seems sensible to emphasise in the first place a few representative species that are found on the Mediterranean but not in the lands lying to the north.

The most spectacular of these is the flamingo. The Mediterranean representative of this species is the greater flamingo (*Phoenicopterus ruber*) and there are breeding colonies in the deltas of both the Rhône and the Guadalquiver. In North Africa it exists in large numbers in Tunisia, and one of the sights of an arrival by sea at Tunis is to pass through the noisy gabbling multitude on the marshes. The species is found in many other parts of the world, but is the only one indigenous to the Mediterranean.

The bird is almost too well known to need description. It is a slender pink and white wader standing some $1\frac{1}{4}$ metres (4 feet), tall with a particularly odd-shaped beak well-designed for dredging up the small crustaceans, molluscs, larvae, and other aquatic food on which it lives. The nest consists of a rough pile of twigs, reeds, and other vegetation which the female straddles to lay and incubate her eggs. The behaviour of the birds in their breeding colonies, with their continual bickering and indignant chatter, is now widely familiar from many first class documentary films, but nothing can replace the excitement of seeing them in the wild.

Quite rightly the breeding sites of the flamingo in Europe are now only allowed to be visited very rarely by a few favoured people with a serious scientific object in view, for the birds can easily be stressed to the point where they stop breeding altogether. But some twenty years ago when the Camargue Nature Reserve on the Rhône delta was an easily accessible piece of wild nature in the midst of almost equally wild country, I remember the great thrill it was to be able to drive one's car to within a few hundred yards of large flocks of flamingoes and photograph them with a telephoto lens. It was, in fact, even more exciting to observe a few hundred of these exotic birds on the soil of Europe than when, in later travels, I saw breeding colonies many thousand strong on the lakes of the African Rift Valley.

Another exotic Mediterranean bird, which comes to southern Europe as a summer visitor from further south, is the bee-eater (*Merops apiaster*). This is not only found in the same places as the flamingo but can be seen over the whole of Spain, the Balkans, and central and southern Italy. It is a long, slender, perching bird measuring just under a foot from the tip of its bill to the tip of its tail. In colour it is quite exquisite, with a chestnut head, yellow throat, light blue-green breast, dark-green tail, brown and yellow back, and wing feathers that range from dark green to a kind of chestnut ochre. On the wing it stimulates the same gasp of wonder as the sight of a kingfisher making its dive, but the bee-eater's colours are, if anything, even more dazzlingly attractive. It is also essentially gregarious so it is common to see several bee-eaters perching at short distances from one another on a telegraph wire. This flight is as graceful as they are elegant, and is characterised by swooping and gliding turns on level

(*Overleaf*) The greater flamingo (*Phoenicopterus ruber*), the most spectacular of Mediterranean birds.

(*Opposite*) An aerial view of
a greater flamingo colony
in the Camargue nature
reserve.

The hoopoe, with its
scimitar-like bill and black
and white plumage.

wings. To complete this catalogue of beauty it has a most distinctive liquid but far-carrying cry which to anyone who has ever heard it will always evoke the atmosphere of its Mediterranean haunts.

Many Mediterranean birds of great beauty have a range that extends far from the sea itself. In fact the majority are found over the greater part of Europe. There is no logical way of selecting any of these for special mention and I shall therefore unashamedly fall back on purely personal and emotional criteria. When I was young I was intoxicated by the beauty of the natural world and used to spend many hours at the London Zoo, particularly in the Bird House there, identifying and watching the birds, enraptured by their dazzling plumage and the thrilling hint they gave of the existence of romantic places far away from the grey skies of London. One of the birds that particularly attracted me was the hoopoe with its long, slender, scimitar-like bill, its proud crest and the handsome black and white markings on its back and tail. Another bird that aroused my delight was the golden oriole, especially the brilliant yellow plumage of the male, with its black wings and black and yellow tail. I shall never forget the wonder with which I first saw these two birds in the wild on one of my Mediterranean journeys – the oriole glowing like a yellow lamp in the green foliage of a south European forest, the hoopoe running about the lawn of a house on Gezira Island when I was living in Cairo. Seeing the cousins of my former zoo friends unfettered by wire cages brought home to me as much as anything in my life the absolute necessity of preserving as much as possible of wild nature for the inspiration of later generations.

Land Animals of the Mediterranean

Birds have always had an immense attraction to men of imagination and have aroused both scientific and aesthetic interest from the earliest times. The Mediterranean particularly, being the place where both western scientific and artistic pursuits were first developed in sophisticated form, has had its general culture much influenced by bird life. One example of an interesting scientific observation is given by Herodotus in Book II of *The Histories* where he talks of a bird which associates itself with the Nile crocodile for the benefit of both animals. The bird he calls the 'trochilus', and he maintains that when a crocodile is lying on a sandbank with jaws agape the bird will enter the mouth and devour leeches and other small animals that adhere to its teeth. This observation, somewhat unlikely as it appears to be, has been authenticated by at least three reliable naturalists and the bird has been identified as the Egyptian plover (*Pluvianus aegyptius*). In the days of Herodotus, who was writing in the fifth century BC, the crocodile, which is no longer found north of the Sudanese frontier, was common in Egypt, so the observation could easily have been made.

More romantically, another Egyptian bird very probably played a role in the development of the phoenix legend. There are many versions of this legend but in essence it can be briefly recapitulated. The phoenix lived in paradise, the land of the rising sun, where nothing ever dies. But at intervals of five hundred or a thousand years or more (the interval varies with different versions of the story) the phoenix felt in need of regeneration and used to fly westwards to the mortal world to die. It gathered spices on the way, and when it came to its destination built itself a platform in the tallest palm tree where it sang a song of such surpassing beauty that even the Sun God, in his westward journey across the sky, was compelled to draw up his chariot and listen. When he set off again the sparks that flew from his horses' hooves and from the blazing corona of fire that encircled his head, ignited the fronds of the palm tree on which the phoenix had taken up its stance, and so the bird was immolated with the herbs it had brought from the east in an aromatic funeral pyre. The story does not end in tragic extinction, however, for from the remains of the phoenix's charred body a little worm eventually grew into a new phoenix. This in turn flew back to paradise and the cycle of life and death began once more.

Several descriptions of the phoenix in the works of ancient writers suggest that it is based on a common Mediterranean bird known as the purple heron (*Ardea purpurea*). This is found today not only on the banks of the Nile and in several places in the Middle East, but has a wide range in Greece, Yugoslavia, Sicily, northern Italy, southern Spain, and western and southern France. Among those who have described the phoenix is the second Pliny who writes in his *Natural History* of the bird's deep purple colour and the tuft of feathers which crowned its head 'right faire and goodly to be seene'. This description would apply very well to the purple heron, and the living bird's association with the phoenix legend is also suggested by one aspect of its behaviour. This is its habit of nesting at the top of very tall trees, a habit shared by herons of many species, including the familiar grey heron of Great Britain. However, even if we do not accept the association of the purple heron with the phoenix, such speculations do show that an interest in Mediterranean birds need not be confined to the professional ornithologist; the antiquarian, or anyone interested in ancient writers and the poetic charm of classical mythology, will also find much bird lore in the region to interest him.

Another aspect of Mediterranean birds, which is by no means irrelevant to the culture of the region, is how best to hunt and eat them. Bird-hunting is one of the most characteristic activities of the Mediterranean, especially in southern Europe, and on Sunday or other holiday mornings the countryside is alive with amateur sportsmen. Dressed in caps and clothing appropriate to the seriousness of their objectives, they make lengthy sorties into the hills and woods and fire away ferociously at anything within sight.

Some twenty years ago this Mediterranean tradition was really somewhat hazardous for the untutored visitor; the peace of the day was shattered by intermittent bangs, and it was not uncommon to hear a bullet whizzing uncomfortably close to one's ear. But since then the growing development of the coastal districts has made it essential to tighten up the rules to some extent. Certain regions have been set apart for hunting and its practise in others has been more rigidly controlled. Nevertheless the Mediterranean sportsman takes a lot of bird species that the northerner, more sentimental at least in this aspect of life, would regard as too aesthetically pleasing to kill. For example, some of the best Mediterranean pâté is made from the flesh of the blackbird and the thrush, and thrushes, particularly, turned on a spit, are a favourite winter lunch

The purple heron (*Ardea purpurea*) may have been the bird which inspired ancient descriptions of the legendary phoenix.

Land Animals of the Mediterranean

The Egyptian cobra
(*Naja haje*).

in many parts of the south of France. Although emotionally disquietening to many people this use of song birds for food does not seem to have reduced their numbers disastrously. They are, indeed, less common than they are in the north, but so much of the coastal belt of the Mediterranean consists of gardens where hunting is not, of course, practised, that the birds have many good refuges.

Apart from such controversial quarry, the more traditional game birds such as pheasant, partridge, quail, guinea-fowl, and so on are very popular in the hunting season in the Mediterranean. In France, as might be expected, they are deliciously cooked and the different birds are served in a variety of most attractive ways. It is interesting to note, however, that the French palate does not seem to respond to the delicious taste of 'high' game in the same way as the British, and in most restaurants the birds are served within a day or two of being shot.

Turning from birds to reptiles, the Mediterranean presents an array of species which must arouse the envy of anyone accustomed to studying reptiles in the colder conditions of the north. Snakes, tortoises, terrapins, and lizards are all common, and some species, especially of snakes and lizards, are dramatic in both appearance and habits. At the eastern end of the sea, for example, lives the Egyptian cobra (*Naja haje*), a large and highly venomous snake which has been responsible for many deaths.

The snakes on the European shores of the Mediterranean are not a serious menace to human life, although venomous species do exist. By northern standards, however, they grow to a large size, snakes $2\frac{1}{2}$ metres (7-8 feet) long being common. Among the largest is the colubrid *Malpolon monspessulanus*, which is the only example of a venomous colubrid in Europe. It grows to a length of 2.30 metres (8 feet) and its body is as thick as a man's wrist. Its poison fangs are placed at the back of its mouth and it is therefore virtually impossible for it to inject its venom into a man, but it is quite otherwise with the frogs and small lizards and mammals which form its main prey. It will stalk these very circumspectly, or lie as if dead so that they wander within a few inches of its mouth, whereupon it will seize them with a sudden lunge.

Although patient in this respect, it is also extremely aggressive and will even attack a large lizard such as the so-called 'eyed lizard' (*Lacerta lepida*), a beautiful green animal with blue spots, which is found along all the shores of the Mediterranean. The eyed lizard grows to a length of at least 60 centimetres (2 feet) and may well be the victor in such a combat, as it, too, has an extremely aggressive nature. Strangely enough this giant amongst Mediterranean lizards is closely related to the green lizard of Great Britain as well as the tiny little wall lizards which can be seen poking their noses out of stone walls and ruined buildings.

A lizard of particular charm is the Mediterranean gecko (*Tarentola mauritanica*) which is widely distributed on every shore of the sea. The name gecko is derived from the chirping and clicking sounds which geckos make, especially when they emerge in the evening from the crannies where they have laid up during the daytime. The geckos have a wide range extending over most of the tropical and subtropical world,

Land Animals of the Mediterranean

and vary in size from the tokay of south-east Asia, which sometimes exceeds 30 centimetres (12 inches), to some West Indian species which, with a length of less than 5 centimetres (2 inches), are the smallest lizards known. The Mediterranean gecko measures from 7 to 12 centimetres or 3 to 5 inches, and is found on rocky terrain, in ruins, and even sometimes in inhabited houses.

My friend Dr Edward Hindle, to whom this book is dedicated, tells an amusing story of a gecko with whom he shared his living room in Africa. The animal used to live in a crevice between the top of the wall and the ceiling, for it was an old house, but at 6 pm every evening when Hindle was pouring himself his aperitif it would emerge, make its way swiftly to the drink table, and take an enthusiastic sip from his glass. It was soon allowed to have a glass of its own and thereafter until Hindle left *l'heure de l'apéritif* for man and gecko became a daily ritual.

The commonest tortoise of the Mediterranean is the Greek tortoise (*Testudo graeca*), which despite its name is not restricted to Greece but is widely distributed along the European Mediterranean shores and in north-west Africa. This is the reptile that is often kept as a pet in northern gardens far from its natural home, and when the weather is warm it can be surprisingly active and amusing. It is also kept as a pet on the Mediterranean itself and in my own apartment in Nice five tortoises live on a rockery on one of the balconies. Tortoises in this part of the world are also one of the more familiar animals that sometimes create newspaper headlines; for instance, recently the local paper in Nice printed a photograph of a tortoise that had been brought into a restaurant on the journey from pet shop to home and had laid a clutch of eggs on the table!

Among amphibians the most noticeable Mediterranean species are the frogs and toads. These vary enormously in size and habits, the best known being the common toad *Bufo bufo*. This is the toad of ancient folk-lore which was supposed to have supernatural qualities and to poison anyone who touched it, even if they stepped on it with the protection of a heavy boot. Vestiges of this belief still remain in southern Europe and cause the toad to be persecuted, even though it is quite harmless, and in fact beneficial to cultivators because of its diet, which includes many insect pests. Another factor that has led to a reduction in its numbers is the ant *Iridomyrmex humilis* which will swarm over the toad in overwhelming numbers and kill it by eating it alive.

The most vociferous of the Mediterranean frogs are the tree-frogs of the family *Hylidae*. These are extremely elegant little creatures about an inch and a half long, as attractive as the toads are gross. The tree frog is notable in its appearance for its brilliant green back and whitish underbelly, its skin glistening from the exudation of moisture which keeps its temperature below that of its surroundings by evaporation. The tree-frogs are widely distributed in many parts of the world, including north of the Mediterranean in central Europe. However the southern European coasts have their own subspecies, *Hyla arborea meridionalis*.

The animal, as its name suggests, can be found clinging to trees and rushes, this habit being aided by the presence on its fingers and toes of

The gecko (*Tarentola mauritanica*) a Mediterranean fixture.

Land Animals of the Mediterranean

little adhesive discs. The croaking uttered by the males throughout the night in March and April is, without exaggeration, quite deafening. Standing by one of the cement-lined cisterns which are present on the land of many small cultivators and are a favourite community centre for Mediterranean tree-frogs, I have literally found it impossible to communicate with my companion. Every word was drowned by the thunderous sounds created by the animals in the huge distended resonance chamber which appears below their chins when they croak.

While the males are putting on this dramatic performance all the females do is grunt. It seems that their vital energies are too taken up with the need to mature their internal sexual organs for them to waste time on external display. It might be thought that the croaking of the males was a kind of love song being sung by numerous individuals to the particular females of their choice, but this is not the case. When aroused by the general noise the female will copulate with any male who attempts to mount her, irrespective of whether he has previously put on a specially good display of croaking or not. As A. N. Brangham amusingly puts it, 'a female tree-frog, stimulated by the explosion of sound about her, will pair off with the first available male, and not necessarily the one who has been bellowing the loudest in her ear.'

All the Mediterranean animals that I have so far discussed are vertebrates. If I were to attempt to give even such a selective account of the invertebrates of the Mediterranean I would be in dire trouble. For instance, the ant alone would need at least a volume to itself, and the same could be said of many other groups. Therefore I intend to conclude this chapter by mentioning only one Mediterranean invertebrate – the cicada. There is, however, perhaps an excuse for this, for no other animal more aptly symbolises the special character and romance of the south.

The cicada is a large insect measuring between 3 and 4 centimetres long (under 2 inches) with a wing span of over 10 centimetres (over 4 inches) in the bigger specimens. Its distribution is wide and there are many species and subspecies even in the comparatively limited region of the Mediterranean. For instance, there are seven in the south of France alone, although only two of these are common. But in the context of this very general survey I certainly will not bore the reader with details of classification; the essential attractiveness of the group is common to all its members.

The characteristic sound, which is first uttered in June and continues during the succeeding two months of what the French call 'la grande chaleur', is produced by a vibrating tymbal in the abdomen and it is then magnified enormously by amplifying cavities and other devices in the cicada's body. Although a single animal can be heard on occasions trying out its voice in a rather tentative way, the characteristic song of the cicadas is a deafening chorus sung in unison. This has been likened to a quantity of fat frying in a pan over a hot flame.

As with the tree-frogs described above, the males have a vertual monopoly of the song, a fact which has inspired the rather trite couplet:

> Happy the cicadas' lives
> Since they all have voiceless wives.

Mating, as with tree-frogs, is also indiscriminate, and after copulation some hundreds of eggs are formed inside the female's body. These she ejects in batches through an ovipositor which is used to puncture a hole in the branches of shrubs and young trees. In the autumn small larvae emerge from the eggs and drop to the ground, where they burrow down among the roots of the plant and remain entirely subterranean for the next four years. When the food supply in one region is exhausted the larva will move on along tunnels which it constructs itself, but it never comes to the surface until it is ready for its final metamorphosis into the familiar flying insect of the pinewoods. The final stage of its life is the shortest. For six or eight weeks only does it live to utter its thunderous hymn to the sun before mating and dying.

To conclude this chapter on Mediterranean animals I cannot do better than quote some verses, translated by Sir Thomas More, from an ode on the cicada by the lyric poet Anacreon who wrote in the sixth century BC:

> Melodious insect! Child of earth!
> In wisdom mirthful, wise in mirth;
> Exempt from every weak decay
> That withers vulgar frames away;
> With not a drop of blood to stain
> The current of thy purer vein;
> So blessed a life is passed by thee,
> Thou seem'st a little deity.

The tree frog has little adhesive discs on its fingers and toes which enable it to cling to trees and rushes.

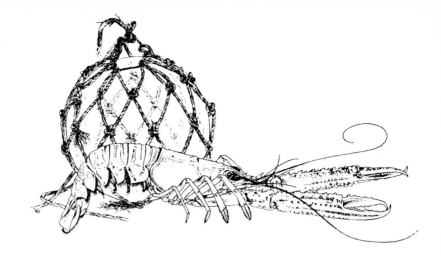

10

Beneath the Waves

So far, except for a few statistics in Chapter 1, I have talked mainly about the shores of the Mediterranean, their plant and animal life, their structure and history, and the story of man and his works in the region. Now I am going to ask the reader to plunge with me beneath the waves of this normally blue and sparkling sea and to spend the next few pages seeing what is going on in these more mysterious regions. This excursion will not be entirely restricted to marine life however, for interesting as this is to the biologist and oceanographer, it is by no means the whole of the story. I therefore intend to include also some reference to more general topics, such as fisheries, skin-diving, and underwater archaeology.

Obviously the ocean is quite a different environment for life from the land, and the Mediterranean has a very special character in this respect. It is not only the most consistently warm of the large expanses of water to be found in temperate regions but, with the exception of the Red Sea, the most salty. The surface temperature of all the world's seas and oceans is, of course, mainly controlled by the amount of radiation they receive from the sun; however, as one goes deeper wide fluctuations may be found. These are largely due to the action of currents, and in general the larger the mass of water the greater the variations are. The stability of the Mediterranean in this respect is quite exceptional. From a depth of 200 metres (650 feet), to the deepest point 4,440 metres (14,435 feet), down off Cape Matapan in the southern Peloponnese, the temperature of the Mediterranean remains at about 13°C (55.4°F), throughout the year. By contrast the Atlantic shows a wide fluctuation, the temperature dropping from 14°C to 2°C (57.2°F to 35°F). Such modifications

(*Opposite*) A Mediterranean fishwife at the market in Menton.

of the environment obviously have a marked effect on underwater life.

The same is true of the Mediterranean's high salinity, which is 3.9 per cent; the Red Sea, which is the saltiest true sea in the world, has a salinity only .1 per cent higher. The cause of this high salinity is partly that the sea is virtually land-locked so that the interchange of waters with the much-less-salty Atlantic can only take place on a very small scale through the Straits of Gibraltar. It is also largely due to the fantastic rate of evaporation from the sea's surface, which is about 100,000 tons a second, and because the inflow of fresh water of rivers into the basin and the limited rainfall are insufficient to keep the salinity down. A third, although less important, factor determining the sea's special character is the virtual absence of tides and the limited extent of the continental shelf. This in general creates a less demanding environment for the rock-dwelling and other littoral organisms than is the case on the shores of large oceans. For instance, in parts of the North Atlantic, where there is a very broad area between the tides, animals must adapt to conditions which may leave their bodies totally uncovered for two periods of about six hours in every twenty-four.

Before I leave this subject, I will recount a piece of historical information that well shows how the hydrology of a sea can have an important effect on day-to-day human life. In the Mediterranean during the winter there is a tendency for the surface water, heavy with salt, to sink and flow westward at low levels into the Atlantic. In fact the presence of this water with its high salinity has been detected no fewer than 3,200 kilometres (2,000 miles) out in the open ocean. Obviously to replace the water lost to the Mediterranean in this way there must be an equivalent inflow, and this is provided by the lighter water of the Atlantic flowing from west to east *above* the westward-flowing current at the bottom which is removing the heavy salt water from the Mediterranean basin.

This purely hydrological phenomenon has had some interesting effects. For instance, right down to the time of the steam vessel the swift-flowing easterly movement of the surface waters through the Straits of Gibraltar was a great impediment to ships attempting to enter the Atlantic. Rachel Carson quotes a ship's log dating from as recently as 1855 which shows how frustrating this current could be to seamen. The entry reads:

'Weather fine; made 1¼ pt leeway. At noon, stood into Almira Bay, and anchored off the village of Roguetas. Found a great number of vessels waiting for a chance to get to the westward, and learned from them that at least a thousand sail are weatherbound between this and Gibraltar. Some of them have been so for six weeks, and have even got as far as Malaga, only to be swept back by the current. Indeed, no vessel has been able to get out into the Atlantic for three months past.'

More recently, and for a more sinister purpose, the current and counter-current flowing through the Straits were used to assist German and Italian submarines during the Second World War. At this time detectors which could pick up the noise of submarine engines were mounted at Gibraltar, and this constituted an obvious hazard for any submarine trying to move in either direction through the Straits. It was the custom of submarine commanders to take their vessels to a depth where they could seek full advantage of the current, whether it was flowing to the west or to the east, and then cut their engines. In this way they were carried through the Straits with a minimum risk of detection. But, although by the standards of normal navigation the currents are quite fast, they were not really effective in the conditions of emergency prevailing at that time, and after some months the experiment was abandoned. Post-war reports do show, however, that in a number of instances the submarines were carried through the Straits as planned.

The submarine fauna of the Mediterranean is a rich one, but differs from the fauna of the North Atlantic, which is geographically so close. The main cause of this, already alluded to, is the consistent warmth of Mediterranean waters and their high salinity, which create a different set of ecological conditions from the wilder and more varied waters of the Atlantic – or indeed of any great oceanic mass. Sometimes the special environment in which Mediterranean marine organisms must survive is of practical benefit to men. To take only one example, the migrations of the Mediterranean tunny, which is the largest quarry of the Mediterranean sea fishermen, at least partially depend on its habit of seeking out the less saline parts of the sea, which vary at different times of year. But more will be said about tunny when I come to discuss the Mediterranean fisheries. Let us look meanwhile at some of the animals that can be seen by the ordinary visitor who takes a stroll along a Mediterranean coast, or is perhaps an amateur diver or fisherman.

Although there are a variety of seaweeds and other plants in the Mediterranean, the animals themselves, especially the invertebrates, are often of surpassing beauty, and when they occur in high concentrations give the sea-bed the aspect of an underwater garden. A rich array of invertebrate animals of every imaginable shape and colour fix themselves to the rocks. The best way of seeing them is naturally to practise skin-diving, a pastime that can be safely enjoyed by anyone up to the age of fifty or even more, provided he is in good health. But for the less intrepid, among whom I number myself, a good way of introducing oneself to many characteristic invertebrates of the Mediterranean is to wander around any fish market and work out the identity of the edible forms. The same process can of course be applied to the edible vertebrates, of which many species differ considerably from the fish obtainable in, say, Britain or North America. Of course, by this means one cannot learn about the more exotic-looking non-edible animals, but one's knowledge can be supplemented at museums and particularly in the aquariums which have been established in many towns along the Mediterranean coast.

The Mediterranean fish market is not only a convenient way of disposing of produce; it is a social institution and a source of much amusement and enjoyment to both residents and visitors. Few vendors of food can attain larger proportions than a Marseilles fishwife, nor blast the housewife into accepting her wares with louder or more insistent shouts. While the women are thus engaged, hands on hips, their husbands, who for some mysterious reason always seem to be as small as their wives are large, tip

Beneath the Waves

The sea-urchin abounds in the rocky shores of the Mediterranean, where it lives in colonies.

new supplies of shellfish into the lattice-wood containers on the stalls, to disappear at intervals to the local *bistro* for an aperitif with their friends.

A common sight on stalls are the edible sea-urchins, of which there are several species. They are gathered along the rocky shores of most of the Mediterranean coast where they attach themselves in colonies. They are like small hedgehogs, about 7 centimetres (just under 3 inches) across, and if a bather has the bad luck to step on one it is quite a business removing the barbed spines. But eaten they are delicious, smelling and tasting of the sea in a subtle way like oysters, of which they are considered by some to be the gastronomical equals. The habitual way of eating them is to cut them in half and serve them with a squeeze of lemon.

Although oysters themselves are eaten widely in the Mediterranean, and are of fine quality, it is not their main habitat. The oysters seen in western Mediterranean restaurants are usually imported from the Atlantic sea-board, especially from the region of Arcachon. But one truly Mediterranean group of invertebrates commonly seen in the markets and on menus is the lobster and its equally delicious smaller relations such as shrimp and crayfish. Although loosely termed shellfish, these animals are not true shellfish such as the mussel, oyster, or clam, but crustacea. This is a zoological nicety that is unlikely to bother the gastronome, however; eaten separately, or mixed together on a sea-food platter, all these 'shell-fish' are equally delicious.

Another invertebrate group of sea animals that provide the Mediterranean markets and restaurants with some of their most attractive fare is that of the cephalopods, or 'head-feet'. These are so called because of the ring of limb-like processes which surround their mouths, and they include such well-known species as the sepia or 'ink-fish', the squid, and the octopus. All of them may be seen in what are admitted rather unattractive piles of slimy-looking flesh in any fish market, but when properly cooked and served they make excellent eating. To many people the octopus is a creature of horror, but this opinion is obviously not shared by the Mediterranean Sunday fisherman who goes down to the beaches to cast his line.

I once saw a phlegmatic individual stroll down to the edge of the water on the shingly beach at Nice and, after slowly coiling a line with a weight and hook at the end of it, throw it dexterously for a hundred yards into the sea. Only a few minutes elapsed before it tautened and, with equal deliberation, the fisherman pulled in a large octopus which must have measured at least 1 metre (3 feet) across the tentacles. This he calmly detached from the hook, bashed its head against a stone, and then threw it up the shore only a few yards away from a crowd of sophisticated holiday-makers who were stretched on mattresses below one of the smarter beach cafés. Except for a few bold spirits who walked down to examine it, the rest hastily beat a retreat as the stunned octopus crawled along the edge of the water in an attempt to regain the sea. By this time the fisherman was casting his line again, pausing only to pick up the first octopus as it approached the edge of the water and throw it again some yards up the shore. He seemed quite genuinely perplexed when the owner of the café

advanced on him shaking her fists and shouting that he must move up the beach to a new site where he would not disturb her clientele.

This octopus was an example of the common species scientifically known as *Octopus vulgaris* which has a universal distribution in the Mediterranean. Apart from being fished from the shore by amateurs it is often brought up in the nets of fishermen who are mainly seeking other quarry. Zoologically it is interesting in many respects, and is a particularly valuable laboratory animal for the study of the brain. Extensive researches in this field in fact attract scientists from all over the world to the famous Marine Biological Laboratories just outside Naples. In a less technical field the octopus is remarkable for its capacity to regenerate tentacles (or 'arms', as they are more correctly called) if these are severed by an enemy. First a little worm-like process grows from the stump and gradually the whole limb is restored almost to its former condition.

It is thought by many people that this capacity of the octopus to regenerate its limbs must have played a part in the legend of the many-headed Hydra. It will be remembered that Hercules was called upon to slay this as one of his penitential labours imposed by the Oracle at Delphi after he had killed his wife and three sons in a fit of madness. The hero, it is recorded, found the monster, which had nine heads, and began to lop them off. But as each one was severed two new ones grew in its place, so with every success he was worse off than before. It was only when his faithful servant Iolaus helped him to destroy eight of the heads by burning and to bury the ninth (in which the Hydra's immortality was believed to lie) under a great stone, that the labour was completed. Even

The octopus, apart from its culinary importance, is of great interest zoologically as a valuable laboratory animal used for the study of the brain.

(*Above*) The octopus, with its capacity to regenerate its tentacles when they are severed, was at the origin of the Hydra legend in which Hercules was called upon to slay the monster.

then, however, it was not allowed to count towards Hercules' penance as he had allowed a second person to help him. A marble tablet in the Vatican shows Hercules in the act of performing what proved to be a rather thankless task, and the Hydra, at least as depicted on the tablet, shows an unmistakable likeness to an octopus, even to the shape of its body and the writhing aspect of its arms.

The squid and the ink-fish are superficially of a very different appearance from the octopus, although if one examines them carefully one will see that they have the same basic design – that is, a mouth surrounded by arms, or tentacles. The bodies of squids and sepias are, however, torpedo-shaped, reflecting their ability to move in a more stream-lined fashion through the water. The arms are also generally of a shorter length, although the two arms of a squid, which are the only processes that are properly termed tentacles, may exceed the arms of an octopus in length. The giant squid (*Architeuthis princeps*), a spectacular species that fortunately, however, does not occur in the Mediterranean, is the world's largest invertebrate animal, and may have a tubular body between 3 and 5 metres (10 and 15 feet) long and tentacles exceeding 16 metres (50 feet).

The octopus and all the smaller relations of the giant squid that live in the Mediterranean are widely eaten, especially in coastal regions where they are obtainable very fresh. The sepia is so named from the ink sack within its body which it discharges to make a 'smoke screen' to escape from its enemies. It is the custom in Spain and elsewhere to cook the smaller sepia in their own ink; this makes a delicious dish with a very special flavour. In France squid is very popular. The body, arms, and tentacles are cut up into suitable lengths and the flesh can be cooked in a variety of ways. A favourite method is to poach or fry it lightly and serve it with a *sauce armoricaine*.

All over the Mediterranean the arms and tentacles of many species of cephalopod are cut up into pieces 4-5 centimetres (2-3 inches), long and lightly fried in oil. These make original cocktail snacks. For the person with an adventurous palate who is not too squeamish after seeing the rather unalluring appearance of these invertebrates in the market, many gastronomic treats are in store.

A wide variety of invertebrates exists in the Mediterranean apart from those that appeal mainly to the eye or the stomach. An example of particular interest is the hermit crab, which although by no means restricted to this sea, is commonly found there. Unlike other crabs, this species has no shell of its own and must therefore spend a good portion of its life moving like a human being from house to house as its various premises becomes successively too small for it. Its body is spirally twisted, which makes it well adapted for taking up residence in any large shell of similar shape. This may perhaps have been the home of another specimen which, finding the pressure on its waist-line becoming excessive, has recently moved out. Having located what it considers to be a suitable home, the first act of the hermit crab will be to give it a thorough inspection, turning it this way and that with its claws, looking inside, and weighing up its possibilities for a lengthy stay. If it is not satisfied it will move on in search of another location, but if it decides to chance it, it will back into the shell, wriggling about like a woman getting into a tight-fitting dress, until finally the contours of its body and the shell seem to fit to its satisfaction. But even then, after an hour or two's trial, things may not seem as snug as it would wish, whereupon it will emerge again and continue its search. In general, however, once the crab has got itself firmly inside the shell it will stay there until it outgrows it, fastening itself to the interior walls by hook-like structures at the end of its body. These can obtain such a grip on the shell wall that the animal will often permit itself to be pulled in half rather than give up its home. When the crab outgrows the shell in the natural course of events it moves on to a larger 'house', a process that is repeated at intervals until it has reached its maximum size.

Although they normally prefer shells as homes, hermit crabs will sometimes take up their residence in other locations. One particularly amusing incident has been recorded in which, during an acute housing shortage on the continental shelf, two hermit crabs occupied different ends of a piece of tubing. This worked perfectly satisfactorily when the crabs were at rest, but as soon as one occupant wished to set off on a foray its intentions were frustrated by the other to the best of its ability.

Of the higher, backboned, animals the waters of the Mediterranean have a good share, but the sill of rock which separates them at a fairly shallow depth from the Atlantic prevents the presence of the deep sea fish typical of the open ocean. Such Mediterranean species as are also found in the Atlantic – the sole, the turbot, the sardine, and so on – are all creatures that live mostly at depths to which light can penetrate. But there are also a considerable number of forms which live in the Mediterranean which are also adapted to its high salinity. To a visitor from the lands bordering colder seas they constitute the sea's main interest, both zoologically and gastronomically.

Some examples of typical Mediterranean food fish are used in the preparation of the famous dish known as *bouillabaisse*. This in my opinion is considerably overrated, but it does provide an excellent talking-point for the student of underwater life. The fishy ingredients may number anything from three to twenty according to the taste and purse of the cook; but these include molluscs and crustaceans as well as such widely distributed vertebrates as conger eel and whiting. The typical Mediterranean fish which every Marseillaise housewife will include in a *bouillabaisse* worthy of the name are red gurnet, hog-fish, and weever, or sting-fish. There are several species of each of these and they are perhaps better known under their French names of *grondin*, *rascasse*, and *vive*. All three are coarse fish, so if the cook can afford it, she adds some of the finer *loup de mer* (*Dicentrarchus labrax*), which is supposed to be one of the finest of all Mediterranean fishes.

I am often asked by nervous bathers whether sharks exist in the Mediterranean. The answer is 'yes', but the common varieties are small and harmless and the larger sharks are encountered very rarely. Even if they are met with, the bather would be extremely unlucky to be attacked. As many skin divers, notably Jacques-Yves Cousteau and Hans Hass, have asserted, even the larger sharks should not necessarily be regarded as dangerous. The trouble is that they are unpredictable and one can never be sure how an individual will behave. In the seas and oceans where, unlike the Mediterranean, large and voracious sharks are common, the main factor that seems to lead to attacks on men is the smell of blood. This may come from quite a small wound in the diver's skin, or even as the result of his carrying a small speared fish. For the ordinary bather it is pretty safe to say that if he enters the Mediterranean with a whole skin then he will leave it in a similar condition. However, in tropical seas, where men and sharks are more closely associated, a shark which has once tasted human flesh may turn man-eater. There are fortunately no instances of this having occurred in the Mediterranean.

One of the most voracious sharks encountered – albeit rarely – in the Mediterranean, is the hammerhead (*Sphyrna zygaena*). In many seas this shark has a very bad reputation but although it is quite common in Mediterranean waters, I have not been able to trace a single instance of an attack on a human being. As its name suggests, this shark has an extremely bizarre appearance, the head having two large outgrowths or processes which cause it to resemble a hammer. It has been suggested that these act as a kind of forward rudder, but a more likely explanation is that to have the eyes, which are situated on the extremities of the processes, widely spaced assists the fish in achieving good binocular vision. Another Mediterranean shark more common than the hammerhead is the white shark (*Carcharodon carcharias*). This is the only Mediterranean shark which can to some extent be regarded as dangerous to bathers, but very few attacks have been reported and the risk of an unpleasantly dramatic conclusion to an afternoon's swim is too slight to be taken very seriously. This shark, incidentally, is much prized for its skin, which is the sharkskin of commerce. It also produces a high quality oil and its liver is superior to that of cod or even halibut in vitamin content. Its flesh is still eaten in North Africa, and during the Second World War was canned and used in Europe as an emergency food supply.

An animal often found in association with the larger sharks, and also with ships, is the pilot fish (*Naucrates ductor*). The more credulous of the ancient writers used to believe that the pilot fish accompanied the shark in order to lead it to calm waters or to food, although what the shark gave it in return is not specified. This fanciful ideas has been perpetuated in later times by many poets and tellers of tall stories. For instance, the English traveller-poet Samuel Martins, writing at the beginning of the eighteenth century, apostrophises the pilot fish as follows:

> O finny comrade of the roving shark,
> Would that we mortals likewise through the dark
> Of life's tempestuous seas had pilot sage
> To bring us safely home to anchorage.

Charming as such concepts are, the explanation of the pilot fish's behaviour is unfortunately quite different from that given by the poet. It is, in fact, simply a scavenger which follows the sharks in order to profit by any bits and pieces that may be left over after they have made their kill. The pilot fish, which measures only between 20 and 30 centimetres long (about 8-12 inches), and is extremely agile, does not interest the shark as prey, and is indeed almost impossible to catch. Thus the animals which the poets regarded as having such generous feelings towards sharks are in reality simply enjoying the amenities of an efficient mobile restaurant where they don't even have to pay the bill.

It is tempting to talk further about some of the more unusual fishes of the Mediterranean, such as the moon-fish, the guitar-fish, the sea-horse, and so on, but in dealing with this rich reservoir of life it is necessary to be even more selective than it was for the animals dwelling on land. However, I must include some reference to the two major classes of vertebrates that have representatives in the Mediterranean – the sea reptiles and the sea mammals.

In ancient geological times the ancestral Tethys sea had a huge and varied population of aquatic reptiles, as I have already stated in Chapter 2. Today, when reptiles have been far overtaken in the evolutionary story by mammals, the only marine forms that exist in the region are turtles. These are by no means common, but it is nevertheless interesting to know that two of the five remaining species of marine turtles in the world make regular – if infrequent – appearances in the Mediterranean. These are the leathery turtle (*Dermochelys coriacea*) and the green turtle (*Chelonia mydas*). These are the two largest of all living turtles, the former having produced specimens weighing 450 kilograms (about 220 lbs), measuring 1-2 metres (3-6 feet) long. The leathery turtle owes its name to the nature of its

(*Left*) A green sea turtle (*Chelonia mydas*) going ashore to lay her eggs.

(*Below*) The leathery turtle (*Dermochelys coriacea*) owes its name to the texture of its carapace.

carapace; this is leathery in texture instead of being made of the horny plates characteristic of other turtles and all tortoises. The green turtle is only very slightly less in weight and dimensions, and is the species used in the preparation of turtle soup – a gastronomic indulgence of man which has gone a long way towards bringing this animal close to extinction. The turtle's own nature has made the process easy, for it is placid, inoffensive, and easily handled – a sad reminder that the meek may not always inherit the earth, and if they are unlucky can turn up in a steaming bowl at a Lord Mayor's Banquet.

Among marine mammals one of the most attractive species to make a permanent home in the Mediterranean is the Mediterranean monk seal (*Monachus monachus*). This has a range extending from the southern Black Sea in the east to the Atlantic shores of north-west Africa beyond the Straits of Gibraltar. In the Mediterranean itself it was formerly very common and is frequently mentioned by such classical writers as Homer, Pliny, and Plutarch. Aristotle examined its anatomy personally and gives an accurate description of it in his *Natural History*. More recently, however, especially since the growth of human population on the sea's shores, the numbers of monk seal in the Mediterranean have declined, and the total population may now only be in the region of four thousand. The animal is quite large, specimens 3 metres (9 feet) long being not uncommon. The adults are an attractive chocolate brown and the pups, which are born in September and October in the few breeding colonies still remaining, have black woolly coats which are moulted at weaning time about six weeks after birth. In French the animal is known as '*le phoque à ventre blanc*', a reference to the large white patch that replaces the chocolate fur of the adult on the underside of the body.

Among many old beliefs concerning the Mediterranean monk seal are that the skins were a protection against lightning and hailstones, that eating the flesh or rubbing the blubber on to the body was an infallible remedy for gout, and that a flipper placed under the head at night was an aid to insomnia. Quite apart from its alleged magical properties the seal was certainly slaughtered – before it was given proper protection – for its fur, which was prized as clothing by the fisherfolk, especially in the east of the Mediterranean.

In spite of the advances in biological education some people still believe that whales, porpoises, and dolphins are kinds of fish. They are, of course, aquatic mammals using lungs to breathe air just as land mammals do. The cetaceans, which is the zoological name for the group to which all these animals belong, nevertheless show some remarkable adaptations to their water environment. The most obvious one is their shape, which has been one of the main factors leading to the confusion with fish. The fish-shaped body of whales and dolphins with its fin-like processes and fluked tail, is, however, a secondary adaptation made some seventy million years ago when a group of land animals re-invaded their ancestral environment, the sea.

Cetaceans are mainly represented in the Mediterranean by the common dolphin (*Delphinus delphis*), but several species of whales are also occasionally sighted, and sometimes stranded on the beaches. The dolphin is one of the most attractive of all animals and it is easy to understand the affectionate regard in which it was held by the ancients, who based many legends on its appearance, character, and behaviour. In all of these the dolphin figured as a most lovable and admirable creature, gay, wise, kind, and always ready either to help others or to deflate the pompous with a little good-natured teasing. Indeed, to contemplate the idea of a wicked dolphin would be unthinkable.

The dolphin of zoology rather than mythology is 1.80 to 3 metres long (6 to 9 feet) and has a beak-like snout projecting from its head. Its back is almost jet black, glistening and shining as it gambols round the bows of ships like a high-spirited escort. The intelligence of dolphins is generally recognised and, although one must discount alleged reports that they have helped drowning bathers to shore, there are at least well-authenticated cases of their using their co-operative skills to kill such enemies of man as sharks. They are particularly aggressive towards hammerheads, and will harass them by striking them with their hard, bony snouts. Sometimes an attack on a shark by several dolphins seems to be the result of a premeditated plan, several of them manoeuvring it into a vulnerable position whereupon one strikes it a fatal blow in a vulnerable region such as the gills. In captivity dolphins can be trained like dogs to retrieve balls thrown to them, to jump out of the water through hoops, and perform all other kinds of circus tricks. They also show a well-developed but quite unspiteful sense of mischief. For instance, in the Marineland in Florida a dolphin used habitually to tease a pelican that came to have a dip in its tank by plucking a feather from its plumage; this it would then toss about or even try to balance it on its own nose as it swam. A turtle, if picked on, may find itself flipped unexpectedly on its back, while there is one recorded instance of a dolphin which was offered a piece of rather high mullet to eat throwing it back in disgust and hitting an innocent bystander on the face. Mediterranean marinelands suitable for keeping dolphins have only recently been created, but as these become established there is no doubt that they will be the scenes of similar impromptu entertainments. In fact, so advanced is the dolphin's mentality that many reputable authorities already rate it with the higher apes in this respect.

Among large cetaceans seen wild in the Mediterranean are the rorqual (*Balaenoptera physales*) and even small specimens of the great cachalot whale (*Physeter macrocephalus*). The cachalot, also known as the sperm whale, is not sufficiently common in the Mediterranean to be exploited there, but the fact that it occurs at all evokes romantic, and also horrific, memories of the great whale fisheries of the past when this fantastic animal was killed at the rate of many thousands a year. After the blue whale, which may weigh as much as 130 tons, the cachalot is the world's largest living animal. It has a battery of twenty to twenty-five pairs of very sharp teeth in its lower jaw and may attain a length of well over 20 metres (65 feet). Many parts of its body are put to human use, especially the intestinal secretion known as ambergris, which is of great commercial value as a fixative for perfume, and the oil of its head, which is used to manufacture a high quality lubricant. When this oil is extracted the material that remains behind is known as '*spermaceti*' which is a waxy substance with a white crystalline texture. It is extensively used in the manufacture of cosmetics and some medicinal creams.

The structure of the sperm whale's head was well-known to the traveller poet Samuel Martins, already mentioned. My friend Dr Harrison Matthews, who until his retirement was Scientific Director of the London Zoo and first brought Martins to my attention, quotes him thus in the epigraph to one of the chapters in his classic work on *British Mammals*. The piece, which is taken from the poet's *Verses upon Several Occasions* reads as follows:

> There spouting whales the billows lash to foam,
> Then plumb the gloomy caverns of their home;
> Relentless there the finny tribe pursue
> Till, bellies fill'd, their gambols they renew –
> The chief among 'em leads his fav'rite spouse
> To coral grottoes, there to hold carouse
> Most strangely in their wat'ry nuptial bed:
> For lo! the spermaceti's in his head.

Although whale fisheries form no part of the economy of the Mediterranean this is by no means the case with many marine animals, both vertebrate and invertebrate. Despite the very limited area occupied in the Mediterranean by the continental shelf, whose waters provide such a rich source of fish for the trawlers operating in more open seas and oceans, several important fisheries nevertheless exist. One of these is the tunny fishery, devoted to the hunting of the giant member of the mackerel group known scientifically as *Thunnus thunnus*. This fish may attain a length of 4 metres (about 12 feet) and weighs 750 kilograms (343 lbs), and is regarded as a big-game fish, to be hunted with rod and line, in many northern waters. In the Mediterranean it has been exploited commercially since classical times and is hunted in a more practical manner. Towards the end of May the tunny shoals congregate in the central Mediterranean whence they gradually disperse to less saline waters. Their migration routes during the summer are generally northwards and are well-known to the local fishermen. They are caught by being shepherded between curtain nets suspended in their path from long boats until they come to a box-like 'death chamber' from which there is no means of exit. This is then hauled to the surface by the long boats where the thrashing mass of tunny is speared to death one after the other. Sometimes, to the great danger of the fishermen, one or two swordfish are pulled up with the tunny and have been known to jump across the barrier of boats, or to land inside them, where they can inflict severe wounds by thrashing around with their sword-like snouts. Even today the tunny fisheries of the Mediterranean are steeped in traditional and magical beliefs which can probably trace back their origins to pagan attitudes. The tunny, when caught and processed, is a valuable source of both meat and oil, as anyone who has studied the menus of even the humblest of Mediterranean restaurants will know. There is also a flourishing industry in the export of tunny,

which is canned in local factories and then sent by road and rail over most
of western Europe.

Second only to the tunny fisheries in importance is the fishing of the
sardine and the anchovy. The term sardine is loosely applied to a variety
of small fish, including the brisling, or young sprat, found in Scandi-
navian waters and fish of superficially similar appearance in South
Africa. Strictly speaking, however, the sardine is the one-year-old off-
spring of the pilchard (*Sardina pilchardus*), the fish which is obtainable in
tinned form in nearly every country in the world and forms such an
appetising and inexpensive item in an hors d'oeuvre. On the Mediterranean the fish are canned with a variety of oils, sometimes with the
addition of tomato purée, but none taste better than those canned with the
simple, unadulterated, olive oil of the region. The fish are also eaten
fresh as a *friture*, being either grilled or dusted with flour and deep fried
in vegetable oil in the same manner as whitebait. When served with
quarters of lemon the *friture* is a most simple and satisfying peasant dish
obtainable on all the Mediterranean coasts.

Sardines are fished for with nets on both a large and small scale. One of the most ancient and interesting methods is that practised by individual fishermen in the coastal villages whose aim is to supply their families and their own little community rather than to participate in large-scale commerce. The little boats go out at dusk equipped simply with nets and one good, bright lamp. The lamp acts as a lure to attract the sardines and other small fish in the vicinity to the boats where they can be netted and hauled out. The practice of this primitive method of fishing is strictly dependent on the state of the weather and the phases of the moon. On a bright moonlight night the lamp is rendered virtually useless, but when the moon is weak or obscured by cloud the fishermen often obtain a fine catch. One of the fascinations of the Mediterranean is the persistence of these ancient methods of fishing, which must date back well before civilisation evolved and were perhaps widely practised in Neolithic times.

Apart from the sardine one of the most prized small fish in the Mediterranean is the anchovy (*Engraulis encrasicholus*). Like the sardine this is eaten both in its natural state and canned in oil or *sauce piquante*. In the south of France a delicious dish consists of anchovies stuffed with olives, and anchovy butter is also sold in the markets of southern Europe. Anchovies are netted in the same way as sardines, but belong to a different zoological group and are different in appearance. They are members of the herring family and can be distinguished from sardines by the length of the upper jaw which projects forward over the mouth. With the tunny and the sardine, the anchovy completes the trio of vertebrate marine animals of most commercial importance in the Mediterranean.

Whereas these fisheries are very much alive, the formerly important sponge fishery that once flourished, particularly in the eastern part of the sea, is in the process of dying. Many non-zoologists mistake the sponge for some kind of aquatic plant, but it is in fact an animal of great evolutionary interest. The group to which living sponges, the Porifera, belong was widely represented in the world's seas in the distant geological past. For instance, in the period known as the Cambrian, which dates from no less than five hundred million years ago, many species of sponges already existed. They were one of the earliest examples in the evolution of life of a large number of single cells being assembled together into one large organism with different specialised parts for different functions. Like modern sponges, these ancient sponges were sessile animals – that is, they remained fixed in one place – and found their food by drawing streams of water through their hollow bodies with the aid of whip-like flagella. The sponges that live in the Mediterranean today are the direct descendants of these ancient forms which even in the Cambrian period were already far too specialised to interbreed with other forms of life.

Sponges are, of course, invertebrates, as might be easily deduced by looking at the homely object in the bathroom. But the bath sponge is only the skeleton of the animal which, in life, is covered with a skin and contains a thick milky substance. There is, perhaps, no more satisfactory device for rinsing the body than a natural sponge, but the sponge fisheries are nevertheless suffering greatly in competition with substitutes made from new synthetic rubbers and plastics. These are made from comparatively cheap materials and do not involve heavy transportation costs.

In spite of this flooding of the market with man-made products, sponge fishing still exists in the Mediterranean to fulfil the demands of a luxury trade. Its centre is the Greek island of Kalimnos in the Dodecanese where the sponge fishing boats have most of their home ports. In the old days the Greek divers who went out on these boats to bring up the sponges used to swim down many metres below the surface without any mechanical aid to assist them. They used to detach the sponges by a twisting motion of the wrist, for even the use of a knife would have damaged the skeleton. Today, the sponges are still removed by hand, but the fishermen have the advantage of modern aids such as the conventional suits of the deep-sea diver and the aqualung equipment invented in France in 1942. Nevertheless when the sponges are brought to the surface they are still hung up in festoons to dry in the traditional manner before being taken to Kalimnos for the final cleaning and processing.

Although much rarer than they were even fifteen years ago, the sponge boats are still a picturesque feature of many harbours in the eastern Mediterranean. Nowhere in the world are sponges of better quality found than here, and there is even a strong regional differentiation between sponge beds separated by only fifty miles or so. In general the better-quality sponges grow further to the east, and North African countries charge the Greeks high prices for the concession of fishing in their waters, on a scale that rises from £100 a season in Tripoli to £1,000 a season in Egypt. After the final treatment at Kalimnos the sponges are shipped all over the world, even to regions where there are already sponge beds. There could be no better proof than this of the superiority of the Mediterranean sponge over all its natural competitors.

Mention of the artificial aids used by the more modern sponge divers in the Mediterranean is a reminder that this was the main sea where the sport of skin-diving was pioneered, and later put to the scientific purpose of biological observation and marine archaeology. Little more than a generation ago the idea that archaeology could be conducted below the sea surface would have been unthinkable, and such finds as were made were more in the nature of treasure trove discovered accidentally by divers using equipment of conventional type. Since then, however, a whole new submarine world has been opened up, mainly as the result of the enthusiastic experiments made by Jacques-Yves Cousteau, the French naval commander who has revolutionised our ideas of what he now calls 'inner space', but first captured the public imagination by his splendid film and book, *The Silent World*. Cousteau has since become Director of the Musée Océanographique at Monaco and continues his work with many books and television films as well as the arduous demands of administration. But following his example in the Mediterranean and elsewhere are a whole team of younger men who have continued and elaborated his techniques for exploring the strange territory beneath the sea.

The term 'underwater archaeology' is strictly speaking inaccurate, for archaeology is archaeology – that is, the study of man-made objects of earlier times as aids in reconstructing human history – wherever it is conducted. But the use of the term is excusable owing to the great difference in the skills and techniques that must be followed under water compared with those followed on land. The Mediterranean, as might be expected, has been a particularly profitable field for investigations into the character of classical and Byzantine civilisation. But even when one takes into account the short time during which the new science has been practised in the region, it would be impossible to give even a summary of the main discoveries that have been made. Once again, therefore, I must rely on a few general observations to conclude my story of the Mediterranean beneath the waves.

The transformation of the hobby of antiquarianism into the science of archaeology had already begun at the end of the nineteenth century. From the time of the great Egyptologist Flinders Petrie, students of the past recognised more and more that to remove finds from their sites, whether these were on land or under water, and to place them in museums or private collections without any proper documentation concerning their origins, was to cause priceless information to be irrevocably lost. As the twentieth century proceeded the recording techniques used by archaeologists became more refined and sophisticated each year. It is now a commonplace of the science that no site should be disturbed without measurements being taken, maps drawn, and proper records made of its stratification. When underwater archaeology began to evolve there was at first some scepticism among the more traditional land archaeologists as to whether the appropriate disciplines would be observed. Indeed, in one or two instances amateur skin divers did plunge in where professors feared to swim, but on the whole the marriage between diving for sport and diving for science was quickly and efficiently consummated. It was found that underwater maps could be drawn on water-resistant paper with the same ease as land maps, that measuring devices appropriate to the liquid medium could be invented without too much difficulty, and that underwater camera and flash could be used in a similar fashion to the photographic equipment used on land to record the appearances of dark caves and the interiors of sand-covered ruins.

It is little more than a decade since underwater archaeology began to be practised with any seriousness in the Mediterranean, but already results of the greatest importance have been obtained. Obvious subjects for investigation are the remains of ports and of submarine wrecks, many of which date from early classical times. From the study of wrecks, in particular, it is possible to learn a great deal about the marine architecture of early Mediterranean peoples and the direction of the trade routes they habitually followed. For instance, by examining and carefully recording the stratification of cargoes it is possible to state with some assurance that such-and-such a ship wrecked off southern Greece had been returning from, say, Egypt, picking up goods in Syria and Turkey on the way. This kind of detective work is obviously much more entertaining as well as instructive than the view of underwater archaeology simply as a diving expedition in search of amphorae.

11

The Future of the Mediterranean

I began this book with an introductory profile of the Mediterranean outlining the territory to be traversed. This introduction was followed by a selection of facts, relating to both the past and the present, which struck me personally as being particularly exciting or interesting. In this last chapter we come to the crystal-gazing department and speculate, perhaps rather rashly, on what may be the future of the Mediterranean during the remaining years of this century. First, however, to give the whole subject perspective, I would like to offer the reader some of the sobering facts revealed by modern science about the future of the region in terms of geological time. Briefly, if we are sufficiently imaginative and interested to think in terms of millions rather than hundreds of years, the Mediterranean as a sea is doomed. This is because the year 1970, when most of this book was written, saw the proof of one of the most important geological theories ever to be proposed. It had been under discussion since the early 1920s and is known as 'continental drift'.

The theory of continental drift is so beautiful and so grandly simple that it seemed inevitable that even before definite proof was forthcoming it must be true. It was first proposed in the second decade of this century by the German geologist Alfred Lothar Wegener in his book *The Origin of Continents and Oceans* and was immediately followed by similar views arrived at independently by the South African Alexander Du Toit, which were set out in a book entitled *Our Wandering Continents*. The theory simply maintains that, instead of being fixed for all time, the continents of the earth are drifting like rafts on a more viscous material which underlies them. They were originally united in a vast single land mass, but after

The pollution of the Mediterranean is becoming an increasing problem. (*Above*) Natural pollution: the Camargue coast is covered with rotting or drying sea-weed. (*Opposite*) The countless yachts which make up the familiar Mediterranean harbour picture are one of the greatest sources of pollution, leaving behind them a trail of tar and refuse.

267

many millions of years this gradually broke into fragments which drifted apart. This is not the place to go into the intricacies of the theory, such as the nature of the processes that led to the fragmentation; it is these problems that have concerned geologists for more than half a century. It is sufficient to say that ever since the theory was proposed only conclusive proof of its truth was lacking and this is what has now been achieved. The reasonableness of the theory, quite apart from this scientific proof, can be demonstrated by a simple glance at the atlas. For example, what better explanation, could be proposed than continental drift of the astonishingly good fit that would be achieved if the western coast of Africa were to be pushed up close to the eastern coast of South America?

The theory also explains with daring vision all the manifestations of major earth movements in the past – the raising of great mountain ranges, the fluctuating shapes of seas and oceans, and even the present geographical distribution of animals and plants. It thus forms the background to most of the geological facts given in the first chapter of this book, and particularly the way in which the modern Mediterranean evolved from the ancestral Tethys Sea. Several whole books could be written on the implications of the acceptance of the new theory, and it would require a total rewriting of the geological history of the Earth. To enlarge on such matters here would take me far beyond the scope of the limited task I have set myself. A word should be said, however, to justify the statement made above that as one of the implications of continental drift the Mediterranean in a geological perspective is a doomed sea.

The movement of the continents now taking place, although at an infinitely slow pace, is proceeding roughly as follows. The remains of the primeval continent, which is known as Pangaea, and which broke up some 225 million years ago, are now scattered about the Earth's surface in the familiar way we know from the atlas or globe. That is to say, there is the great northern land mass of Eurasia, extended in the New World by North America and only separated from it by the narrow Bering Strait; a large frost-bound island known as Greenland, which partially fills the gap between North America and western Europe; two large southward-pointing projections, or giant peninsulas, which we know as South America and Africa respectively; and two enormous islands known as Australia and Antarctica. It seems that all these land fragments are continuing movements that probably originated when Pangaea broke up. They 'float' on the more viscous substratum referred to above, which is warm and now technically referred to as the 'asthenosphere'. The movement of the continents varies in speed and may attain the pace of 10 centimetres (4 inches) a year; this is the rate at which it is believed western Africa and eastern South America, where the most obvious congruity occurs, are believed to be receding from each other.

But other movements are also going on, and among these is the one which will eventually affect the size and even the existence of the Mediterranean. The whole continent of Africa, it is believed, is gradually moving northwards, and will eventually push its way into the southern coast of Europe, crushing the present southward-pointing projections in Spain,

Italy, and Greece, and at best leaving the Mediterranean as a gigantic duckpond or a chain of lakes. The twenty odd million years this will take is unlikely to mean that the process will cause concern to the modern resident or visitor, but it does underline the poetry of geological processes and, as an aid to humility, reminds us that even the eternal hills of the poets are as ephemeral as a human life in the grand context of cosmology.

But although such vast perspectives seem a little unreal to the ordinary Mediterranean traveller, there is another discovery of modern geology which certainly has vital relevance to one of the problems in the region today. This concerns the accumulation and subsequent melting of snow on the polar ice caps. It is now known that between ten thousand and a million or more years ago the Earth was in the grip of an ice age. This was not continuous however; it occurred in four major phases separated by three warmer 'interglacials'. In the cold phases the glaciers came down close to the fringe of the Mediterranean itself; in the warmer phases tropical animals such as hippopotamuses, hyenas, and crocodiles lived quite comfortably in what is now Italy, Greece, and France. The causes of these extreme fluctuations in temperature are controversial, although it is believed by a study of astronomy that they may be connected with the sun-spot cycle, which makes the sun radiate more heat at periods of peak sun-spot activity than at other times. This would, of course, account for the warmer conditions on earth at certain periods. But however this may be, there is no doubt that the fluctuations occurred. It is possible to examine, not only in the Mediterranean but in many parts of the world, raised beaches lying far above the present sea-levels which indicate that the water was sometimes much higher than at present. These times obviously coincided with the melting of the polar ice caps, in which water was otherwise trapped but then became released to swell the volume of the oceans.

Now what of the relevance of this to the modern Mediterranean and the possible course of its history over the next few decades? It seems that we are entering a new warm phase, and that the sea-level of the Mediterranean, as that of oceans all over the world, is gradually rising. One dramatic instance of this is connected with the sea-level in Venice, where there has been a great deal of alarm at the prospect of even more serious inundations than occurred in 1966. The melting of the ice cap was certainly one factor in the tragedy of the 1966 floods and underlines the importance of major geological factors in influencing human affairs. But other aspects of Earth science also played a part. For instance, the events at Venice were not only influenced by a global rise in sea-level but by the subsidence of the land itself and the special behaviour of the tides in the peculiarly-shaped Adriatic at the head of which Venice stands. As the fate of Venice is one of the most urgent problems in the immediate future not only of Italy and the Mediterranean but even the world itself, which recognises it as a unique cultural heritage, I shall go into the story, and especially its scientific aspects, in a little more detail.

The major crisis that first called the attention of the world to the very real danger that Venice might cease to exist occurred, as I have already

One of the many dangers which beset Venice is the erosive action of the water on the foundations of the houses.

said, in 1966. At the beginning of November of that year a violent storm hit the city. The greater part of its island site was completely flooded to a depth of several feet. Ancient monuments were severely damaged, private dwellings were inundated, and many people had to abandon their homes. The climax was reached on 4th November, when the façade of St Mark's Basilica itself was bombarded by huge waves, and there was a danger that the whole structure would be undermined by water percolating through to the foundations. As the fierceness of the sea – but not the height of the water – subsided, some remarkable photographs were taken of gondolas and other hand-propelled craft cruising about St Mark's Square, which had been transformed into a lake. It would have been perfectly possible for these craft to have sailed through the doors of the Basilica itself to the very steps of the High Altar.

Now, what was the cause of this disaster which befell Venice, and is there any means by which a repetition can be avoided in the future? Measurements have shown that the whole city has subsided in the last few centuries by a foot, or even more. I use the word subsided because there has indeed been a down-warping of the earth in this part of the Mediterranean. But, as stated above, the effect has been increased by the

rise in the sea-level now taking place more rapidly with each decade due to the melting of the polar ice caps. These phenomena, important influences as they were, do not account for the full extent of the inundation however. It was greatly aggravated by the shape of the Adriatic itself and the behaviour of the water within it.

The Adriatic is shaped like a huge bath and a similar phenomenon takes place there as can be seen in an ordinary bath tub at home. That is to say, when set in motion, the water will slosh in a vast wave across the bath with a swaying motion quite distinct from the smaller waves that may be set going by local disturbances. Now if in a 'bath' the size of the Adriatic this 'slosh' should happen to coincide with a high tide (for the Adriatic is one of the regions of the Mediterranean where some tidal action occurs), *and* a heavy on-shore wind producing large waves, then all is set for the sea to come well above its normal level and inundate the land. It is a rare phenomenon that such forces should coincide, but this is just what happened at Venice in November 1966.

To safeguard the future of Venice and of other vulnerable parts of the Mediterranean shore is a problem that is now greatly concerning scientists and administrators. Where Venice itself is concerned, the Italians have

St Mark's Square, Venice, was transformed into a lake by the 1966 floods, and gondolas were used to convey worshippers to St Mark's Basilica.

271

The 1966 floods in Florence were responsible for the destruction of countless works of art. Here the rain-swollen Arno pours over its banks, engulfing cars and transforming streets into rivers.

set up under the auspices of the National Research Council of Italy an elaborate laboratory in the Palazzo Papaopoli on the Grand Canal. Here a whole team of scientists from different parts of the world is studying the interactions of water masses and of the likely effect they may have again on flooding in the area. It may be necessary eventually to seal off all the neighbouring lagoons, and construct locks for the passage of ships. Local subsidence of the sub-soil through industrial pumping is another danger that must be watched. Such activities do not, of course, constitute the whole of the work of the Palazzo Papaopoli laboratory, for research goes on in subjects bearing on air pollution, water pollution, and destruction by environmental fouling of the city's works of art, but it is obviously an aspect of the laboratory's work that has a vital interest for the whole future of Venice.

This book is being completed in 1970, which is Conservation Year, and in discussing the future of the Mediterranean I feel it would be especially appropriate to refer to some other aspects of conservation, apart from that of cities, which deeply affect the region. One of these is

272

The Future of the Mediterranean

obviously the growing pollution of the sea. In his recent voyage across the Atlantic, Thor Heyerdahl observed that even in the midst of that vast ocean he sometimes sailed for hundreds of miles through sea polluted with all kinds of man-made objects – so common were they, in fact, that he was seldom out of sight of them. If this degree of pollution can occur in the Atlantic, how much greater is the danger of the fouling of such a comparatively small sea as the Mediterranean? This is indeed apparent to the casual visitor to its shores with no special knowledge of the subject. For instance, whereas it was possible to swim with great pleasure on the beaches of the south of France, even in the height of the season, as recently as five years ago, a great deal of the surface is now polluted with floating plastic containers, sewage, used rubber contraceptives, and similar distasteful objects that the bather in search of pleasure could well do without. Oil is another menace, especially with the growing number of small motor cruisers. The great liners and warships that come into Mediterranean ports are comparatively guiltless in this respect, for the discharge of their waste is governed by strict and enforceable laws, but the irresponsible yachtsman can entirely destroy the sea surface for many square miles. For instance, at Villefranche and off Beaulieu in France, when the yachts are occupied by their owners for the season, it is necessary to pick one's bathing spot most carefully if one is to avoid contamination by tar or by sharing the water with the kind of objects mentioned above. The proof that the sources of this pollution is yachts rather than the big ships lies in the presence out of season of many visiting warships to the port of Villefranche with no detriment to the coastal facilities. It is only in July and August that the condition of the sea becomes virtually obscene.

Although it is on the shoreline itself that pollution is mainly noticeable to a casual visitor, we should not forget that these contaminating materials must in due course drift somewhere – that is to say, out to the open sea. At present the process has not been going on long enough for there to be great evidence of this kind of pollution more than a mile or two from the shore, but this is only temporary; if unchecked, pollution will soon turn the Mediterranean into a vast sink of sewage, a kind of floating rubbish dump for all the unsavoury wastage from the land. Oil, insoluble plastic cartons, and most serious of all, unwanted poisonous gases and atomic devices used in war time, constitute the main threat. Sewage, although one of the most disagreeable forms of refuse close inshore, is not a menace if carried far enough out to sea. Some conservationists have even asserted that it is advantageous as a fertiliser for the marine plants which form part of the diet of the sea animals useful to man, although this I personally doubt. In any case the deposition of *all* forms of refuse in the sea requires the strictest supervision backed by stringent and enforceable laws. Especially in the case of poisonous chemicals and atomic waste, these call for international agreements that are by no means easy to achieve.

Fortunately, as the result of the efforts of conservationists there is now a strong public awareness of the problems, and local authorities – if only yet on a small scale – have begun to take action that should have happened many years ago. For instance, in many parts of the Mediterranean

The Future of the Mediterranean

the sewers are being modified at considerable municipal expense to carry waste much further out to sea than was formerly the case. Stricter controls are also being imposed on yachtsmen who jettison oil or tip waste indiscriminately into the waters of harbours. But, as is always the case with such problems, the most important single aim to work for is an enlightened public opinion; in other words, education. Far more than any legal safeguards or authoritarian measures to enforce them, what will eventually win the pollution war is the realisation by man that he is at present squandering his own environment. By so doing he is not only destroying the resources that will make for his future health and happiness, but also in some instances fatally defacing the beauty which is our human heritage and is one of the most important legacies we can pass on to future generations.

The conservation of the environment, as reflected in the war against pollution as well as in many other ways, does not, of course, mean that either land or sea should not be properly exploited for human benefit. There is still some confusion in people's minds that conservation means only preservation and that the person interested in such things is simply repeating the mistake of the character in the biblical parable who believed that the proper use of talents was to bury them without putting them to any constructive use. Exactly the opposite is the case. The conservation of the environment is of prime importance in rendering it suitable for production, provided that this production is intelligently controlled and carried out in such a way that the riches of land and sea do not become defaced or exhausted.

As regards all forms of production, the future of the Mediterranean looks extremely good. The visitor who simply visits the region on holiday thinks of it as almost entirely agricultural, but this is not correct. A look at the industrial production figures of many Mediterranean countries comes as a cause of surprise, and some of the goods produced are, to say the least of it, unexpected. For instance, who would immediately associate Israel (known mainly for its Jaffa oranges), with the production of artificial teeth? And would most visitors to Turkey, while enjoying the magnificent scenery, wondering at the ancient Bronze Age monuments, or simply enjoying a drink in a café at Istanbul, realise that the country possesses immense mineral wealth, a great deal of it as yet unexploited? Turkey produces, for example, some ten million tons of coal each year for domestic consumption alone, and exports almost two million tons of iron ore. Similarly unexpected figures could be produced for several other Mediterranean countries in different fields of industry.

Even in those regions famous for their scenic beauty, such as the south of France, light industry is of growing importance. New production techniques have shown that industrial products can be manufactured without excessive pollution and a great deal of energy is going into the design of buildings and the landscaping of whole areas to see that the increased wealth resulting from industrial activities does no violence, or as little violence as possible, to the visual aspect of the environment. Alongside these developments there is an immense growth of learned and

General view of the Aswan dam site before the construction of the High Dam.

particularly scientific institutions. New universities are being created, just as they are in Britain and North America, and the standard of higher education is steadily increasing. During the next decade the Mediterranean will undoubtedly see a return to its classical role as one of the main centres of learning in the western world.

Although such developments have their bad side, such as was referred to earlier in connection with the Camargue, where commercialism was allowed to run away with itself, they are not only inevitable, but must in the long run be a great power for good. It is natural enough for those of us who remember earlier times in the Mediterranean to think nostalgic thoughts about its former wildness, but it would be grossly selfish to indulge these thoughts beyond a reasonable point. Such developments as the Montdragon hydroelectric scheme in the Rhône valley and the increasingly efficient irrigation of the Nile have brought great happiness and a greater degree of comfort to many millions of people who could not formerly enjoy it. On the Nile particularly, the difference between

The Future of the Mediterranean

efficient and inefficient irrigation is a matter of life and death. A tendency to accuse those who are responsible for these developments as being simply worshippers of mammon because they are sources of wealth to their initiators must therefore be restrained. There is no worse example of sentimental self-indulgence than unbridled nostalgia.

Now, to complete this book, what are my own feelings about the Mediterranean during the next thirty years? If we are spared another major war, and signs in this respect are not, in my opinion, as gloomy as some people would have us believe, then this great land-locked sea with its bordering lands, so full of romance, history, and possibility, should become an earthly paradise. In spite of my own passion for wild nature and the excitement to be gained from re-creating the atmosphere of man's past from ancient remains, I recognise that the Mediterranean, if properly developed and managed by the authorities in the various countries bordering it, can offer even greater delight than it did formerly in these respects. As man learns more about the techniques necessary to preserve ancient monuments and can educate himself through the efforts of the most enlightened individuals on the necessity for this, then they will be enabled to survive longer and in a better state of repair than ever before. Proper means of access will be provided even to the most remote sites and greater numbers of people will be able to acquire knowledge of their significance and be able to appreciate the interest and wonder of ancient times.

The same principles will apply to man's appreciation of nature. Instead of indiscriminate building by exploiters who think only of immediate profit, it will be possible for new towns and villages to be harmoniously adapted to the natural environment. Certain areas will become urban agglomerations – not we hope the confused jumbles of the past but properly designed cities in which as much care has been taken about the happiness of their inhabitants as their suitability for processing the world's goods for human use. National Parks for the preservation of rare and vanishing animal and plant species have already been established in Spain, France, Italy, and elsewhere and although these at present are of unequal quality their importance is being more fully recognised each day. If wise policies are pursued, the nature lover will be able to enjoy his special form of relaxation better than ever before.

Such optimistic predictions could be continued indefinitely and are far from mere wishful thinking. The only factor that can prevent their coming to fruition is human self-centredness, which could make man put his pride, his prejudices, or his emphasis on personal whims, above the good of the community. Some pessimists believe that man is essentially of this self-centred nature, but I do not personally think that a study of history gives support to this view. Whether the Mediterranean is going to be a region where such ideas, already pioneered, are to be further developed remains to be seen. It is certainly a unique environment for the task. Perhaps some of my readers, whether they be visitors or residents, who share my love for this enchanted sea and agree with my way of thinking, will also share the effort.

(*Opposite*) Construction of the first and second generating units of the hydroelectric power plant of the Aswan High Dam.

277

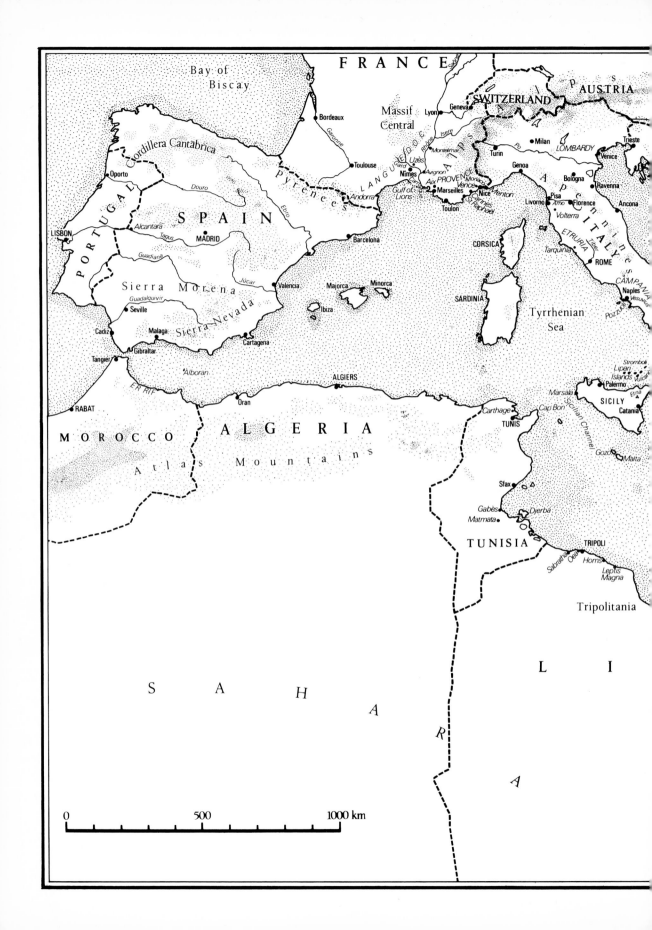

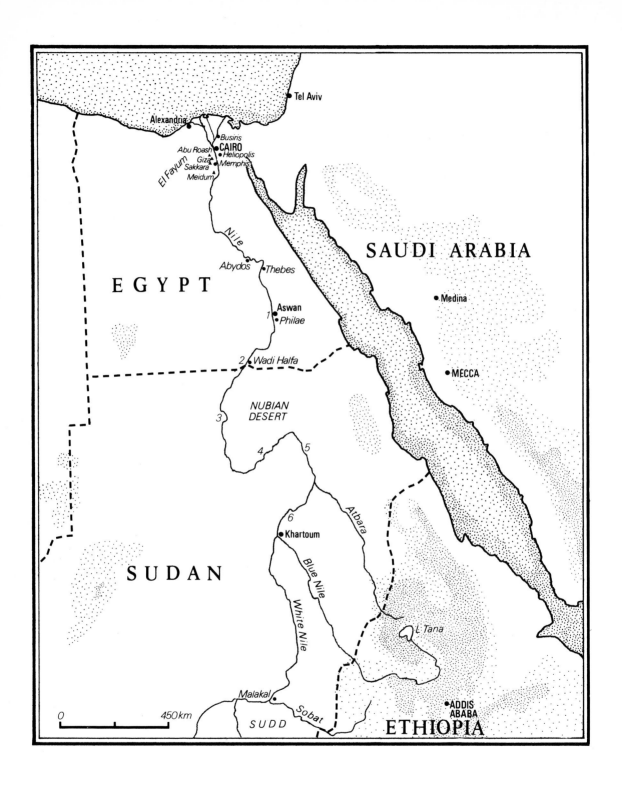

Tel Aviv

Alexandria

Busiris
Abu Roash
CAIRO
Heliopolis
Giza
Memphis
El Fayum
Sakkara
Meidum

Nile

SAUDI ARABIA

EGYPT

Abydos   Thebes

Medina

1   Aswan
    Philae

2   Wadi Halfa

MECCA

NUBIAN
DESERT

3

4   5

Atbara

6
    Khartoum

SUDAN

Blue Nile

White Nile

L Tana

Malakal

Sobat

ADDIS
ABABA

SUDD

ETHIOPIA

0   450km

Appendix: A Guide to Further Reading

The Mediterranean was the first region of our planet to be written about. Indeed the craft of writing itself grew from the scratched signs, ideograms, and picture symbols scratched by the first true members of the human species who rose from savagery to civilisation on the lands bordering its eastern shores. To give a bibliography of the Mediterranean would therefore be to give a complete bibliography of early human history as well as the names of many thousands of books written on or about Mediterranean life in more recent times.

Instead of this obviously impossible task I propose in this short Appendix to mention first in an informal way some of the source books for following up different aspects of the subject, all the books referred to are available either in English or French. Secondly I propose to mention some companionable books which my wife and I have particularly enjoyed for the fun and entertainment they have given us on our many travels in the region.

To begin with the guide books, which at their best will give both the resident and traveller a vast amount of clearly assembled and scholarly information and numerous clues to more specialised reading. Many series are available in many languages but I personally regard the splendid *Blue Guides*, available everywhere and constantly being updated, as the pick of the bunch.

Equalling the *Blue Guides* in quality, but more limited in scope are the softcover *Michelin Green Guides* to southern France, and their companion volumes to Spain and Italy. These are at present mainly available in French, but translations into English and other European languages are gradually appearing. These guides should not be confused with the well-known hardcover *Michelin Red Guides* to France and Italy which, although admirable, are confined mainly to information about hotels, restaurants, and roads and are not intended to provide any historical or scientific background.

For general information, entertainingly written, about the Mediterranean two books now out of print are well worth consulting in a library. The first is *The Geography of the Mediterranean Region: its relation to Ancient History* by Ellen Churchill Semple, published by Constable, London, in 1932. This is much better reading material than its rather austere academic title suggests.

The other book also has rather a forbidding title but is equally rewarding. This is *The Mediterranean Lands: an introductory study in human and historical geography* by Marion I. Newbiggin, published by Christopher, London, in 1925.

Two more modern books still in print which are packed with up-to-date information are: *The Mediterranean Lands* by D.S. Walker (Methuen, London, and John Wiley, New York, 1965), and *The Western Mediterranean World: an introduction to its regional landscapes* by J. M. Houston, with contributions by J. Roglic and J. I. Clarke (Longman, London, 1967).

Neither of these books makes any claim to popular appeal but, especially with such a subject, it is almost impossible for good geographers to be dull. To anyone seriously interested in the Mediterranean today these books are indispensable, especially as they give much simple geological and climatic information which is otherwise difficult to find outside severe technical monographs.

For the archaeological story of many ancient Mediterranean lands there is no better series than *Ancient People and Places* edited by Professor Glyn Daniel. He has always rightly regarded archaeology as a subject concerned with the lives of human beings rather than the academic study of pots and ruins. The series originated with the British publishers Thames and Hudson, but many volumes have also appeared in the United States and been translated into the major European languages. Individual works by lively scholars deal with ancient Egypt, ancient Greece, ancient Rome, the Etruscans, islands such as Crete, Sicily, Malta, and Sardinia, and many other subjects. An up-to-date contribution entitled *Archaeology Under Water* by George F. Bass gives a clear account of the techniques of this new science.

Incidentally, a more personal volume on marine archaeology is *Under the Mediterranean: marine antiquities* published by Routledge and Kegan Paul. This recounts the submarine adventures of the woman diver-scholar Honor Frost who was one of the pioneers of serious work in the field.

There is no existing book on the geological history of the Mediterranean as such, but many out-of-the-way facts can be found in such works as the following: *The Succession of Life through Geological Time* by Dr Kenneth P. Oakley and Dr Helen Muir-Wood (Trustees of the British Museum [Natural History], London, 1964). *The Procession of Life* by Dr Alfred S. Romer (Weidenfeld and Nicolson, London, 1968). *The History of Man* by Carleton Coon (Penguin Books, Harmondsworth, 1962).

A Guide to Further Reading

Two books of my own also give part of the background. These are *A Guide to Earth History* (Chatto and Windus, London, 1956) and *A Million Years of Man: the story of human development as a part of nature* (Weidenfeld and Nicolson, London, 1963). I have also, incidentally, written about some Mediterranean national parks in my *Great National Parks* (Weidenfeld and Nicolson, London, and Random House, New York, 1967). Translations of all these books are available in many European languages.

When one comes to the earliest Mediterranean civilisations there is an almost infinite choice of readable modern books as well as the works of the major writers of the time. Of these I can only mention very few, limiting myself purposely to books that are not only exciting to read in themselves, but which will give clues to further reading in their special fields.

Three standard works on ancient Egypt are J. H. Breasted's *A History of Egypt: from the earliest times to the Persian Conquest* (2nd. ed. fully revised. Hodder and Stoughton, London, 1921); W. B. Emery's *Archaic Egypt* (Penguin Books, Harmondsworth, 1967); and Margaret Murray's *The Splendour that was Egypt: a general survey of Egyptian culture and civilisation*. (Sidgwick and Jackson, London, 1949).

To understand the ancient Greek contribution to Mediterranean civilisation Sir Maurice Bowra's *The Greek Experience* (Weidenfeld and Nicolson, London, 1957) is virtually essential. It compares with another famous classic, *The Greek View of Life* by G. Lowes Dickinson (Methuen & Co., London, 1896), which is also superbly written. A book intended to give more practical information about the travels of the Greeks in the Mediterranean is John Boardman's *The Greeks Overseas* (Penguin Books, Harmondsworth, 1968), an authoritative and interesting recent contribution.

But some of the most readable material about the Mediterranean was written by the ancient Greeks themselves. The Homeric legends can be a source of enormous pleasure to the least academic reader, and no one who lives on or visits the Mediterranean should miss the delight of reading *The Histories* of Herodotus. For those who do not know his work, Herodotus could be best described as the first journalist. As well as many personal experiences *The Histories* give in completely unpompous form many humerous sidelights and speculations about nature and life in the eastern Mediterranean in the fifth century BC. His work is available in many translations, one of the best in English still being Sir George Rawlinson's, first published in four volumes as *The History of Herodotus*. This appeared between 1858 and 1860 and has been often reprinted in two

volumes in the Everyman Library (Dent, London). Another admirable and more up-to-date version is simply entitled *The Histories* (Penguin Classics, Penguin Books, Harmondsworth, 1968), translated by Aubrey de Selincourt and has a helpful introduction.

Another ancient Greek author from whom much pleasure can be derived in translation is Aristotle, most humane and approachable of men. To any lover of the natural world in general and the Mediterranean in particular his *Natural History* makes the best starting point. There are numerous translations. But one should read Aristotle more for the pleasure of his intellectual speculations than the narrative interest that makes Herodotus a sheer delight.

Ancient Rome also produced a fine crop of approachable writers whose lively style may come as a surprise to those who recall struggling with Latin declensions at school. The paperbacks published in the Penguin Classics are the best introduction in English to Roman writers on the Mediterranean, and in this admirable series the translations are as readable and vivid as one could wish. The volumes by Plutarch and Caesar are perhaps the best to start with and Caesar's *The Conquest of Gaul* is particularly the kind of book which a modern critic would call 'unputdownable'. The cavalry officer Pliny wrote a *Natural History* which unfortunately is not available in Penguins. But it is well-worth looking at in its first English translation, by the Elizabethan Scholar Philemon Holland, and published in London in 1607 under the title *The Historie of the World*. It is a huge leather-bound volume only to be seen in specialist libraries, but to handle such a book and dip into it will give the book-lover a marvellous feeling of what the Mediterranean world meant not only to the Romans but also to our Renaissance ancestors.

There are, of course, hundreds of good modern books about the role of the Romans in Mediterranean history from which I will single out only two that have given me special pleasure. These are *The World of Rome* by Michael Grant (Weidenfeld and Nicolson, London, 1960) and a most lively work by the French scholar Jérôme Carcopino entitled *Daily Life in Ancient Rome*. This became available as a Penguin book in 1967, translated from the French by E. O. Lorimer, and is a fine starting point for the understanding of the Romans as human beings rather than a 'dead' race and has much to say about the activities that went on in the circuses and arenas as well as the construction of roads, ports, sewers, private dwellings, and other buildings which the Mediterranean visitor will encounter wherever he goes.

Finally, in connection with the Greeks and

Romans a very useful, very inexpensive, and easily portable reference book is *A Shorter Atlas of the Classical World* by H. H. Scullard and A. A. M. van der Heyden. Within its 238 pages a vast amount of information is compressed, and there are 234 half-tone plates as well as many good maps, drawings, and diagrams. It was published by Nelson in 1962 and despite its impressive coverage could be easily tucked into a small beach bag or even a large pocket.

To keep this short and very personal 'guide' within manageable proportions I must now skip forward to the nineteenth century, during which many authors were writing on different aspects of Mediterranean life.

Many of these books are now delightful period pieces, and here are the names of a few that have given me much pleasure and entertainment.

A Thousand Miles up the Nile by Amelia Edwards (London, 1877). The first part of this book gives a most amusing picture of Lower Egypt as seen by one of those intrepid Anglo-Saxon ladies who explored the Mediterranean in the early days of tourism.

Notes of a Naturalist in the Nile Valley and Malta by Andrew Leith Adams (Edinburgh, 1870). A splendid account with descriptions of the first fossil elephants and other prehistoric animals to be found on Malta.

Proceedings of the Expedition to explore the Northern Coast of Africa, from Tripoli eastward in MDCCCXXI and MDCCCXXII comprehending an account of the Greater Syrtis and Cyrenaica; and of the ancient cities composing the Pentapolis by F. W. and H. W. Beechey (London, 1828). In spite of its forbidding title this book is packed with lively experiences and vivid descriptions of North Africa a hundred and fifty years ago.

The History and Description of Africa and of the notable things therein contained by Leo Africanus (ie Hassan Ibn Mohammed el Wazzan el Fasi), (Hakluyt Society, 3 vols., 1896). This and the Beecheys' book listed above were much used by my wife and myself during our own travels in North Africa. The translation of Leo into English by J. Pory was done in 1600 and is in itself an Elizabethan period piece.

Winter and Spring on the Shores of the Mediterranean by James Henry Bennet (4th ed. John Churchill and Sons, London, 1870). A charming book by a distinguished British lung specialist who went to Menton to die but 'under its genial sky' lived there for many years and created it as a winter health resort. His studies of Mediterranean microclimates, pursued through botanical investigation, are still of great interest and value.

A Winter at Mentone by Augustus Hare also appeared in 1861, and we can join this lively author on mule rides into the mountain villages of the Alpes Maritimes.

The list could be continued indefinitely, and many other titles are referred to in the second chapter of a recent naturalist's work on the Riviera which is essential reading for every visitor to the south of France. This is *The Naturalist's Riviera* by A. N. Brangham (John Baker, London, 1965).

Among other twentieth-century Mediterranean reading the visitor should greatly enjoy: *The Riviera of the Cornishe Road*, a *jeu d'esprit* by the famous surgeon Sir Frederick Treves, Bt (Cassell, London, 1921); *Etruscan Places* by D. H. Lawrence (Secker, London, 1932); and *The Colossus of Maroussi*, a classic personal reaction to post-war Greece by Henry Miller (Penguin Books, Harmondsworth, 1950). My own *East from Tunis* and *The Tears of Isis*, published by Chatto and Windus in 1957 and 1959 respectively may also pass an idle hour.

But whether or not the Mediterranean enthusiast should ever open some of the books referred to is of no importance. If the present volume should have stimulated him in however small a degree to pursue his own interests and researches in the region its modest aim will have been fulfilled.

Index

Index